IRA
JAILBREAKS
1918–1921

IRA
JAILBREAKS
1918–1921

FOREWORD BY
FLORENCE O'DONOGHUE

MERCIER PRESS
IRISH PUBLISHER – IRISH STORY

MERCIER PRESS

Cork

www.mercierpress.ie

Trade enquiries to CMD BookSource,
55a Spruce Avenue, Stillorgan Industrial Park,
Blackrock, County Dublin

First published by Anvil Books Ltd, 1971

This edition published by Mercier Press, 2010

© Mercier Press, 2010

ISBN: 978 1 85635 689 3

10 9 8 7 6 5 4 3 2 1

A CIP record for this title is available from the British Library

Printed and bound in the EU.

Contents

Foreword

by Florence O'Donoghue

Imprisonment is, and for a long time has been, the commonest form of punishment for crime. The long series of British laws which sought to make patriotism a crime in Ireland made no distinction between the prison treatment of the ordinary criminal and the patriot, except that in the case of a person imprisoned for trying to serve his country the comparative severity of the sentence was often greater.

The attachment of the brand of criminality to breaches of British law imposed a double punishment on those convicted: the deprivation of liberty and the imputation of crime to deeds or words not inherently criminal, but, on the contrary, done or spoken in the cause of national freedom. For the patriot, that was the more grievous wrong, and it was a fate suffered by thousands of Irish men and women in all the generations of the struggle for liberty. It was a condition against which they revolted with a remarkable consistency whether their place of detention was one of the grim bastilles in Ireland or Britain, the convict settlements of Van Diemen's Land, or the internment camps at Frongoch, the Curragh or Ballykinlar.

'In warfare,' General Eisenhower has said, 'morale is everything.' Ireland's war has been a long and bitter one. It has been waged in many fields and under many forms, but always morale has been the key to the extent of its success or failure.

In no aspect of the conflict has morale been put to a more severe test than in the prisons, and in no period of the struggle has it been maintained on a higher level than during the War of Independence. Either alone and isolated as individuals or in small groups, without contact with the outside world, the prisoners often had to find in their own hearts the spirit to resist and go on resisting the attempt to brand them as criminals. In that resistance they incurred the relentless discipline of the prison code and its barbarous punishments.

In every age since the conquest, examples of that unselfish loyalty shine out of the dark and sinister record of the prisons, and emerge in any circumstances where the freedom fighters found themselves in the hands of the enemy. Recall just a few: Bishop Boetius MacEgan of Ross defying Cromwell's Lord Broghill before Carrigadrohid Castle in 1650 and dying for his defiance; faithful Anne Devlin half hanged and brutally maltreated because she would not betray Robert Emmet; Tom Clarke's fifteen years, much of it in solitary confinement in Millbank and Chatham; O'Donovan Rossa, hands manacled behind his back, obliged to eat his food off a dish on the cell floor; Tom Ashe killed by forcible feeding in Mountjoy; Terence MacSwiney dying in Brixton; Michael Fitzgerald and Joseph Murphy in Cork jail. They are typical of many others. Their fortitude is the triumph of the human spirit over adversity and death itself.

Since jails became part of the machinery of British domination here, resistance by political prisoners to the prison code with its imputation of criminality became inevitable. Official reaction to resistance was invariably unsympathetic and envisaged no response other than the infliction of savage punishments sometimes bordering on the sadistic. The foul and overcrowded prison hulks in Cork harbour, the dark, cold underground cells in Spike Island, the punishment pit in Kilmainham, remind us of how ruthlessly the prison system was used to break the spirit and destroy the manhood of its victims.

The factual accounts of conditions in jails and internment camps, of hunger strikes, escapes, rescues and rescue bids, which are recorded in this book, cover the period from 1916 to 1921. They record events which are in historic succession to the struggles and sufferings of earlier patriots, events which were, as the War of Independence itself was and of which they are an integral part, a continuation and an effort to complete the unfinished task of former generations.

The conditions which these accounts record differ in two respects from those of earlier periods. Because the conflict was nation wide and of longer duration than any previous similar effort, there were more prisoners and they had better training in organisation and discipline. The prison code had undergone some reform and was less harsh than in the days of the United Irishmen or the Fenians.

Nevertheless, the old brand of criminality still applied, and it was against this and for the great principle of political treatment that the prisoners made their most dramatic and successful stands. It was not a battle won once and for all. Over and over again it had to be fought for in different prisons and by different groups of prisoners – sometimes, as in the case of Paddy Fleming in Maryborough, by one lone man.

Many of the events recorded here will recall similar occurrences in earlier times. They affirm the continuity of the struggle and the consistent attitude of resistance and defiance which Irish political prisoners have maintained against the injustices of prison treatment. The rescue of Éamon de Valera from Lincoln will recall that of James Stephens from Richmond in 1865. Hugh Ruadh O'Donnell and Art O'Neill escaping from Dublin Castle in 1591, had their counterparts in the escape of Simon Donnelly, Frank Teeling and Ernie O'Malley from Kilmainham. The rescue of Seán Hogan at Knocklong has echoes of the rescue of Kelly and Deasy in 1867, for which the Manchester Martyrs died.

Even if no rescue of the War of Independence was as long-range or costly as that of the seven Fenian prisoners from their penal exile in Fremantle, Western Australia, 10,000 miles from their homeland, the spirit of the prisoners and their rescuers was the same. Of that daring and brilliantly executed rescue, John Boyle O'Reilly, who had himself escaped a little earlier, wrote: 'It will be remembered of Irish patriots that they never forgot their suffering brothers. The prisoners who have escaped are humble men, most of them private soldiers. But the principle was at stake – and for this they have been released.' The principle was the same in the War of Independence; the national organisations did not forget the prisoners.

In one way or another contact with the men and women in jails and internment camps was maintained. J.J. Breslin, who made the Stephens' escape possible, had his counterpart in many a prison. The Cumann na mBan organisation did magnificent work in supplying food and comforts to the prisoners, in tracing their locations and keeping their relatives informed. The prisoners remained under the discipline of the organisations to which they belonged when free. Wherever possible they organised themselves in the jails and camps under the senior officer of the group and they maintained a discipline which often compelled the unwilling admiration of their captors.

The only really new weapon used by the War of Independence prisoners was the audacious and formidable one of hunger strike. This desperate form of protest was not an official policy of any of the national organisations in the sense that anybody was ever ordered to adopt it. Prisoners were free to decide to hunger strike, either individually or in combination, but volunteers were instructed that once embarked upon, it should not be abandoned until victory was won or death intervened. It was an elemental conflict between the individual prisoner and the power that held him captive. Frequently, he was also untried.

The early British reaction to hunger strike was the application of the Prisoners (Temporary Discharge for Ill-Health) Act 1913, wittily known as the Cat and Mouse Act. This was a statute passed in England at the time of the Suffragette agitation. The Act permitted the release of hunger strikers and their rearrest for completion of their sentences after a lapse of such time as the authorities assumed had enabled them to recover from the effects of their fasting. But when Irish political prisoners so released disappeared and could not be rearrested, or when, as was usual, they refused to give the required undertaking to return to prison at the end of a specified period, use of the Act was discontinued.

There followed the inhuman process of forcible feeding which resulted in the tragic death of Thomas Ashe. So great was the public outcry against this outrage that it put an end to any further attempts to forcibly feed the hunger strikers. From that point onwards British reaction became progressively more ruthless. Although the great hunger strikes in Mountjoy, Dundalk and Belfast were successful in obtaining a temporary measure of political treatment, the later one begun in Cork jail was confronted by a relentless determination on the part of the British government to let the hunger strikers die. Deaf to all humanitarian appeals (and they were worldwide and influential), Lloyd George and his cabinet encompassed the deaths of Terence MacSwiney in Brixton and of Michael Fitzgerald and Joseph Murphy in Cork.

After these sacrifices there were still nine men at the point of death in the hospital section of Cork jail. When, on 12 November 1920, they had sustained a record fast of ninety-four days, Arthur Griffith, Acting President of the Republic, suggested to them that they should discontinue the strike. The manner in which he did so is evidence of the official attitude to hunger strikes and shows that even in their extreme exhaustion the right of decision still remained with the prisoners.

'I am of opinion,' he wrote, 'that our countrymen in Cork prison have sufficiently proved their devotion and fidelity and that they should now, as they were prepared to die for Ireland, prepare again to live for her.' The hunger strike, in this case as in all others, was a voluntary acceptance by the prisoners of the most severe ordeal to which men could subject themselves in assertion of their inalienable right to work for national independence. The decision to end the strike was their own, and happily all of them survived.

Even before the Rising many workers in the independence movement had seen the inside of prisons. It was a continuation of British policy since the Act of Union. In 100 years there had been eighty-seven coercion acts, with a Perpetual Crimes Act in 1887, under which 1,500 persons were given hard-labour sentences in the following fifteen years.

Many of the charges against Irishmen in the period 1914–21 were brought under the Defence of the Realm Act, popularly known as DORA. It was enacted as a war measure in Britain in August 1914, but its provisions were so comprehensive that it became an effective weapon of coercion in Ireland. By the regulations made under this Act any person merely suspected of having committed an offence could be held in custody indefinitely until the competent military authority decided how he was to be tried. This could be either by a civil or a military court. The Crimes Act still operated and these measures were reinforced in August 1920, by the even more drastic Restoration of Order in Ireland Act. That made the whole population potential jailbirds.

Some of the early prosecutions, allegedly in defence of the British realm, must sound a bit absurd today. Pádraig Ó Conaire was jailed and Claude Chavasse fined £5 for answering a policeman's questions in Irish. Men were fined for singing *God Save Ireland*. Liam Mellows, Denis McCullough and Ernest Blythe were banished out of the country. Many others were prohibited from living in certain areas. Desmond Fitzgerald was ordered out of Kerry and Seán O'Hegarty out of Cork. Volunteers in any branch of the public service or in the national schools were deprived of their livelihood. Austin Stack was one of the victims. By June 1915 forty persons, including Seán MacDermott, had been sentenced to terms of imprisonment under DORA. A common charge was that of having made statements likely to prejudice recruiting for the British forces.

After the Rising the number of prisoners in British custody was 3,430 men and 79 women. 1,424 men and 73 women were released. Of the remaining 2,006 men and six women, 159 men and one woman, Countess Markievicz, were sentenced by courts martial and eleven were acquitted. Ninety were sentenced to death and fifteen of them executed. Ten were sentenced to penal servitude for life, one to twenty years, thirty-three to ten years, three to eight years, one to seven years, eighteen to five years, fifty-six to three years, two to two years, and the remaining twenty-three to shorter terms of imprisonment with hard labour. 1,836 men and five women were interned without being sentenced. The sentenced prisoners were taken to various prisons in England, there to wear the broad arrow and associate with criminals. The male internees were confined in a prisoner-of-war camp at Frongoch in north Wales.

Unwittingly, the British authorities gave the internees an opportunity of creating a school for revolution and national resistance – an opportunity which was fully availed of. From all over the country they had gathered into Frongoch, with some of the survivors of the Rising, men who had been active in building up the Volunteer organisation in their own areas, giving them opportunities of becoming better acquainted, of planning the lines of future action, and of laying the foundations for the policy of organisation and resistance in jails and internment camps which formed the basis of all subsequent prisoner activity.

In each of the two camps at Frongoch the internees appointed their commandants, established a chain of command with group and hut leaders, and, in effect, controlled the camps under their own discipline. Irish language classes, lectures on military subjects and recreational activities were organised. Morale was sustained. Incipient capacity for organisation and leadership was fostered and developed, and from it emerged many, including Michael Collins and Tomás MacCurtain, who played notable parts in the subsequent struggle.

The internees were released at Christmas 1916 and the

sentenced prisoners in June 1917. And at once the great reorganisation and expansion of the Volunteer organisation commenced, side by side with the build-up of the political arm, Sinn Féin. Once again the prisons began to be filled; the demand for political treatment was made and refused, the first hunger strike began in Mountjoy. From then until December 1921 the number of prisoners continued to grow and the ceaseless struggle in jails and camps became ever more bitter and intense.

As part of the general policy of resistance, Volunteer prisoners were instructed to refuse to recognise the right of British courts to charge or try them at all. In many a so-called court the prisoner's contemptuous reply to the charge was: *Nil meas madra agam ar an gcúirt seo.* This occasionally provoked a few outbursts of infuriated response from scandalised British officers and provided a moment of light relief for the prisoners, although undoubtedly it did nothing to mitigate their sentences.

In the spring of 1921 the number of prisoners had grown to over 7,000. The majority were Volunteers and although the capture of active men was a grievous loss, it did not significantly limit the extent of operations against the occupation forces in most areas. There were always more men ready and willing to fight than there were arms with which to equip them. In the peculiar circumstances of the struggle the prisoners and internees were not completely cut off by capture from contributing to the overall effort. Their sustained resistance to treatment as criminals focused public attention on the national claim to freedom. Their high morale and steady discipline imposed continuous strain and frustration on the troops and officials in whose custody they were held. The hunger strike deaths of Ashe and MacSwiney received worldwide publicity and evoked the sympathy of freedom-loving people in every land. The recurring rescues and escapes of prisoners, bringing, as they did, discredit and ridicule on the prison and camp authorities, were also indications of the undaunted spirit of the captives and of courage and resourcefulness in the organisations to which they belonged. The British authorities needed the equivalent of eight battalions of troops to guard their internment camps and prisons.

Casualties amongst the prisoners were relatively few. Pierce McCan died in Gloucester prison on 6 March 1919, as a result of long confinement and an epidemic of influenza. Two Westmeath Volunteers, James Sloan and James Tormey, were shot dead by a sentry at Ballykinlar camp, County Down, in January 1921. In the same camp Tadhg Barry of Cork died from a sentry's bullet on 15 November 1921. Another prisoner was killed by a sentry in Spike Island.

Of the 7,000 odd prisoners at the Truce of 11 July 1921, only those few who were members of Dáil Éireann were released. Even for them the British government sought to make one exception – they held Seán MacEoin. It was only after President de Valera had threatened to discontinue the negotiations unless he was released that they relented. In the months between the Truce and the signing of the Articles of Agreement in December, the prisoners, having no means of knowing how the negotiations would end, continued to plan escapes. A great many attempts succeeded, including one on a large scale from the Curragh.

As a factual record of prison conditions and of the contribution made by the prisoners in the War of Independence, this is the most comprehensive collection of first-hand evidence which has been published. Not alone to the men and women whose names appear in the record, but also to the unnamed thousands of prisoners and internees whose loyalty and discipline sustained the struggle, it will stand as a well-deserved tribute.

Cork, 1967

Chapter 1

Rescue of Donnchadha MacNeilus from Cork jail

by Florence O'Donoghue

The escapes of Irish political prisoners from British jails in this country and abroad are a part of the thrilling story of the nation's long struggle for freedom. Some, like the rescue of prisoners from British convict settlements, were accomplished after long and careful preparations and with the co-operation and assistance of the prisoners themselves; others, like the rescue of Colonel Tom Kelly and Captain T. Deasy at Manchester, were successful and tragic for the rescuers, but called forth that noble spirit of self-sacrifice in the interests of a comrade which caused the names of the Manchester Martyrs to be remembered forever in song and story. In the more recent phase of the nation's struggle, from 1916 onwards, there was scarcely a jail or fortress in the country from which some Irishman, held there for his part in the fight for liberty, had not escaped or been rescued. Among those, one of the earliest and most successful was the rescue of Donnchadha MacNeilus from Cork jail on 11 November 1918. It was, perhaps, unique in that it was planned and carried out entirely from outside and without any assistance from inside the prison.

Donnchadha MacNeilus was a Volunteer officer who was attached to the Cork Brigade since he had come from his native Donegal. At the date of his arrest he was captain of the cyclist company attached to brigade headquarters. An expert toolmaker, he had studied mechanical and electrical engineering, and acted as armourer for the city companies. There was rarely a time when he did not have a number of revolvers and pistols on hand for repair. On the morning of 4 November 1918, five men of the RIC, one of them armed with a .38 Webley revolver, raided his lodgings at the home of Denis Kelleher, No. 28 Leitrim Street, and attempted to arrest him. MacNeilus was armed and resisted arrest. In the desperate struggle which followed Head Constable Clarke was very seriously wounded, and it was only on the arrival of reinforcements with carbines and in the charge of a district inspector that MacNeilus was finally overpowered.

When the news spread it was realised, not alone by his comrades in Cork, but in every part of Ireland where Volunteers were armed, that a lead had been given in armed resistance to capture at a time when such a lead was needed. The armed might of the British army of occupation was then so much in evidence everywhere that many doubted the wisdom or feasibility of challenging it in arms. Nevertheless, the militant spirit of the Volunteers was growing steadily with the growth of their organisation and their proficiency in the use of arms; and this valiant defence of his liberty and his arms by one man, alone and against superior numbers, set a standard for his comrades and put the respective positions of the Volunteers and the British army of occupation again in their proper perspective.

The wounded head constable was in danger of death and if he died the fate of MacNeilus was inevitable – unless a rescue could be effected. The prisoner had been taken to Cork jail, unhurt except for some minor scratches. With him was arrested Denis Kelleher, who had gone unarmed to the assistance of MacNeilus in resisting the raiding party.

One thought was uppermost in the minds of his comrades from the moment of his arrest – he should be rescued. But when they came to consider how the attempt was to be made they were faced with the situation that they knew practically nothing of the position inside the prison, except that there was an armed military guard always on duty; they knew nothing about the supervision of visits to prisoners or the internal organisation of the prison. The Volunteers had no contact with any person in, or employed in, Cork jail. They started from scratch and in six days completed their arrangements and brought them to a successful issue. The operation was a good example of that careful attention to detail in planning and audacity in action which were features of so many subsequent Volunteer operations and which contributed largely to their success.

On the night of 4 November a hastily summoned meeting of the available members of the brigade council was held at the house of the acting Brigade Commandant, Seán O'Hegarty, who was in charge of the operation. The available information amounted only to this: that the wounded head constable was in danger of death and that untried prisoners were allowed one visit of ten minutes' duration each day between 10 and 11 a.m. or between 3 and 4 p.m. Two visitors were allowed in together and no visits were allowed on Sundays. It was decided to send Florrie O'Donoghue on a visit to MacNeilus on the following morning, in the course of which he was to observe the disposition of the guards, the method of supervising the admission of visitors and interviews, the nature of the gates and locks, and any other details that might be useful. He was, if possible, to suggest a plan for the rescue and convey to MacNeilus that the effort would be made. Owing to the vigilance of the warders on duty he was unable to convey the message at the first visit, but he did so on the following day when he again visited the prisoner, accompanied by Rev. Father MacNeilus – the prisoner's brother.

The jail was surrounded by a high wall, standing clear of the buildings within. The entrance was closed on the outside by a pair of heavy iron-bound doors, in one of which was a small wicket. The outer doors gave access to a small space closed on the inner side by a pair of heavy wrought-iron gates which extended the full height of the archway. Opening off the space between the two gates, and to the left, was the visitors' waiting-room in which a warder was always on duty. Not more than six persons were allowed in the waiting-room at the same time. The visiting cell was situated near the centre of the prison and was approached from the main gate by a path running inside the outer wall and past the main gate into the prison buildings, at which the military sentry was on duty. These circumstances governed the decision as to the choice of plan for the rescue, and, when the council had considered them, the plan was quickly decided upon.

Then began a systematic consideration of every minute detail, a close examination of every point at which the plan might break down or miscarry. A time schedule was decided upon because the success of the plan depended to a great extent upon synchronising the movements and the actions of two and possibly three pairs of ostensible visitors and a group of Volunteers acting outside the prison without any means of knowing what was happening inside. MacNeilus himself should receive two Volunteer visitors on the afternoon of the day decided upon; any proposed visit by friends of his on that day should be prevented without occasioning comment, and two other prisoners had to be got to reserve visits for the afternoon of the same day. Seán Scanlan visited MacNeilus on the Wednesday and, in shaking hands with him across the barrier, managed to pass a small note: 'Be prepared for anything', and said 'Friday'. The rescue was first planned for Friday 9 November but, owing to arrangements not being complete, it was postponed to Monday 11 November. O'Donoghue made another visit on Thursday to convey the change of date and check up the proposed plan against the prison routine.

Then came the afternoon of Monday 11 November. At 3.25 p.m. two Volunteers, Joe Murphy and Martin Donovan, presented themselves at the prison gate and asked to see MacNeilus. They were admitted through the wicket to the waiting-room and the gate locked behind them. Their request was telephoned to the main prison buildings by the warder on duty, and they sat down to wait. Five minutes after the first pair had been admitted, a second pair of Volunteers, Christy McSweeney and Paddy Healy, presented themselves at the main gate and asked to see a prisoner from Tipperary, whose name they had. They were admitted to the waiting-room. Three minutes later a third pair of Volunteers, Frank McCarthy and Jerome Donovan, walked to the main gate, asked for another prisoner and were admitted. So far all was well and according to plan – there were no other visitors. If only four of the six had succeeded in getting in, the plan would have gone on. It was all the better that the six had got inside. One of the Volunteers was in clerical attire in order to allay possible suspicion.

Meanwhile the remainder of the rescue party took up their allotted positions in the neighbourhood of the prison, watching carefully for the time when, in accordance with their instructions, they should hold up all persons approaching the prison. The last pair had been five minutes inside the prison when the outside party came into action. Paddy Varien cut the telephone wires leading into the prison and the isolation of the building was completed. Father Dominic, Brigade Chaplain, arrived in the vicinity and remained until the end. Just at the moment when the outside party was coming into action the first unexpected incident happened. A party of military with a horse and cart drove up to the prison gate. The outside party was in a terrible predicament. If their comrades inside had not gone into action and they on the outside held up this party, the whole job might be ruined. Varien was actually at the top of the pole cutting the wires when the military arrived. On the other hand, if our men inside had come into action and the soldiers were admitted, there was a chance of dealing with them at the gate before the alarm could spread to the main buildings. It was decided to let them pass. This was a usual time for police to arrive with prisoners; they would be armed and that contingency had been provided against.

Inside the prison a warder had just come down from the main buildings to take Joe Murphy and Martin Donovan to the visiting cell when the soldiers knocked at the main gate. They had actually been taken through the inside gates and these were being locked behind them when the warder stopped on hearing the knock, to see who was at the outer gate. The other warder opened it and the six Volunteers inside the prison saw the soldiers. Was it a trap? Had someone dropped an incautious word and was the whole plan known to the enemy? Had they waited until six men were inside the prison only to swoop on them? Six men waited tensely, guns ready for instant action, while the soldiers filed in. Would they turn into the waiting-room? No. They continued into the prison grounds, and the warder taking Joe Murphy and Martin Donovan to the visiting cell admitted them through the main gate on the path to the prison buildings. He then continued with his two visitors to the visiting cell and locked them in.

MacNeilus was brought in on the other side of the cell and locked in. The visiting cell had a double barrier between the prisoner and his visitors, and between the two barriers the warder walked up and down during the interviews. The visitors spoke to the prisoner across the barriers. MacNeilus' visitors this evening appeared to be in a hurry to get away (they knew their four companions were inside the prison). After chatting with him for a few minutes they said they had to catch a train and bade him goodbye. MacNeilus, bewildered, tried to prolong the interview. They were insistent. The warder inserted the key in the lock to let them out and then MacNeilus saw the point of their actions. They were waiting for the right key to be inserted in the lock. In a flash they were upon the warder, sandbags in hand; he was down and unconscious without more than a groan. The key turned in the lock, the door opened. 'Jump Mac,' and MacNeilus was over the barrier into the visitors' side of the cell and through the gate into the prison grounds. A revolver was passed to him and all three started to walk at an easy pace towards the main gate by the path inside the prison wall. They had to pass the sentry. Just then they remembered that they had left the visitors' cell door unlocked behind them. Joe Murphy went back and locked it. This was fortunate because just as they arrived at the gate opening into the centre of the prison the sentry was at the end of his beat and within a few yards. If the three of them were together his suspicions might have been aroused, as only two visitors were allowed up together. He had turned and was facing the other way on his beat when Joe Murphy passed behind him. Once past the sentry all three ran towards the main gate.

In the visitors' waiting-room the four Volunteers waited until five minutes had elapsed after the first pair were taken to the visiting cell. Then they suddenly closed on the warder, felled him and disconnected the telephone. They tied the warder securely and took his keys. With these they unlocked the outer wicket gate, but though they found the right key on the bunch they could not open the inner wrought-iron gate. If that key failed to turn the whole job was a failure and neither the two men who were inside nor MacNeilus could get out. They took turns at wrestling with the key but the gate could not be opened. Every second was important. If all had gone according to plan in the visitors' cell MacNeilus and his two companions should appear at any moment round the bend of the path. Another effort. Suddenly the lock shot back! Round the bend came MacNeilus and his two companions at the double; in a second they were through the inside gate and it was locked behind them. Through the wicket gate filed the whole party and that, too, was locked. All the prison gates were locked. No one could get in or out; the rescue party had all the keys – and MacNeilus was again outside the prison walls.

And here the plan broke down. Elaborate arrangements had been made for getting the rescued man safely away. They collapsed because in the tense and rapid sequence of events from the moment of the attack on the warder in the visitors' cell until the whole party were outside the gates, it had not been possible to convey to MacNeilus the arrangements made for his getaway from the vicinity of the jail. The natural jubilation and congratulations of his comrades caused some slight confusion, and a Volunteer had left a bicycle standing outside the prison gate. MacNeilus asked somebody: 'Is this for me?' This particular Volunteer was uncertain, as he was not one of those detailed to cover the getaway. MacNeilus mounted the bicycle and rode away in the direction of Thomas Davis Bridge.

From that moment until after 7 o'clock he was completely lost. He had eluded not only his captors but his rescuers. Later he sent word to brigade headquarters at Wallace's, St Augustine Street, that he had arrived at Walsh's at Clogheen, outside the city. What happened was that he had gone some distance before he realised, not seeing any Volunteers, that he was not on the road it was intended he should take. He turned back and cycled almost to the prison entrance again only to find that everybody had left. He decided to make for Ballingeary, forty miles away. However, after going a short distance his bicycle punctured; he put it inside a fence and started across the fields for Walsh's.

He ran into a Volunteer funeral going to Currikippane graveyard and escorted by a body of armed police. When they passed he got to Walsh's and sent a message into town.

That night he left Walsh's with Dominic Sullivan and Florrie O'Donoghue about 11.30 and, travelling on foot and avoiding the roads as much as possible, arrived next morning at O'Mahony's, Berrings, where the 6th Battalion took over his protection. As he said that night, the little journey illustrated the spirit and national character of the Volunteer movement, for this Donegal man had for his companions a Corkman and a Kerryman.

Head Constable Clarke did not die. Although very seriously wounded he made a good recovery.

MacNeilus had been one of the first to join the Cork Volunteers on their formation, and when the split with Redmond occurred he was one of the minority in the city who remained steadfast in allegiance to the Volunteer executive. He was one of those who paraded under arms on Easter Sunday 1916 and travelled to Macroom with the Cork City Battalion. In all his service he was one of the most active and consistent workers for the ideal of a free Ireland. He was an enthusiastic student of the national language and spoke it fluently.

After his rescue MacNeilus continued in the service of Cork No. 1 Brigade and took part in many activities, including the Dripsey ambush. In the Civil War he was divisional engineering officer, 1st Northern Division, and later commandant of the division. He died at Rosses Point, Co. Sligo, on 15 December 1954. A committee formed in his native Glencolumbkille, County Donegal, has erected a worthy memorial to him near Saint Columba's church, Cashel, where he attended Mass as a boy.

Chapter 2

The 'German Plot' arrests

by the Editor

The British conspiracy against separatist Ireland, known as the 'German Plot', was translated into dramatic action on 17–18 May 1918, with the arrest of scores of leaders of both Sinn Féin and the Irish Volunteers. Seventy-three were immediately deported and jailed in England and Wales. Amongst them was Éamon de Valera, President of Sinn Féin and Executive President of the Volunteers.

Field Marshal Sir John French, who had succeeded Lord Wimborne as Lord Lieutenant and who had arrived in Ireland on 11 May, gave the reason for the arrests in a proclamation in which he stated:

> It has come to our knowledge that certain subjects of his Majesty the King, domiciled in Ireland, have conspired to enter into, and have entered into, treasonable communication with the German enemy ...

In fact, the only evidence of German interest in Irish affairs at that time was the putting ashore of Joe Dowling from a German submarine, on the Clare coast, on 12 April. Dowling, who was arrested immediately on landing, had been a lance-corporal in the Connaught Rangers. Captured by the Germans on the Western Front, he had joined Roger Casement's Irish Brigade in 1915 while a prisoner-of-war in Germany. Two years after Easter Week 1916, he was sent to Ireland by the German general staff to report on the prospects for another Irish rising. Since this was wholly a German idea it was hardly evidence of a plot involving Sinn Féin and the Volunteers. Dowling was court-martialled, sentenced to penal servitude for life and held in jail in England until February 1924 despite resolutions by the Irish Free State Oireachtas.

Before de Valera was arrested and deported he had rallied the nation in face of the threat of conscription. It was he who had drafted the declaration issued by the Mansion House Conference of 18 April 1918 in which it was stated that 'the passing of the Conscription Bill by the British House of Commons must be regarded as a declaration of war on the Irish nation'. The conference was attended by representatives of Sinn Féin, the Irish Parliamentary Party, the parliamentary minority and the trade unions. He had won over the support of the Catholic hierarchy against the measure on the evening of the day on which the conference was held.

The trade unions organised a one-day general strike in protest against conscription, on 23 April, the first general strike in western Europe. With the exception of the north-east, the stoppage was complete and it demonstrated most effectively the chaos that would prevail if the British government attempted to enforce conscription.

'Be calm and confident' was the message de Valera gave the nation as the British took him on board a gunboat at Dún Laoghaire (then Kingstown) en route for Gloucester jail. A week later he and other prisoners were removed to Lincoln jail.

The idea of the 'German Plot' was conjured up by David Lloyd George, the British Premier, and some of his cabinet colleagues soon after the arrest of Dowling. Their immediate object was twofold: to strike a blow at Sinn Féin and the Volunteers from which neither could easily recover, and to injure seriously Ireland's cause in the Allied nations, especially the United States.

It was clear at the time that conscription could not be enforced in Ireland without the use of troops which could not be spared from the Western Front. In fact, any attempt to enforce conscription would deplete rather than augment the British forces aligned against the Germans. The country was largely united in resistance to the measure. Sinn Féin, the organised and disciplined man-power of the Volunteers, the Irish Parliamentary Party, the nationalist parliamentary minority, the Catholic bishops, the trade unions, all stood four-square against conscription. The British government sought to break this solidarity and in the landing of Dowling they saw a ready-made means towards that end. Soon they put in train a sequence of events that culminated in the arrests of 17–18 May and the release of 'news' of the 'German Plot'.

On 24 April, quietly and without notice, the Defence of the Realm Act was altered. There had been serious doubt as to whether it was legal to deport political prisoners from Ireland under the provisions of this Act, and sometime after the 1916 Rising its legality was to be tested in the courts. The proceedings were abruptly dropped when the 1916 deportees were released and permitted to return home from England.

Now the Act was altered so as to ensure the legality of future deportations without trial.

Next the Dublin Castle executive was reorganised and purged of all personnel suspected of Irish leanings. On 1 May Edward Shortt was appointed Chief Secretary for Ireland in place of Henry Duke, who had never liked the idea of conscripting the Irish. 'We might as well enlist Germans,' he said. And on 6 May Lord Wimborne was replaced by Field Marshal Sir John French who was appointed 'His Majesty's Lord Lieutenant-General and General Governor of Ireland'. French, somewhat discredited as a soldier at this time, had been commander of all the British armies in France. He had a simple programme for the application of conscription to the Irish. 'Home Rule will be offered and declined,' he told Lord Riddel, 'then conscription will be enforced. If they will leave me alone I can do what is necessary. I shall notify a date before which recruits must offer themselves in the different districts. If they do not come we will fetch them.' The whole thing was going to be just too easy. Or so French thought.

It did not matter a button that Britain had no moral right to press the issue of conscription. Lloyd George and his colleagues had made up their minds to enforce military service on the Irish (which they had as much right to do as the Germans would have had to conscript the Belgians). They had worked overtime occasionally preparing touching homilies on the rights of 'small nations'. The elegant dialecticians, Arthur James Balfour in particular, had expended a considerable amount of verbiage which touched the justice of a nation's demand for what he termed 'self-determination'. Ireland did not count at all in any of this.

But the conscription of a whole country, so unitedly and resolutely opposed to the measure, constituted a proposition which proved too much even for the talents with which the Lloyd George cabinet was furnished. Whilst a sincere, even fervent desire to subject Ireland to military service was no doubt in existence, a long distance and a rugged road separated the desire from its fruition. And so the British plotters got to work.

The next move in the plot was made on 8 May when Sir Edward Carson, not a member of the Cabinet, issued a statement that 'the Government had the closest evidence in their possession that the Sinn Féin organisation is, and had been, in alliance with Germany'. Such a statement from such a source was ominous.

The removal of the Irish-born General Sir Bryan Mahon from his command and his replacement by General Sir F. Shaw as General Commanding the British troops in Ireland, on 10 May, was the final preparatory step. Sir Bryan, who was to become a Free State senator, took leave of his troops 'with deep regret'.

The arrests followed on 17–18 May and on 24 May the official version of the affair was issued through the Press Bureau in Dublin Castle. It was so phrased as to prove useful to the British-controlled Reuter Press Agency in linking de Valera to Dowling for the purpose of anti-Irish propaganda, particularly in the United States. The Germans had unleashed their spring offensive on the Western Front. Paris was threatened. The French were being bled to death by their terrible losses in manpower. Young American soldiers were sailing to the slaughter. At such a time, the British decided, publication of news of the 'German Plot' would be disastrous for Ireland's aspirations.

Millions believed the story. Millions did not. Soon the plot started to come undone.

It fell to Edward Shortt, the new Chief Secretary, to explain to the House of Commons how it happened that, with Ireland said to be so deeply implicated in a German plot, the Lord Lieutenant was calling for still more recruits from the treasonable Irish. Shortt admitted that 'the number of Irishmen and women who are in active co-operation with the German enemy is very small, but many of them might unwittingly become involved'.

Demands poured in asking Lloyd George to produce proof of the existence of the 'German Plot'. 'Sinn Féiners here are saying that it is a concoction,' said *The New York Times*. An embarrassed British Press began to ask for a public trial of the deported men, but a trial was the last thing that Lloyd George wanted. 'A sad unpleasant story to any friend of Ireland – but it cannot be published,' he countered with customary hypocrisy. The demand for proof continued and at last the British felt constrained to issue a statement. The best that they were able to manage, however, failed to connect Sinn Féin or the Volunteers with any German plot.

The gaff was really blown by Lord Wimborne, the recently deposed Lord Lieutenant, who said he knew nothing of a German plot and did not believe there was one. He addressed the House of Lords on the Irish situation, on 20 June 1918, and was thus reported in the London *Times* of the following day:

Lord Wimborne said that in the present grave condition of national defence, when unity was imperative, it would not be right to embarrass the government in the prosecution of the war.

It was only in so far as the Irish question was, as it had repeatedly declared it to be, a vital war issue that comments and suggestions were justified.

He intended to make no reference to any personal matter, and certainly he would not offer any explanation of the circumstances in which his connection with the Government of Ireland was terminated recently. Amid the confusion of events, one fact which stood out was the change of personnel of the Irish executive. That change was not confined to the offices of the Lord Lieutenant and the Chief Secretary; it included the Lord Chancellor, the Lord Chief Justice, the Commander of the forces, and other functionaries, great and small.

As far as one could see, the changes had removed from the Irish Government all or nearly all who had sympathy with Irish nationality. The change had been so complete and dramatic that one was entitled to ask the Government what it might portend.

In partial explanation, the Government had alleged a German plot; but it seems strange that in view of the highly-specialised means of obtaining information which recently existed in Ireland, neither he nor, as far as he was aware, any member of the Irish Executive had been aware of the existence of the plot until it was discovered by the British Government.

Years afterwards, de Valera said: 'Lord Wimborne, not Mr Lloyd George, told the truth on this matter.' Not until Wimborne had been replaced and the Irish executive purged of all officers held to be in some sympathy with Irish nationality was the 'German Plot' uncovered.

At Dowling's trial it was proved that no documents whatever had been found upon him – yet a statement alleging that documents had been taken from him by the RIC was put forward in justification of the arrest and deportation of more than ninety Irishmen (others were deported after the first swoop of 17–18 May). Men who had been in jail in Ireland for periods covering the time of this alleged plot were rearrested as they emerged from jail and were hastily deported. John Dillon, leader of the Irish Parliamentary Party, said in the House of Commons on 28 July:

> We were told in Dublin that on his [Dowling's] person were discovered documents of the most dangerous and incriminating character, but I am told that the only thing he had were Rosary beads and £35 in money.

After Wimborne's speech in the House of Lords and the trial of Dowling, less was heard of the plot, even from Shortt. He changed his story, too, but not his mind about holding the deportees and deporting others without showing cause. 'The first person to call the attention of the Ministry to incidents connected with the arrest of the soldier Dowling [the man in the Tower, as he came to be called] was Edward Carson,' declared Tim Healy in the House of Commons on 5 August. Mr Healy said:

> Documents were said to have been found on Dowling to implicate de Valera, and which were put forward in justification of the arrests and deportation of nearly 100 Irishmen ... This raised a very serious question of propaganda, because there was immediately issued by the Reuter Press Agency for circulation in America a statement to the effect that documents had been found on Dowling which warranted the arrests of the men now interned. I want to know from the Government which of their officials in the Irish Office was responsible for the issue of these untruths, because it was proved at the trial of this man that not

a single document was captured on him. And yet upon the faith of that story over ninety men occupying important positions in Ireland are now in custody.

On 5 August the *Times* reported as follows:

Mr Tim Healy in the House of Commons urged the appointment of a select committee to examine the documents which, the Government declared, justified the internment of Irish prisoners.

'The others [Irish prisoners] are there under suspicion,' Edward Shortt told the House of Commons on 4 August. 'Supposing they were found innocent of that [i.e. conspiring with Dowling], do you imagine that that would let them out? Of course it would not. They may not be the individuals, but they may be equally dangerous to the State.'

It would appear that Shortt had belatedly shifted ground to some extent since an MP named McKean had stated on 24 June:

Is not this plot, this bogus plot, because it is nothing else, a most humiliating position for honourable men to occupy; to stand over such a monstrous imposition as this? What the Government has got to do is to throw over this whole business of the plot because, after that declaration of Lord Wimborne's, there is no man who will believe in the reality of the plot.

But while the 'plot' was gradually abandoned as a reason for the deportation of the leaders this other reason was put forward for their continued detention: They may be dangerous to the state! In what respect could they be dangerous? As the leaders of a constantly growing national party voicing a claim for the complete freedom of Ireland? As possible victors at the next general election? (Nearly all the most capable and experienced electioneering agents and platform speakers had been deported.)

Two of the most sensational episodes in the 'German Plot' drama were yet to come. On 22 January 1919 four 'German Plot' prisoners escaped from Usk jail in Wales. And on 3 February President de Valera and two others vanished from Lincoln jail. The stories of these escapes are told in the chapters which follow.

Chapter 3

The break-out from Usk jail in Wales by four 'German Plot' prisoners

by Frank Shouldice and George Geraghty

The passengers poured out of the train on platform 2 at Lime Street station, Liverpool, and went swarming towards the barrier. It was 6 o'clock in the morning of Wednesday 22 January 1919. Four travel-weary young men, keeping close together and trying to be as inconspicuous as possible, mingled with the crowd, their probing eyes on the look-out for danger. They were fugitives from one of his Britannic Majesty's jails out of which they had moved without permission about ten hours earlier. For all they knew, every policeman and detective in Britain could be on the look-out for them.

A sudden disturbance broke out at the barrier and the four men tensed. This was the last thing they wanted – but there was worse to follow. A police constable pushed his way through the crowd and, without hesitation, put his hand on the shoulder of one of the four – Frank Shouldice, a 'dangerous' man in the eyes of the British government. Shouldice had fought in the Rising of 1916 and, in and out of jail, had been under surveillance by British agents for the past three years.

Joe McGrath, George Geraghty and Barney Mellows, the companions of Shouldice, moved unobtrusively towards the policeman. But relief for Shouldice came unexpectedly from another quarter. A coloured man, the centre of the commotion, rolled his eyes and shook his head violently. 'Nunno, nunno,' he shouted, 'not that man.' The policeman removed his hand, courteously proffered his apologies to Shouldice and moved off through the crowd in search of someone who had robbed the coloured man on the train. And the four most wanted men in Britain moved through the barrier towards the streets of Liverpool.

They were not out of danger yet. Their pre-arranged hide-out was Murphy's pub at Sefton, Clover Street, and they had to hang around the city streets until opening time an hour later. It was an hour of great anxiety for them. The fates were kind to them, however, and just after seven o'clock that morning they slipped into Murphy's and out of harm's way for the time being, reasonably safe until they began the journey home to Ireland and resumed the dangerous work which had been interrupted, eight months previously, by their arrest in the 'German Plot' round-up of 17–18 May 1918 – the work of winning the independence of their country.

In the months preceding the escape, a mass break-out by the twenty Irish political prisoners in Usk jail had been planned, but the great flu of 1918, which ravaged Britain and Ireland as well as the rest of the world, had set that plan awry. Too many of the prisoners had been ill and were still too weak to go over the wall on 21 January. Ultimately, only McGrath, Shouldice, Mellows and Geraghty went out. They were no strangers to British 'restraint'. Shouldice, after the Rising, had been interned in Frongoch, but no more than any of the others did he intend to endure imprisonment for a moment longer than was necessary. Almost from the day they arrived in Usk jail, which is in the town of Usk, near Monmouth in south Wales, the prisoners had been seeking ways of escape.

From Wednesday 22 January 1919, there was a hue and cry for the four Irishmen, but they lay low in Liverpool until arrangements had been made to bring them back to Ireland. Meanwhile, their descriptions were published in the British newspapers:

WANTED

Sinn Féin prison breakers. George Geraghty (40), dark complexion, heavy dark moustache, weight 11½ stone, 6 ft in height; Joseph McGrath (28), clean shaven, pale complexion, loose lipped and drawls, 6 ft in height, 12 stone; Herbert Mellows (28), clean shaven, hair long and light brown, pale complexion, wears glasses, his overcoat is rather too long for him, 10 stone; Frank Shouldice (25), round boyish face, fresh complexion, appears shy, has little Irish accent, 6 ft in height, 12 stone. The others have much accent.

Frank Shouldice had been arrested near Ballaghaderreen, County Roscommon, where he was reorganising the Volunteers. McGrath and Mellows had been picked up in Dublin, and Geraghty had actually been taken from the spire of Roscommon cathedral, on which he was working at his trade of mason.

The so-called 'German plotters' were put on board a British gunboat at Dún Laoghaire, on the evening of 18 May 1918, and taken to Holyhead. On board the gunboat they were served with an order for their internment at Frongoch but, on arrival at Holyhead about 10.30 p.m., they were marched under heavily armed guard to a disused army camp. They were held there until Monday morning when they were ordered to move once more, and they learned then that they were to be separated and sent to various prisons in Britain. Shouldice, McGrath, Mellows and Geraghty were in a party of twenty which included W.J. Brennan-Whitmore, Paudeen O'Keeffe, Frank Lawless, Éamonn Moane and Dick Coleman. After a day-long train journey they found themselves in the little town of Usk. Again, under armed escort, they were marched through the winding streets to the jail. Townspeople looked on and wondered who they were.

Resistance by the prisoners to an attempt to treat them as convicts began almost immediately the jail gates had closed on them. After a bath they were ordered to wear prison clothes. They refused. Well experienced in the art of obstructing British 'justice' as administered to Irish political prisoners, they stood on their rights. They were not convicts. They were political internees.

Governor Young was nonplussed. His experience was limited to controlling convicts. At a loss as to how he should deal with the stand taken by the Irish, he telephoned the Home Office for instructions. The outcome was that, before they entered their cells for the night, the internees had won their first victory: the right of association, of receiving and sending letters and parcels; the right to smoke and wear their own clothes. Nevertheless, conditions were bad enough for a few weeks. Smokes and food were scarce until parcels began to arrive from home. With the parcels came the first hope of escape.

When the summer had given way to autumn, however, the prisoners seemed to be no nearer to freedom. Then their cook, Billy Loughran, relinquished his job. He had grown tired of it.

George Geraghty took over from him, with McGrath, Shouldice and Mellows whom he insisted he needed as helpers.

The new kitchen staff had their eyes open for a means of escape. A corridor off the kitchen had to be kept clean by the kitchen staff. On the first duty-day of the new staff a door in the corridor slammed and a key dropped out of the lock. Quick as a darting snake Joe McGrath's right hand flashed to the floor and he had the key in his pocket. Though it was not a key to the cells, their possession of it might be a stage on the way to freedom, they felt. But would the key be missed and the jail authorities thus be alerted to the possibility of an escape bid? To learn the answer they had to find out whether the door was frequently used and locked at night; as they had to be in their cells by eight o'clock they obviously could not keep watch. So Joe McGrath put the key back in the lock and smeared the door hinges with some soap that had been softened in warm water. He left the door open. If it was closed the hardened soap would crack.

For three days the four men resisted the urge to take a look at the hinges, until at last McGrath and Geraghty sneaked over to the door and made an examination. The soap was intact. So it seemed that the door was rarely, if ever, used. Now they could chance taking the key.

The next step to freedom was taken when Frank Shouldice and McGrath persuaded a schoolmaster to bring them in some shaving soap and nail files. Files are traditionally associated with jail breaks, but anything less likely than a nail file as an instrument of escape is hard to envisage. Yet the prisoners intended to fashion their key to freedom by using the nail files on the key to the door in the corridor.

The political prisoners in Usk spent a lot of time in the

exercise yard where they were closely watched by a warder. That was the way they wanted it, for the warder carried the key to the cells on his belt, and they needed to sketch his key before they commenced to file their own key. The warder took no notice of the art-work, and once it was finished McGrath and Shouldice filed with a will, shaping their key to fit the locks on the cell doors. To make sure the key would be cut correctly they removed a lock from a disused cell, using a screwdriver which they had made from a kitchen poker, another tedious task that involved hours of rubbing the poker against the sandstone floor of the kitchen.

At long last the key was ready to be tested under operational conditions. Opposite the kitchen was a cell which was used as a potato store from which a warder drew rations every morning. The lock on the door of that cell would be ideal for the purpose of the test. The hearts of the four prisoners leapt with excitement when they tested the key in the lock and found that it worked. They tried it a second time – just to make sure. And their luck ran out. The key broke in the lock. Dumbfounded, they looked at each other and at the broken part of the key in McGrath's hand, shocked in the realisation that not alone had their immediate hopes been dashed but also, if the warder could not open the cell next time he tried, the lock would be examined, the broken key discovered and measures taken to prevent an escape.

In quiet desperation McGrath set to work with his nail file and a pocket knife, and by picking the lock he managed to retrieve the other broken part of the key. Despite the success of this salvage operation, it was four rather dispirited men who moved away from the potato store door. But their dejection did not last long; soon they were trying to make another key, this time from the blunt block-tin knives which were issued to the prisoners. Nothing came of this effort. The tin was too soft.

Having racked their brains in vain for some other means of getting a key, or making one, they saw no possibility of their opening the doors that mattered. Then, following the lapse of a few weeks, fate was kind to them again. One of their regular warders, Williams, went on vacation and his place was taken by a talkative friendly ex-British soldier who had served in Ireland with a cavalry regiment. Softened up by tea, tobacco and talk of horses, the ex-soldier agreed to bring out letters from them. In this way McGrath, through friends in England, established a line of communication with his home in Ireland. Confirmation that the line was working was given in code in the *Irish Independent* which was sent in to the prisoners every day. 'Found, outside the Tivoli, a bunch of keys' was the wording of an advertisement in the 'Lost and Found' section. The boys in Usk got the message and soon they were busy. A copy of the key to the cells was cut in cardboard, the dimensions of the keyhole were carefully drawn, and these were taken out by the friendly warder, in all innocence of what he was doing. Within a few days the prisoners had received gifts of a number of pan-loaves in which were baked a blank key and three files. For four determined men it was a labour of love to file the blank. The new key worked. Now they could open the cells.

Possession of the key, however, was not a passport to freedom. The British government did not hold the view that iron bars did not a prison make, or that stone walls did not do likewise. And so Usk jail was bounded by a stout high wall.

Nor did the British Government provide measuring instruments for the use of prisoners. As a mason, however, George

Geraghty was able to estimate the height of the wall without difficulty. He knew that rubble mason work was built of standard fourteen-inch courses, and by counting the courses he calculated the height of the wall. He found that the prisoners needed a twenty-foot ladder. Where were they going to get it? In solving that problem the prisoners once more showed their ingenuity. From roller towels of very strong material they made the two sides of a rope ladder. Wood chips were provided for the fires in the jail. Some of the chips were of ash about nine inches long, and from them the prisoners made rungs for the ladder. The finished ladder fitted nicely into a boot box which was easily concealed from the jail authorities.

Curtains on the kitchen windows hung from half-inch iron bars. McGrath put in a request that they be permitted to remove the curtains to allow more light into the kitchen. The request was granted and the iron bars were made into hooks.

Handball was played by the prisoners, and Governor Young, who had never previously seen the game, became an enthusiastic fan. Geraghty was given permission to build side-walls at right angles to the wall they used for the games, to make a proper ball-alley. In this task some of the other prisoners acted as labourers for Geraghty whose thoughts were ranging further than the side-walls of a ball-alley. Amongst the rubble he was using for his building work he found a piece of the coping from the top of the outer jail wall. It was a most useful find as it showed the exact shape of the coping – the hooks had to fit the coping tightly, otherwise the ladder would come down on top of the escaping prisoners.

The first test of the ladder was unsuccessful. They tried out the hooks on a lower wall but they stretched badly when Joe McGrath put his twelve-stone weight on the ladder. Somehow they found two more pieces of iron and, having fashioned them and bound them together with an old singlet, they used them to reinforce the hooks.

Winter was sweeping its icy hand across Wales, and the terrible 1918 influenza was raging in Britain and Ireland as Shouldice and his comrades made their preparations for escape. Christmas had come and gone without the prisoners having an opportunity to get out of Usk jail. Geraghty had been given ten days' parole to visit his home in Ireland because his sister was dangerously ill with flu. She was dead before he reached Roscommon. When he returned to Usk he found that McGrath, Mellows and seven other prisoners were down with flu. Two bottles of Jameson which he had brought back were used as medicine; it was the only medicine available because the local doctor in Usk was too busy to attend Irish prisoners. Eventually, a doctor arrived from London and ordered the invalids to a sick ward. Geraghty acted as night nurse to his comrades.

In the meantime Shouldice and the others who were well had removed about twelve feet of piping from an old lamp standard which stood at the edge of the ball-alley. It was an obstruction to the handballers, they claimed, and they were allowed to shift it. A good length of piping was just what they needed to lift the ladder to the top of the jail wall.

Because of the flu epidemic and the dangerous illness of many of the prisoners, the Volunteers had been demanding release from Usk or transfer to another jail. Dick Coleman had died in Usk in December. The authorities became alarmed. On 20 January news came through that all the Usk prisoners were to be transferred to Gloucester almost immediately. The escape bid had to be made without further delay. It was then or never.

McGrath and Mellows were still weak after the flu but, with Shouldice and Geraghty, they decided to make the attempt the following night. The plan for a mass break-out had to be abandoned because of the illness of the other prisoners.

On Tuesday 21 January the prisoners sought the permission of the governor to have the cells left unlocked all night, so that packing could be finished and everything in readiness for the transfer by the following morning. The governor granted permission and the conspirators chortled with glee. No more need to bother about a key. The permission also meant that there would be no roll-call when the prisoners went to their cells at eight o'clock. And so the escape would not be discovered, they hoped, before breakfast the following morning.

As the other prisoners went in from the yard that evening, Shouldice, Geraghty, McGrath and Mellows hid themselves and, after a short wait, sneaked across the yard to the wall. It took but a moment to fix the rope ladder to the coping, and with Shouldice, the fittest of the four, acting as ballast, Geraghty shinned up to the top. Next went Barney Mellows, still so weak that he felt the wall was shaking under him. Then McGrath climbed. When Shouldice climbed, the ladder no longer had ballast and it swayed violently, but he swarmed up, hand over hand, like a sailor. The ladder was quickly drawn up and let down outside the wall. Then they climbed down. Next the ladder was pulled down and hidden in a cabbage patch. It transpired that the cabbage patch was in Governor Young's garden, and they left him the ladder as a farewell present.

The escapers had their first brush with danger immediately they were clear of the precincts of the jail. Approaching them were four warders, including one named Lovell who knew them well and whose voice they now recognised. The warders were making their way back to the jail. Brazening it out, the four fugitives carried on, trusting to the darkness and the unexpectedness of the encounter to see them through safely. Lovell, no doubt believing that all his charges were secure in their prison beds, passed them by without recognising them. Two of the four warders had come from Gloucester that day, to form part of the prisoners' escort during the transfer next morning.

Once clear of the town the escapers headed towards Pontypool railway junction where they hoped to catch the Fishguard express. At a crossroads Shouldice had to climb a signpost and light a match to read directions.

Bravely they strode on, their pace the best that could be managed by the least fit. At last they saw the lights of the junction. But disappointment awaited them: the Fishguard express, they were told, would not stop there. They had no alternative but to push on towards the nearest place where it might stop. This was Pilemile, about four miles distant. Doggedly they pressed on, their steps more urgent, anxiety welling up within them. Pilemile, when they reached it, had nothing to offer them. The station was deserted and the gates securely locked. It was heartbreaking. As one, the four vented their feelings on British travel facilities, the British government, and Pilemile in particular, in strongly turned phrases.

Their position was becoming desperate, for they had to reach cover before daylight. The receptionist at an hotel in Pilemile where, posing as Americans they inquired about a car, was not encouraging. She told them that all the young hackney drivers were in the army, and that the old men would not travel by night. There was one slight hope, she added by way of afterthought: a Mr Evans of the Mews, although an elderly man, might be willing to undertake a journey to Newport. He was willing, following some persuasive talk by Joe McGrath. He would drive the four Americans to Newport, to catch a train to Shrewsbury. Having first caused the four some moments of suspense while he produced a pocket-watch and studied it carefully, Mr Evans said: 'Aye, Oi think we can moike it.'

Soon the exhausted escapers were lolling back in the Evans automobile, three drawing contentedly on cigars which had remained from their Christmas stock. Geraghty was the odd man out of character with the part of an American; he insisted on smoking his old clay pipe. Evans, intent on getting the journey finished and returning to his bed, gave no attention to his passengers.

The Liverpool train was already in the station at Newport when the Evans party arrived on the platform. Also on the platform was Tom O'Loughlin, a draper of Parliament Street, Dublin. He was a Volunteer and the four escapers were well known to him. It is a moot point whether he was more surprised to see the fugitives than they to see him. He was in England to study train times in connection with another escape project. (Plans were in train to get Éamon de Valera out of Lincoln jail.)

This unscheduled escape of four men from Usk might lead to more stringent security measures in other jails and upset the de Valera project. So Tom O'Loughlin thought, but Frank Shouldice, Joe McGrath and the others brushed aside his fears on this account, and they also got sufficient money from him for their journey. Then, with the train about to move out, they divided into pairs and bought tickets to Shrewsbury. At Shrewsbury they booked to Liverpool, again in pairs, and dozed through the journey. At Lime Street station they had the worst moment of their escape when the policeman put his hand on the shoulder of Shouldice. By seven o'clock on Wednesday 22 January 1919, they were under cover in Murphy's pub.

McGrath and Geraghty remained a few days in Murphy's before they were smuggled aboard a boat by Steve Lanigan, an IRB man who handled more 'goods' for the organisation than most others. (He held an important post in the Liverpool Custom House.) They arrived safely at the North Wall and went to Billy Byrne's house on the North Circular Road, where a jubilant Billy greeted them and placed a bottle of whiskey before them. Next day they went to Doherty's, No. 4 James Terrace, Dolphin's Barn, and soon the city had swallowed them up.

Mellows and Shouldice had to remain in Liverpool until Lanigan had made arrangements for their passage some little time later.

During that period they changed their hide-out twice. A week after their escape Lanigan brought them two suits of dungarees and, disguised as seamen, they were aboard ship in Liverpool an hour before sailing time.

None of the crew spoke a word to them, but they were shown to the forecastle where they lay down quietly in the bunks. As they lay there, two detectives were searching the ship for them. At one stage they overheard the detectives talking to an officer, but no search of the crew's quarters was made and, after a calm sea voyage, the two jail-breakers arrived in Dublin. The Liverpool detectives must have reported to Dublin that they had made a thorough search of the ship, for there were no police to meet it on its arrival. Frank and Barney simply went ashore with the crew.

They hired a side-car and, following the trail of their

comrades, turned up at the hospitable house of Billy Byrne near Mountjoy jail. There they lay low for a couple of days, after which they crossed to the south side of the city, to friends of Barney's who lived near Francis Street, in the Coombe. After another couple of days they parted, Mellows to stay elsewhere in the city, and Shouldice to head back to Ballaghaderreen, there to resume his work of organising the Volunteers.

The release of the 'German Plot' deportees, which followed on 8 March, allowed all four who had escaped from Usk to walk boldly in the open as free men – for a short time, at least. But in the meantime three more 'German Plot' men were to take 'French leave' of their jailers.

Chapter 4

Escape of de Valera, McGarry and Milroy ('German Plot' prisoners) from Lincoln jail

by Bill Kelly

It was a moment of despair for Michael Collins. 'Dev,' he whispered, 'the key's broken in the lock!' Beside him in the darkness of a winter evening, outside an outer gate of Lincoln jail, Harry Boland was aghast. Could it be that the careful planning of months had just been wrecked?

Two of the three men on the wrong side of the jail gate, Seán McGarry and Seán Milroy, froze, shocked by the impact of the whispered words. The third man paused a moment, then slowly inserted a skeleton key in the lock, pushed out the head of the broken key, turned the skeleton key smoothly and pushed the gate open. He was Éamon de Valera. With McGarry and Milroy he walked out of Lincoln jail and into freedom. It was 3 February 1919. All three had been 'German Plot' prisoners since 17 May of the previous year.

Much had happened since the British invented the 'German Plot', swooped on prominent Sinn Féin and Volunteer leaders in Dublin and the provinces, and deported scores of them to England and Wales – and almost anybody could have faked a better excuse for the arrests. The First World War had ended and Sinn Féin had swept the country at the general election in December 1918. Dáil Éireann had met in the Mansion House, Dublin, on 21 January 1919, and adopted the Declaration of Independence, Ireland's address to the free nations of the world, and a democratic programme. De Valera himself, whose election address had been seized by the authorities in Lincoln jail, had not only been re-elected for East Clare but had also received twice the number of votes cast in East Mayo for John Dillon, his Irish Parliamentary Party opponent. Home Rule was dead and Sinn Féin, reconstituted under the influence of its militant elements, had openly defied the British Empire. Tar barrels had blazed and republican Ireland was jubilant. Ballad-makers were busy, and the youth of the country sang a new song of insuppressible extravagance:

> *Up de Valera, he's the champion of the right,*
> *We'll follow him to battle 'neath the orange, green and white;*
> *When next we challenge England, we'll beat her in the fight,*
> *And we'll crown de Valera King of Ireland.*

The Sinn Féin Ard Fheis met in the Mansion House, Dublin, on 25–26 October 1917, and elected de Valera (unopposed) to be president of the party. The committee which drew up the agenda unanimously accepted this formula, devised by de Valera, to reconcile divergent views as to the form of government of Ireland:

Sinn Féin aims at securing the international recognition of

Ireland as an independent Irish republic. Having achieved that status, the Irish people may by referendum freely choose their own form of government.

Arthur Griffith and Father Michael O'Flanagan were elected vice-presidents of Sinn Féin. Two days later, at a secret convention held in the buildings of the Gaelic Athletic Association headquarters in Jones's Road (now Croke Park), Dublin, de Valera was elected president of the executive of the Irish Volunteers which body was independent of Sinn Féin.

On 17 May 1918, de Valera attended a meeting of the executive of the Volunteers at 44 Parnell Square, Dublin. Michael Collins, Director of Organisation of the Volunteers, attended the meeting and warned the executive that the British were preparing to seize the leaders of Sinn Féin and the Volunteer movement. He had already sent Joe O'Reilly, one of his resourceful lieutenants, by bike to warn as many as possible of the Sinn Féin leaders in the city and advise them not to sleep at home for a while.

Another warning was given to the Sinn Féin executive which met the same night. A few heeded the warning. Most of the others did not take it seriously; they did not yet know Collins and could not appreciate the value of the intelligence service that he was even then creating. Also, some of the Sinn Féin leaders took the view that the arrests would stiffen the national resistance to conscription. The news of the arrests would shock and arouse the country, they argued, and so they made no attempt to escape.

A long list of the leaders who were to be arrested that night had been handed to Collins that very day. It was provided by Joe Kavanagh of the political branch or 'G' Division of the

Dublin Metropolitan Police. He gave the list to Tomás Gay, the librarian in the Corporation library in Capel Street, on 17 May. Gay rushed it to Harry Boland who then had a tailoring shop in Middle Abbey Street. In his office in Bachelor's Walk Collins got the list from Boland. On 15 May he had been given a similar warning of impending arrests, by a young detective named Éamonn Broy who was attached to police headquarters in Brunswick Street, now Pearse Street. Broy was not sure when the swoop would take place – he thought it would be on Friday 17 May. Kavanagh confirmed the date: it was the night of 17–18 May.

President de Valera, already in his early thirties, was older than the majority of his colleagues in Sinn Féin and the Volunteers and he was a family man. He decided to ignore the warning. After the meeting of the Volunteer executive on 17 May, he set out by train for his home in the little village of Greystones, some fifteen miles south-east of Dublin. But he never made it home. At Greystones station two of his fellow travellers, who had joined the train at Bray, introduced themselves. They were RIC men. On the platform they were joined by an inspector of the force and de Valera was a prisoner within seconds of alighting from the train. The RIC handed him over to the military who conveyed him to Dún Laoghaire where they put him on board a man-of-war.

Most of the leaders of Sinn Féin and the principal Volunteer officers were swept into the British net. During that night and the following day they were rounded up and brought into police barracks in many parts of the country. Michael Collins, to whose warning such little heed had been paid, actually cycled past the raiding party that was arresting Seán McGarry, General Secretary of the Volunteers, at his home in Clontarf.

He had cycled from Vaughan's Hotel, Parnell Square, to warn McGarry, but arrived too late. He waited until the raiders had searched the house and carried away McGarry. He then decided that it was the safest place in Dublin in which to spend the remainder of the night, went in and slept soundly. For some time afterwards he stayed frequently in the house of Joe McDonagh who was another of those taken in the swoop.

In addition to de Valera, those arrested included Arthur Griffith, Count Plunkett, Countess Markievicz, Frank Fahy, Seán Etchingham, Joe McGuinness, Maud Gonne MacBride, Paudeen O'Keeffe, Mrs Tom Clarke, Pierce McCan, Mick Spillane, W.T. Cosgrave, Dick Coleman, Dr Richard Hayes, P. Ó Siochfhradha ('An Seabhac'), W.J. Brennan-Whitmore, Seán McGarry and Seán Milroy. They also included Joe McGrath, Frank Shouldice, George Geraghty and Barney Mellows whose escape from Usk jail is described by Shouldice and Geraghty in the preceding chapter. Seán McEntee and Denis McCullough were arrested in Belfast; Tom Hunter and others in Cork.

By the evening of 18 May there were seventy-three prisoners on board the man-of-war. They were told that they were about to be deported and interned in Britain under a regulation of the Defence of the Realm Act. At six o'clock the ship sailed for Holyhead. Following some days in an internment camp near Holyhead, the prisoners were divided into two groups. One group was sent to Usk in Wales and the other to Gloucester. De Valera and Griffith were amongst the prisoners sent to Gloucester and, after a short time there, de Valera and others were changed to Lincoln.

Éamon de Valera was no stranger to British jails. Sentenced to death after the Rising of 1916, his sentence was commuted to penal servitude for life and he was successively held in Dartmoor, Maidstone, Lewes and Pentonville, until his release on 17 June 1917.

From his barred cell-window high up in Lincoln jail, de Valera could see a pleasant green countryside. Six months after his arrest he knew that the menace of conscription had ended with the collapse of the Central Powers and the end of the war, following more than four years of holocaust in which 50,000 Irishmen had given their lives 'that small nationalities might be free'. He knew also that the British had no intention of releasing the 'German Plot' prisoners in the immediate future. The dreary days in the jail he spent in the study of mathematics, reading works such as Wolfe Tone's autobiography and eventually reflecting on the problems of Sinn Féin, especially since the party's overwhelming success at the general election in December. From these reflections the urge to escape evolved. He must get out of Lincoln and speak for Ireland at the Peace Conference. Inevitably, the British would do all in their power to block the presentation of Ireland's case; on recognition of the validity of the case by the United States, in particular, seemed to rest the sole hope for an Irish republic. 'Government with the consent of the governed' was the famous principle of self-determination enunciated by President Woodrow Wilson of the United States. And where could it be applied with more justice than in the case of Ireland, thought de Valera.

In their walks around the exercise grounds in Lincoln jail, de Valera and his close comrades, Seán McGarry and Seán Milroy, noticed a door in the wall of the grounds, which seemed to give on to the surrounding fields. If only they could open their cell doors, they thought, and the doors in the corridors also, then one of the jail gates and finally this door in the exercise grounds. And if only their colleagues outside could organise a party to spirit them away – they could escape. There were many hypotheses involved. But there was a splendid IRA organisation being developed also, both in Ireland and Britain, and there was the determination to free de Valera.

De Valera served Mass for the prison chaplain, and some time before Christmas he had the opportunity to take a wax impression of the chaplain's key. The key had been left carelessly on a desk in the sacristy and it was a comparatively simple matter for de Valera to press it into a lump of warm wax from the butts of altar candles. With the taking of the impression, the first move in the escape bid had been made. The problem then was to get a key cut to match the impression, or so the prisoners thought; they believed that with the key they could open all the doors and gates that barred their way to freedom. What they did not know, however, was that the chaplain's key was not a master-key.

Seán Milroy was an excellent black-and-white artist and he had a brilliant idea which resulted in Mrs Seán McGarry in Dublin receiving a humorous Christmas card. The card was as subtle as it was humorous, for it depicted one of the prisoners, filled with the stuff of seasonal good cheer, outside the door of his house, making the most ineffectual use of a minutely-drawn latch key. Above the sketch were the words: 'Christmas 1917; I can't get in'. In another section of the card the prisoner, holding a huge key, was shown in his cell, above the legend: 'Christmas 1918; I can't get out'. No doubt the jail censor had smiled in appreciation of the grim humour of a prisoner. What he did not realise was that the huge key in the sketch was one of the jail keys, exact in every detail. And so the card was allowed through to Mrs McGarry who did not understand its significance. De Valera and his friends sent out veiled messages, one of which reached Michael Collins. About the same time an explanatory letter in Irish reached Paddy O'Donoghue at his home in Greenhayes, Manchester. Paddy, then in charge of the IRA in Manchester, made haste to Dublin to give the letter to Collins. Michael Collins and Con Collins got busy. A key was made by Gerald Boland, Harry's brother, once a fitter in the employment of the Dublin Corporation. In the time-honoured method the key was inside a cake baked for the prisoners. The cake was brought into the jail and presented to the prisoners by Fintan Murphy who had been sent over by GHQ in Dublin. Amazingly, the key escaped the most intensive exploration of the cake by a warder – but it did not fit the lock; it was too small.

Another Milroy postcard arrived in Dublin. This one featured a beautiful Celtic design and the words: 'Eocair na Saoirse' (The Key to Freedom).

In the meantime Collins had sent over Frank Kelly from Sinn Féin headquarters in Harcourt Street, Dublin, to collaborate with Paddy O'Donoghue in spying out the land about the jail. They saw immediately that the gate in the exercise grounds did, in fact, give on to the surrounding fields, and they reported also that it faced the main gate of a military hospital from which there were always considerable comings and goings by convalescent soldiers and others. The prison gate was sheeted with corrugated iron.

The Key to Freedom postcard was relayed to O'Donoghue and he had a matching key made by a Manchester locksmith. And so the prisoners got another cake that contained another key. The second cake was brought in to them by Frank Kelly. It had been baked in Manchester by a Mrs O'Sullivan and taken to Lincoln by a Miss Talty, an Irish girl who resided in Manchester. When the prisoners tried out the key they found that it opened some of the doors only; it was then they realised that the chaplain's key was not a master-key.

Despite these setbacks, plans for the escape of de Valera, McGarry and Milroy, by their colleagues on the outside, were well advanced when the Dáil sat on 21 January 1919. At the roll-call other teachtaí answered for Michael Collins and Harry Boland, who were in England and in the vicinity of Lincoln jail where they had established communications with the prisoners through an influential local man who had the right to visit them.

The escape of the president of Sinn Féin and of the Volunteers demanded their presence on the spot. Boland, with Seán T. O'Kelly (afterwards president of Ireland), was secretary of the Sinn Féin executive and a bosom-friend of Collins. He was also a man of brains, and boundless energy and determination. Gay and kindly, and utterly devoid of self-interest, he had been through the Rising of 1916 and was afterwards imprisoned in Dartmoor and Lewes. His father was a member of the IRB in Dublin and his uncle was a Fenian organiser in America. Harry Boland was himself a member of the GAA and had been in the Volunteers since before the 1916 Rising.

When the first Dáil assembled in the Mansion House, in January 1919, one of its decisions was to appoint three envoys to place Ireland's claim to freedom before the Peace Conference in Paris. They were Éamon de Valera, Arthur Griffith and Count Plunkett, all three of whom were in British jails. It was believed that no one else could make a greater impact on the conference or speak for Irish freedom with the same authority as de Valera. And so the entire resources of the

IRA headquarters in Dublin and of the IRA in Britain were at the disposal of Collins in the planning and organising of the escape, which involved three cakes, three keys, many blanks, files, key-cutting tools, a rope ladder and relays of motor cars.

In the meantime the prisoners had not been pinning their hopes exclusively on help from the outside. Alderman Paddy de Loughrey of Kilkenny, one of the 'German Plot' men, had an interest in locks. He succeeded in dismantling a jail lock which was found to be a multiple lock. The key that would open this lock would serve as a master-key, so he asked for blanks and files. In a short time the blanks and files, together with key-cutting tools, got through to the prisoners, inside a third cake. De Loughrey got to work.

Frank Kelly had been loitering in the vicinity of the jail, drinking in the local pubs and assimilating the casual talk of warders and soldiers. He was able to report to Collins that the presence of so many people near the main gate of the hospital, far from being a hindrance, might even be an advantage to the rescue party. The fields around the jail were a popular place for courting by the convalescent soldiers and their girlfriends, and strolling figures in the darkness of a February night might be thought to have no more sinister purpose than a little romance.

To get the prisoners out of Lincoln jail was but part of the overall escape problem, and it might not prove to be as difficult as getting them away from Lincoln and out of England. There were military restrictions, including restrictions on the use of petrol and, even though the war had ended, strangers were still looked upon with suspicion.

Then came the news of the escape of McGrath, Shouldice, Geraghty and Mellows from Usk on 21 January. Would this mean a closer watch on the men in Lincoln jail? There was a hue-and-cry and the newspapers were full of the Usk escape story. It was the sensation of the time.

Nevertheless, Collins and Boland were satisfied that the prisoners could be taken to safety after they had got out of jail and, having completed the arrangements for the escape, they returned to Dublin. Some days later Seán Etchingham was released from Lincoln on grounds of ill-health. He had a message for Collins who searched Dublin to find him. The message received, Collins and Boland re-crossed the Irish Sea at once. This time the job was definitely on.

Immediately that they arrived in Lincoln, Collins and Boland contacted Paddy O'Donoghue and went over the final details of the plan with him, to make sure that everything was in order. O'Donoghue was letter perfect. Liam MacMahon, Chief of Communications and in charge of funds, had organised the escape transport. A relay of cars, under the direction of Fintan Murphy and two other reliable men, was in readiness from the jail to Worksop, and from Worksop to Sheffield and from Sheffield to Manchester. The escape route had been carefully studied and a hiding-place had been prepared in Manchester. Satisfied that the escape must succeed unless their luck was out, Collins and Boland waited for darkness. Then, accompanied by Frank Kelly, they arrived at the jail which stood a few hundred yards from the outskirts of the town. All three were armed. Kelly also carried a rope ladder which had been sent over from Dublin on the mail boat. The ladder, which had been made by the Belfast IRA, had been taken secretly to Dublin and tested by Collins.

Like stalking Indians the three men made their way through the fields. The night was cold and damp, and every now and then they could hear voices and the sound of footsteps swishing through the grass; they could hear but not see the British soldiers and their lady loves, a number of whom were grouped by a stile which straddled the line of escape. This made the prospects for the getaway chancy enough. Collins took the ladder from Kelly and sent him into the darkness to scout for a safer alternative route across the fields to where Paddy O'Donoghue had a taxi waiting.

Collins and Boland lay down on the wet grass and awaited zero hour, their eyes fixed in the general direction of a window high up in the deeper darkness that vaguely indicated Lincoln jail. About 7.30 p.m. Boland flashed a torch that Collins had handed him. An interval of a second or so, then another flash and yet another. Three staccato flashes. He dare not hold the light longer in case an alert warder should notice it and become suspicious. Anxiously, they awaited an answering signal. It came, a peculiarly vivid flash that lit up an upper-storey window for a few moments. Milroy had ignited a whole box of matches to indicate that all was well and that de Valera, McGarry and himself were about to come out.

Cautiously, Collins and Boland approached the gate in the wall of the exercise grounds. When they reached it, however, they found it was protected on the outside by a vertically barred gate, sheeted with corrugated iron. Then they heard the approaching footsteps of the three prisoners. Collins inserted his duplicate master-key in the gate lock and attempted to turn it but, to his horror, the key stuck fast. Desperately, he tried to free it but the head broke off and remained in the keyhole just as the inside gate swung open and de Valera, Milroy and McGarry arrived at the other side of the outer gate. In an agonised whisper Collins urgently told them of the catastrophe.

McGarry had already broken a key in another lock but de Valera's key opened it. On their way through the jail and into the grounds they had re-locked every door and gate which they had opened. The keys used were master-keys made by de Loughrey.

What was to be done now? All seemed to be lost. Rescuers and prisoners exchanged whispers through the gate, and they could see each other dimly through holes in the corrugated iron sheeting. Then de Valera stepped forward, thrust his de Loughrey master-key into the lock and, by the greatest of good fortune, pushed out the head of the key that Collins had used. The gate creaked open and the prisoners stepped into the field and freedom. Time only for hurried expressions of relief, a warm embrace and a buoyant thump of Collins' hand on Dev's shoulders before all five were off through the fields. With a cheery 'good night' to the courting couples by the stile, they walked past the hospital gate and across a field to a place where Paddy O'Donoghue was waiting with a taxi. There had been no need of the rope ladder and they left it behind in one of the fields. Nor was there any question of waiting for the return of Frank Kelly with his report on alternative escape routes.

The prisoners were out of Lincoln jail. Would they also succeed in getting out of Britain and back to Ireland? That was the question. The most difficult part of the escape bid lay ahead.

All five crowded into the taxi with Paddy O'Donoghue and were driven to Lincoln city centre where Collins and Boland dropped off to catch a London-bound train. On to Worksop the taximan was told. To throw trackers off the scent, O'Donoghue had given the name of a certain hotel as their destination and, on arrival there, the taxi was paid off and all four walked into the foyer. No sooner was the taxi out of sight than they left the hotel and crossed the road to where Fintan Murphy had another taxi waiting. When the second taxi-man was told to drive them to Sheffield, he argued about regulations and petrol rationing. O'Donoghue was persuasive, however, and soon they were on their way. On their arrival in Sheffield he took them to where Liam MacMahon awaited them in a private car, and within a couple of hours they were driving through the suburbs of Manchester. O'Donoghue dropped off to resume his normal shopkeeping, and MacMahon took the prisoners to safe hide-outs – Milroy and McGarry to his own house, and de Valera to the house of a Father Charles O'Mahony.

The escape was discovered about 9.30 p.m., two hours after the prisoners had got out of jail. The hue-and-cry was started and the hunt was soon in full swing. Cars were stopped and searched and their occupants interrogated. A watch was kept on ports and railway stations, and trains were searched. All in vain. The fugitives had vanished without trace.

Boland returned to Manchester from London and, within a few days of the escape, Milroy and McGarry, having joined the crowds travelling by train to the Waterloo Cup coursing meeting, arrived in Liverpool. They had been passed along this section of the escape route by IRB agents. In Liverpool they were taken in charge by a veteran IRB man, Neil Kerr of the Cunard Line. He lodged them safely with a Mrs MacCarthy who lived near the docks. Soon afterwards they were on board a B & I steamer bound for Dublin. Boland followed. Collins had already returned to Dublin from London via Liverpool. De Valera remained hidden for a week in the house of Father O'Mahony and for another week in a house in Fallowfield, on the outskirts of Manchester. On 18 February, dressed as a priest and escorted by two Irish girls, he was taken to Liverpool to the house of Mrs MacCarthy. Next night he went on board the *Cambria* and he arrived in Dublin in the early hours of 20 February.

In the meantime the two sensational jail escapes within eleven days had made the British look silly in the eyes of the world, and nowhere was their discomfiture appreciated more than in Ireland. Complete strangers greeted one another in the streets and exchanged expressions of joy and jubilation. Only the Dublin Castle executive was red-faced with confusion and embarrassment, and there were angry questions in the House of Commons. The British Press raged and sought to track down de Valera in particular. It was reported that he was seen on a boat to France, on a liner to the United States, on a Southampton-bound train, on a fishing smack in the Irish Sea; it was even reported that he had escaped by balloon to France, to meet US President Wilson. A strong guard was placed on the House of Commons lest he should turn up and claim his seat. Never before was there such a hue-and-cry, never such a hunt for an escaped prisoner. For weeks nothing was heard of him. It was as though he had vanished from the face of the earth.

Of the many dramatic escapes from British jails by Irish political prisoners, there had been nothing quite comparable with the escape of de Valera from Lincoln. The British had refused to free the 'German Plot' prisoners for the general election even though the war had ended and they were being held on trumped-up grounds. They refused to free them for the first session of Dáil Éireann, and their meanness touched a new low when they held the sick prisoners in prison hospitals that were inadequately staffed while the great flu was raging.

And now de Valera, the one prisoner above all others whom they most wanted to hold, had walked out of Lincoln jail. Not to mention the other six who had vanished from Usk and Lincoln within the space of eleven days.

Then the British shifted ground in their attitude to the escape of de Valera. The ranting was eased off and, instead, the Press was used to imply that he was one of the Sinn Féin moderates and that no great obstacle had been put in his path to freedom. He would counter the more militant elements who had not been gathered in by the 'German Plot' arrests, and who had since gained control of Sinn Féin and the Volunteers. 'If they only knew what was in Dev's mind,' said Michael Collins, 'they wouldn't have acted like that.'

On 6 March, Pierce McCan, a Tipperary TD and another of the 'German Plot' prisoners, died of flu in Gloucester jail. He had feared the flu. 'We will,' he wrote shortly before it attacked him, 'be bad subjects after our long confinement, and the danger will be great.' McCan was a well-loved patriot, a noted rider to the hounds, a fine swimmer and all-round athlete.

The escape of de Valera and the death of McCan forced the British, on 8 March, to decide upon a general release of the 'German Plot' prisoners in England and Wales. For one thing, public opinion in Ireland was at boiling point after the news of McCan's death had been learned.

On 9 March the first batch of the liberated prisoners arrived in Ireland, headed by Arthur Griffith, and they brought with them the remains of McCan. Following the escape of de Valera and the other six, the prison gates had been opened by the hand of a dead man. So ended the internment of the 'German Plot' prisoners.

In the meantime, de Valera, who had arrived in Dublin on 20 February, was taken first to the house of Dr Robert Farnan in Merrion Square, and then to the gate-lodge in the grounds of Archbishop's House in Clonliffe Road. He remained in the gate-lodge until a short time before the general release of the 'German Plot' prisoners. Then he had occasion to cross to Liverpool where he again went into hiding in Mrs MacCarthy's house. Following the general release of the prisoners, the leaders of Sinn Féin and the Volunteers decided that de Valera could safely return openly to Dublin.

On Saturday 22 March the following announcement from Sinn Féin headquarters was published in the Dublin newspapers:

> President de Valera will arrive in Ireland on Wednesday evening next, the 26th inst, and the Executive of Dáil Éireann will offer him a national welcome. It is expected that the home-coming of de Valera will be an occasion of national rejoicing, and full arrangements will be made for marshalling the procession. The Lord Mayor of Dublin will receive him at the gates of the city, and will escort him to the Mansion House, where he will deliver a message to the Irish people. All organisations and bands wishing to participate in the demonstration should apply to 6 Harcourt Street, on Monday the 24th inst, up to 6 p.m.
>
> H. Boland
> T. Kelly (Honorary Secretaries)

Dublin Castle was foaming mad. A public reception to de Valera as President of the Irish Republic. The very idea of it! Not since Queen Victoria had made her state visit to Dublin, in 1900, had such an entry through the gates of the city been made. And so it came as no surprise when the meeting and reception were banned by a military proclamation. The decision to ban them was taken by Ian MacPherson, the new Chief Secretary who had succeeded Shortt, and the proclamation was signed by General Shaw, the Commander-in-Chief of the British forces in Ireland.

The more militant elements in Sinn Féin, notably Collins, Cathal Brugha, Harry Boland and Austin Stack, were all in favour of defying the Castle and going ahead with the reception, regardless of the consequences. It looked odds on for a showdown. British troops were rushed into the city. Then de Valera intervened and insisted on the reception being called off. In his name another announcement was published in the newspapers, on 25 March, to the effect that the occasion was not one on which he could call the people to incur any danger, and that the public reception should, therefore, be abandoned.

Sullenly, the young men agreed, and some of them talked of 'another Clontarf'. De Valera was then re-elected president of Sinn Féin. At a private session of the Dáil, on 1 April, he was elected president of Dáil Éireann and, on 2 April, he appointed his ministers. Satisfied that Ireland would not be permitted to present her case for freedom to the Peace Conference, he decided to set out on a bid to win over the United States to the Irish cause. Towards the end of May 1919 he vanished from the Irish scene and, following many adventures in Liverpool and as a stowaway on a transatlantic liner, he outwitted the British and arrived in New York. Harry Boland, who had gone on ahead of him to make arrangements for the visit, announced the arrival of the president in the American Press. The date was 12 June 1919.

Chapter 5

Twenty got away in the big daylight escape from Mountjoy jail

by Piaras Béaslaí

When the first public session of the first Dáil was held, in the Round Room of the Mansion House, Dublin, on 21 January 1919, most of the elected members were prisoners in Britain. They and other prominent Sinn Féiners and Volunteers had been arrested by the British on 17–18 May 1918, on the pretext that they were found to be engaged in a conspiracy with Germany, a fable usually referred to derisively in Ireland as the 'German Plot.'

Two members of the first Dáil who were at liberty were not present at that public session. They were Michael Collins and Harry Boland. When the roll was called other members answered in their names so that their absence would not be generally noticed – for Collins and Boland were then in Britain, engaged in the business of engineering the escape of Éamon de Valera and two other 'German Plot' prisoners from Lincoln jail.

Also on the day of the first public session of the Dáil four prisoners escaped from Usk jail without assistance from outside. One was Joe McGrath, a member of the Dáil; the others were Frank Shouldice, George Geraghty and Barney Mellows. On 3 February Éamon de Valera, Seán McGarry and Seán Milroy escaped from Lincoln jail with the assistance of Collins, Boland and others.

Prior to the Rising of 1916 it had been customary for the IRB in Dublin, under the guise of the 'Wolfe Tone Memorial Committee', to hold an annual Emmet commemoration concert.

It was decided to revive the concert and 4 March 1919 was fixed as the date. An announcement was published that, in addition to the concert programme, a lecture would be delivered by 'a well-known republican'.

The audience who thronged the Round Room of the Mansion House on the night of 4 March had a thrill when, after the doors had been securely locked, the lecturer came onto the platform and proved to be none other than Seán McGarry, one of the prisoners who had recently escaped from Lincoln jail. He delivered his lecture and disappeared. Detectives who had been locked out of the Mansion House and who had waited outside until the concert ended did not learn of his presence there until the following day.

I was at the concert and while I was in the Mansion House two of my GHQ colleagues handed me material they had promised me for *An t-Óglach*, the secret underground journal of Óglaigh na hÉireann, which I edited. The Director of Engineering, Rory O'Connor, gave me notes on blowing up bridges; the Director of Training, Michael W. O'Reilly, gave me notes on musketry. When on my way home that night with these papers in my pocket I was intercepted by Detectives Smith and Wharton, G-men of the political branch of the Dublin Metropolitan Police. I resisted arrest as strenuously as I could, but reinforcements arrived from the police headquarters close at hand and I was overpowered. I had no weapon. The papers I carried were most incriminating.

Smith and Wharton arrested me on a charge in connection with a speech which I had made at a proclaimed meeting at Rhode in County Offaly. J.J. Walsh, who also spoke at Rhode on the same occasion, was arrested on a similar charge. The charge was trivial and in all probability would have meant only a month or two in jail, but the papers I carried and which had been found on me by Smith were much more serious. So Michael Collins and Harry Boland approached him and offered him a bribe not to produce the papers at my court martial. He obstinately refused to accept the offer and they warned him he would produce the papers at his peril. In the event, I got a sentence of two years' imprisonment. Smith was shot and mortally wounded on 30 July. He was the first detective to be executed in Dublin for having continued to engage in political work for the British government after he had been warned against doing so.

Before my trial I was lodged in Mountjoy jail where my fellow prisoners included Robert Barton, William Sears and J.J. Walsh – all three, like myself, members of Dáil Éireann. Barton had been arrested for a speech in which he had threatened reprisals and mentioned the names of prominent persons against whom the reprisals would be taken – because of the reported ill-treatment of prisoners in Mountjoy.

In deference to our status as elected representatives of the people, the governor had us put in cells in the hospital, a detached building at the rear of the jail. Mine was a corner cell on the ground floor, and I had not been in it a day when I realised that all I needed for an escape was a file to cut through a window-bar. Accordingly, I wrote to Collins to inform him of this and I included an elaborate description of the jail together with plans of its interior. Collins' reaction was conveyed to me verbally by Barton who explained that, as he had been working on a similar plan himself and had already got in a file and a coil of rope, GHQ thought it better for him to proceed with his project without any added complications. Before I was arrested I was aware that a plan for a general escape of prisoners from Mountjoy was under consideration, and so I readily agreed to wait for this and, meanwhile, to help Barton make his individual escape.

Barton's cell was on the top storey and consequently the coil of rope was necessary for the escape. An outbreak of flu among the prisoners in cells adjacent to his, however, gave us a good excuse for demanding his removal to the ground floor. The demand was conceded by the jail authorities. Barton was then placed in a cell between the cells of J.J. Walsh and Sears. I occupied the cell next to that of Sears.

At the time Mountjoy was in a state of almost continuous uproar, and once again there was great agitation on the outside because of the treatment of political prisoners inside. These disturbances had commenced with the arrival in the jail of Padraic Fleming, a remarkable young man whose extraordinary fight for treatment as a political prisoner in Maryborough (Portlaoise) jail is described fully in another chapter.

In Mountjoy Fleming found himself associated with a number of other political prisoners who were being accorded all the privileges won by the 1917 hunger strike. He speedily became their leader and, though he had scarcely recovered from an illness brought on by his long personal struggle for political treatment, he initiated a fresh agitation to secure political treatment also for four political prisoners in the jail, who were being treated as criminals. On behalf of the four he organised the other prisoners in strike action against the jail regulations; smashing-up tactics were resorted to with the result that all the prisoners were kept in handcuffs for several weeks. Ultimately, it was decided to halt the strike, at least for the time being, so that the plan for a general escape might be put into effect in the more favourable circumstances of a quieter atmosphere.

It was at this time that I arrived in the jail. Although the strike had been called off then, scenes between prisoners and jailers were of daily occurrence nevertheless, and the jail authorities, under the strain and stress of the prolonged conflict, were inclined to avoid trouble by allowing the prisoners considerable latitude. This improved the prospects of escape.

Barton, having been removed to the ground-floor cell and having sawn through a window-bar in about three nights, without attracting attention, escaped on the night of 16 March. He gave the final touch to his work that evening while having tea with Sears, J.J. Walsh and myself in Walsh's cell. This was to rig up a dummy figure to be placed in his bed so that a warder who looked through the spy-hole during the night would imagine that he was in bed.

The hospital in which we were confined was just beside the rear wall of the jail, a twenty-foot-high wall which cut off Barton from the Royal Canal; he made his escape on a night of bright moonlight, yet no warder, policeman or soldier (there was a guard of police and soldiers in the jail) saw him scale this wall. He threw over a piece of soap as a signal, and Volunteers on the other side responded by throwing him a weight with a rope attached. Barton caught the rope and pulled over a rope ladder with the aid of which he climbed the wall. Then he jumped from the top of the wall into an outspread blanket. He landed without mishap and was taken to the house of Batt O'Connor at 1 Brendan Road, Donnybrook. All the arrangements for his escape had been made by Michael Collins.

O'Connor has recorded that when he expressed his delight in the achievement to Collins, Michael replied: 'That's only the beginning. We're going to get Béaslaí and Fleming out next.' In fact, at the time, he was sending letters to me in which he outlined the plans of escape.

The original plan had been devised specially for the benefit of Fleming and the four prisoners who were being treated as criminals. It envisaged the use of explosives to breach the wall near the canal bank at a time when the prisoners were exercising in the field immediately inside the wall. It also included provision for transport to a safe place once they had got out. The objection to this plan was that the explosion was certain to bring the guard of soldiers and armed policemen hurrying to the scene. It was decided to try a less noisy method.

Amongst the political prisoners were some who had only short sentences to serve. It was agreed that they would remain inside when the break-out was made and, on a given signal, hold up the warders while the others scaled the wall by means of a rope ladder thrown over from the outside. A list of the prisoners who were to escape was made in the order in which they were to go. I was to go first, then Fleming, then J.J. Walsh and then the four prisoners whose treatment had been the cause of the strike action. I do not think that the list exceeded twelve. It was not thought that so many would get away before the alarm was given and the guard arrived to interfere with the business, but it was believed that the first five or six had a good chance. One of the prisoners, Paddy Daly, afterwards the commanding officer of 'The Squad' and later a major-general in the National Army, was placed by Fleming in charge of those prisoners who were to remain in Mountjoy.

As a prisoner awaiting trial I was entitled to see a solicitor privately, and I availed of this privilege to have a number of interviews with Éamonn Duggan. Various details of the escape were arranged during those interviews.

The escape was fixed for 29 March, just thirteen days after Barton's departure, but there was an unexpected complication as that day drew near. As has been mentioned, the strike against the jail regulations had been called off with a view to creating conditions in which the escape would be easier. The four prisoners who were being treated as criminals had reluctantly agreed to accept such treatment without protest for the time being. At length, not being aware that a definite date for the escape had been fixed, they grew restive and, on the Monday, broke away from the warders in charge of them during exercise, and gave them a long chase around the field before being recaptured. For the next few days they had to take their exercise inside a kind of iron cage while they were guarded by no less than eleven warders. If these precautions were continued their chance of escape would be very slight, while the presence of so many warders would also present a serious obstacle to the escape of the rest of us. It was decided to go on with the attempt nevertheless, and the four prisoners declared that if the rope were thrown over the wall they would undertake to break through their guard of eleven warders and get to it.

So desperate a break was not required. The four prisoners, on Fleming's orders, behaved so well for the next few days that the jail officials were lulled into a false sense of security.

Saturday was the day fixed for the escape, and the hour 3 p.m. All the prisoners were locked up for their meal at 1 p.m. At 2.30 they were allowed out to exercise and during this period one of them signalled from a window to a Volunteer stationed in Claude Road, to let those outside know that all was ready.

During meal-time a snowstorm had come on and, for a time, it looked as if the prisoners would not be let out for exercise at all. Fortunately, the storm cleared up about half-past two and we were all allowed out. There were three parties of us: J.J. Walsh and I, who exercised in front of the hospital; the bulk of the political prisoners under Fleming, who exercised in a field just inside the wall; and the four prisoners in the iron cage. When we came out we found to our delight that the guard of eleven over the men in the cage had been reduced to three. The military guard and police were stationed in front of the jail and, as it would take them some time to get round to us, we had only seven unarmed warders to deal with.

Fleming crossed over from his comrades to J.J. Walsh and myself, and the three of us took up a position where we had a view of both the wall and the iron cage. The rules did not allow the different parties to associate with one another, but the jail officials had long given up all hope of compelling Fleming to submit to rules. Not five minutes before the escape the deputy governor passed by and made some remark to Fleming and the rest of us about being out of bounds. Fleming replied with a jest and the deputy governor passed on, obviously having thought it wise to say no more. He was hardly out of sight when the escape signal, a whistle from the outside, was heard.

The main body of the prisoners ran to the selected point in the wall at the rear of the hospital. Fleming, Walsh and I joined them, and the four men in the cage broke through their guard and raced towards us. Meanwhile, five prisoners, who had been told off for the purpose, went up to the warders and, hands in pockets, pretended to be covering the warders with revolvers. They ordered them not to speak or move. The warders obeyed, although the 'revolvers' were simply horn spoons which were served out to the prisoners.

While this action was taking place on the inside, Peadar Clancy, who was outside on the canal bank, threw over a weight with a rope attached, and we pulled over a rope ladder. Paddy Daly took his place at the foot of the ladder and called out the names of the prisoners in the order in which they were to go. I went first, followed by Fleming and J.J. Walsh. We ran along the canal bank and down an entry into Innisfallen Parade where Seán Nunan and others were awaiting us with bicycles.

The escape exceeded our most sanguine expectations. No less than twenty prisoners got out. Several who had only short sentences to serve and who had made up their minds to remain were unable to resist the temptation of the dangling rope ladder. Only seven prisoners were left inside – one to take care of each warder. Just as the last of the escaping prisoners had crossed the wall the military guard came rushing up on the inside with fixed bayonets. Daly lined up his men and they greeted the soldiers with a derisive cheer.

All the men who escaped got away safely, some on bicycles, some by tram. Once we were out among the people our safety was assured, for we were befriended by all with whom we had contact. Such was the famous daylight escape from Mountjoy. Dick McKee and Rory O'Connor had charge of the arrangements on the outside.

Chapter 6

Padraic Fleming's personal fight for political rights – a horror story with few equals in prison annals

by Lochlinn MacGlynn

When Padraic Fleming went over the wall of Mountjoy in a big break-out, on 29 March 1919, he left behind him a record of courage and defiance that belongs to the classic struggles of history. It was difficult for contemporaries to have a clear idea of the classic proportions of his struggle at the time when it was going on, but Piaras Béaslaí, who was in the same break-out, gave it its true value shortly afterwards in a foreword to an account (written by a priest) of the inhuman experiences of Fleming.

At that time there were about 35,000 British regular troops in Ireland. There were also the other aids to 'order', such as jails and the Royal Irish Constabulary.

Fleming fought a personal battle for political rights. He went naked in his cell in winter rather than submit to wearing the uniform of a convicted criminal, and he fought for his rights with such violence and defiance that he exhausted the wits and resources of the British authorities in Ireland. The fight involved his being kept handcuffed for long periods and kept in straitjackets, and in an even worse contraption called 'muffs' which is generally reserved for the dangerously violent insane.

The killing of Thomas Ashe by forcible feeding while he was on hunger strike in Mountjoy, in September 1917, shocked the world. After that experience the authorities did not want Fleming to die also in such circumstances that his death would be another blow to their prestige. He was to be subdued and kept alive behind prison walls. Instead of being subdued, however, he eventually became known as 'the Republican Governor of Mountjoy jail' where the prisoners elected him to be their commandant. But, prior to that, he was to pass through the hell of Maryborough (now Portlaoise) jail to which he had been sent to serve five years' penal servitude. That sentence was based on a suspicious set of circumstances: there is evidence of machinations by the British to trap him into a position where he would receive a long prison sentence; he was aware of this intrigue, and so it is unlikely that he walked blindly into the sort of trap which he knew was being set for him.

After the Rising of Easter Week 1916, Fleming was staying with his parents at 'The Swan' in Queen's County (now Offaly), and, while there, he was questioned in such a way by the RIC that he believed he would be arrested soon. Early in 1917 there was a statement issued by the British authorities in Ireland that no further arrests in connection with the Rising would be made, a device which, on occasion, was used by them to lure wanted men into the open. Fleming went to stay with some friends at Bandon, County Cork, and there, it is believed, the trap took the form of a frame-up which led to his being charged with attempting to buy arms from British soldiers.

He was arrested at Kinsale on 16 February 1917 and brought before a court martial on 9 March.

The charge: That he had attempted to purchase arms and ammunition from British soldiers, that he had in his possession a clip of cartridges, and seditious literature consisting of two original poems and an extract from an Indiana newspaper containing a sermon preached in a church as a panegyric on those who lost their lives asserting the Irish cause in Easter Week.

The evidence: A soldier testified that Fleming had offered him £10 a rifle. This, wrote the priest who recorded his experiences, was not a good commentary on Fleming's business capacity 'as, at the time, British soldiers in Ireland were freely selling rifles at rates varying from 5s to £2 each'. Another soldier swore that Fleming had offered £5 each for revolvers, a story which did not stand up to cross-examination.

The sentence: Five years' penal servitude. Fleming was sent to Maryborough jail where he was refused political treatment. Thereafter he followed a course which, marked by his courage, defiance and iron will, led to humiliations which still shock the reader after more than fifty years.

By hunger strike he won an offer of political treatment, but it was an offer with a condition attached: he must wear prison clothes. Fleming would not accept this condition and his battle against it led the British authorities in Ireland into conduct which is a horror story with few equals in prison annals.

For twelve days Fleming went naked. Then hunger strike again. After another two days without food and fourteen without clothes his condition caused fears that, in the event of his death, the blow that Ashe (by his death) had just struck at British authority in Ireland would once more echo around the world. So, at 10.30 p.m. on 20 November 1917, Fleming was released under the Cat and Mouse Act. He was to have the same struggle imposed on him again six months later, in May 1918, when he was rearrested. This time the excuse for his arrest was involvement in the so-called 'German Plot.'

Back in Maryborough, Fleming was again told he would not be given political treatment. His reply was the same: he would fight. He fought with all the ingenuity and utter disregard for himself that anyone could imagine, and every humiliation which he knew would be imposed on him by his jailers became, in the perspective of history, exactly what he intended it to be: the humiliation of a mighty pressure machine which Piaras Béaslaí described soon afterwards as 'the cold-blooded formalised cruelty of officialdom in power'. These, incidentally, were brave printed words in those years, for the machine was at its most powerful, processing hundreds of prisoners in its courts and jails.

Fleming refused to change into prison clothes. He remained in his own clothes; the prison authorities said they could 'rot off him'. After three weeks, when he badly needed a change of some clothes, he asked to have it from a valise which he had brought with him when arrested. The request was refused. He then wore only his suit, but by 'stratagems' even this was taken from him and he was left with only the bedclothes.

As the bedclothes were removed from his cell from 6 a.m. to 8 p.m., there was the long period of fourteen hours every day when Fleming had no clothes at all. He was a strong, agile young man of twenty-three, over six feet tall, and from now on he pitted his mind and strength against a British system of torture and degradation that was maintained by tens of thousands of men armed with modern weapons.

The warders in Maryborough again ordered him to put on the prison clothes which branded the criminal. He still refused. By weight of numbers (in the struggle one of them stamped on his stomach) they got the clothes on him. They went on doing this in the same way, day after day, and it took so many warders to accomplish the task that he was given the name 'Samson' although there was nothing amusing about this grim ritual.

For three weeks the forcible dressing went on. Each day about eight warders struggled to overcome their prisoner and dress him in the hated clothes of the criminal, which he refused to wear voluntarily. But how to ensure that he continued to wear those clothes for the rest of the day? It would be a full-time job for a whole staff of warders, so they put him into iron manacles, with a body-belt which kept his manacled wrists and his upper arms strapped tightly to his body.

In this position he couldn't use his hands to eat and so he was fed by a warder. Even these restraints and privations didn't prevent him from keeping up the fight, and there was a high rate of damage to prison clothes. He worked out stratagems by which, even when trussed up like a Christmas turkey, he could damage prison property.

The forcible dressing required a new suit every day, so it was necessary to work out new tortures that would bring this courageous man into line. At this stage came the muffs, which practically paralyse the body.

Fleming had been able to break out of the manacles. He achieved the same with the muffs but, by weight of numbers, the warders had him back in his trussed-up condition, not easily because he fought every inch of the way. The miracle was that he had the strength to go on resisting when, at best, he could take no more than a half-pint of coffee or a few spoons of soup each day. He was strapped so tightly across the stomach that his whole digestive system was disrupted. Then he went on hunger strike again.

Fighting for a simple right, he had lost his great strength and, when it seemed that the prison system could do no more to him, he was taken to a hospital cell, again that the British authorities might escape the odium which had been expressed so strongly in the worldwide reaction to Ashe's death – and was to be expressed again when Terence MacSwiney died in Brixton prison, on 25 October 1920, after a hunger strike of seventy-five days.

After eight days without food, Fleming, because of his terrible ordeal prior to the latest hunger strike, was regarded by the prison doctor as being in his death agony. He was expected to live only a few hours, and all the necessary preparations were made for his death. Then came an authentic message that his leaders had ordered a general cessation of hunger strikes.

Fleming recovered and found there was still much which he could do, besides hunger striking, to assert his rights. He continued 'active agitation', a renewal of the campaign that led to some of his most harrowing experiences. Perhaps, thought the prison authorities, there was one way to both subdue him and forestall public sympathy. It was not a new way. He was to be certified insane. For this purpose the superintendent of an asylum for the insane was called in, but doctors, as a rule, do not lend themselves to nefarious practices, and the doctor in this case followed the principles of his profession: he could find no sign of mental disease and would not issue a certificate.

Fleming, coming out of the age-long religious background

of Ireland, was a man of deep spiritual conviction. Could this be used against him? Could he be persuaded, for religious reasons, to lend himself to treatment as a criminal? Find, then, a priest who would counsel him to abide by the inhuman and degrading prison conditions which the authorities sought to impose on him. This plan was, of course, doomed to failure.

Then what about a son's love for his mother? If he were confronted by his mother, and if she took the attitude that some mothers were frightened into taking towards what their sons were risking for Irish independence, would he yield to her entreaties and accept the prison system? Send for his mother and try this stratagem. He would take her advice, the jailers believed.

But that brave woman, like many another, would give no advice to compromise her son with his captors. She had not been allowed to know the horrible conditions in which he had spent the previous months, she said, and she would give no advice at all. She would leave her son to his sense of what was right. And both knew what was right in this case.

Torture, his religious convictions, his love for his mother – all were used in the attempt to break this man of iron will. The one that could be used again with any hope of success, his jailers believed, was the physical method: torture. This they resumed by not allowing him to take off the straitjacket even for the elementary needs of nature unless he would promise to give up 'active agitation'. They knew they could trust any promise made by an Irish political prisoner. Fleming refused to give the promise.

The straitjacket stayed on, even for those occasions when he had to obey the call of nature. This placed him in a disgusting, cruel situation which the authorities had the power to end by granting him the elementary political rights which, by tradition, belong to 'prisoners of conscience'. Justice was in his cause, not in that of the authorities, and he was paying a high price to sustain it not only for himself but for all political prisoners. Even now, more than fifty years later, the ordeal of this man, who in eighty-six days in Maryborough was only twenty-four hours in the open air, stands out as a supreme illustration of what escape could mean.

Meantime structural alterations were going on near his cell. He complained to the doctor that this work gave him no chance to sleep during the day. These alterations, incidentally, were in his honour: the authorities were making a special cell to subdue this utterly fearless man.

The structural alterations followed a visit by the Chief Secretary, Edward Shortt. The specially altered cell was to be warm enough in winter for a man with no clothes. The idea was not to provide for Fleming's comfort, but to remove the need for having a large number of warders available to confine him in a normal cell and prevent him from destroying prison property, for which he had no respect. It was two cells (one above the other) knocked into one. The intervening floor/ceiling was taken away, to present Fleming with a roof which he could not reach, a gas-jet which he could not smash while in a straitjacket, a cell in which he could injure himself but not damage prison property in his fight for political rights.

In what had been the lower cell, the window was built up. The customary spy-hole, through which the peeping warders might observe the prisoner, was in the upper part of the new cell. How Fleming spent his first day in his new cell is a study in fearless ingenuity. Part of it was spent tearing up the bedclothes which, to avoid another Ashe tragedy that would, inevitably, revolt public opinion far beyond Maryborough, the authorities had again supplied. For nature's needs a rubber pot was provided in the cell. Fleming used the pot as a football at times, and, at other times when he had got out of his straitjacket, to smash the cell fittings. This use of the pot did not please the prison governor and he complained that each pot cost half a guinea.

Fleming, on his second day in the new cell, launched an assault on the radiator casing. He had, obviously, a plan of campaign to reduce this special cell to chaos. The plan was successful. Indeed, he announced that, each morning, he would let the warders know his 'dispositions for the day' or, in other words, what piece of prison property would be his target for the day.

To carry out this campaign he first got rid of the straitjacket by jumping at the gas-jet sufficiently often to set the straitjacket on fire and, as it burned, he got it off. He was then trussed up in the muffs which were designed to defy even the super-human strength of the violently insane, but he disposed of these also.

In the December frost his target was to dismantle the radiator which was supposed to keep him at survival temperature while he rotted almost to death in his special cell, designed for economy of prison staff and supplies.

The radiator he took apart with the handcuffs on his wrists. He was then dragged in a straitjacket to an ordinary punishment cell. Here the rubber pot came in useful again. He managed to use it to smash the window.

Fleming, like the prison authorities, was economical in using his resources. He wished them to go as far as possible in registering his protest, these chance 'weapons' such as hand-cuffs, straitjackets and pots.

By breaking the window with the pot he got a supply of

broken glass. With the glass he cut the fastenings of the strait-jacket. But how did he manage to do this without the free movement of his hands? He manoeuvred the glass until he was able to grip it with his teeth and use it as a knife to cut the straitjacket fastenings. Straitjackets, the governor found, were almost as expendable as rubber pots when it came to a man of Fleming's ingenuity. So they had to make a super straitjacket. How to keep it on him? They tightened it so much that Fleming fainted under the fierce pressure. The doctor ordered that it be loosened. Fleming had not used all his supply of broken glass from the smashed window. He had hidden some of it for situations such as this, and during the night he cut his way out of his new harness.

Perhaps if his hands were handcuffed behind his back and he were returned to the special cell, the jailers' troubles with Fleming would be at an end? They tried this, but he managed to get his hands to the front again and was put back in the deadly muffs.

He soon broke out of the muffs again and used them to splice the planks of his bed into a sort of ladder designed to get him towards the ceiling which, it will be remembered, was twice the height of a normal cell. The ascent was discovered in progress by a warder who immediately went to summon help. Meanwhile Fleming climbed higher. He climbed until he was out of the lower cell, but up top where there was no heating he would undoubtedly freeze as his sole attire was a form of loin-cloth. So he came down to the warmth of the lower cell, his immediate mission accomplished.

The variety and ingenuity of this naked man's protests could raise a smile now, but there was little for him to smile about in those grim days. He fought on: another attack on the radiator, which became known as 'Fleming's piano'. Chief Secretary Shortt's special cell for the prisoner was known as 'Shortt's stronghold'.

A period of truce in his 'active agitation' was agreed, covering from Christmas Eve until 7 January. Fleming's terms for the truce were that he should be offered no provocation. In fact, however, he didn't get his clothes back for the truce. This, he said, was a provocation and he would resist it.

He had a few passive, or, at least, less active forms of protest. With remarkable ingenuity he made a badge in the national colours from materials he found on the floor. A warder seized the badge. Fleming made his usual strong protest, he was asked by the authorities to apologise, and, of course, he didn't. The authorities, for the sake of harmony, might have allowed the incident to pass. But the warder, no. He insisted on a disciplinary charge. Fleming was back in muffs. He treated them with the same respect as before, and then he was 'dragged head foremost down four flights of iron stairs to the punishment cells', in the words of the priest who set down Fleming's experiences. His hands were manacled behind his back 'as the supply of muffs and straitjackets was exhausted'. And during these terrible experiences he was 'practically nude'.

He was left in this condition from 9.30 p.m. until the following afternoon, in what was to have been a time of Christmas truce. He was then due to be tried before an inspector of the Prisons Board for his alleged breach of discipline. But the British government decided that he was a political prisoner.

Fleming had won. He had won his personal battle against all the forces of restraint which were at the command of the British at the time. Originally, he had been sentenced to five years' penal servitude. As the regulations for the treatment of political prisoners, introduced after the hunger strike in 1917, applied only to prisoners sentenced to two years or less, Fleming's sentence placed him in a different category. To get over this difficulty his sentence was reduced to two years and he was sent to Mountjoy. Thus, winning his way to political rights was a double victory.

He had been allowed to receive only one letter during his first term in Maryborough; in his second term, which lasted seven months, no letter or communication of any kind. A letter to his parents to visit him was never posted.

And the struggle was still not over. The jailers wouldn't allow him to receive any warm clothes from his friends, even for the winter journey from Maryborough to Mountjoy. He had only a summer suit and a light waterproof in which to go under escort to the train which left Maryborough for Dublin at 8 p.m. that cold night of 1 January 1919. He refused to be manacled for the journey. Following one of his usual fierce struggles against such means of restraint, the blood was still dripping from his wrists in the train. Touched by sympathy, a passenger insisted on giving his coat to Fleming.

In Mountjoy they put him in a basement cell that night but, after the grim ordeal of Maryborough, it was hospitalisation he needed and to a hospital cell he was taken next morning.

Later, when out of hospital and back in the jail proper, his fellow republican prisoners elected him to be their commandant. As prisoners' commandant, Fleming gave the governor an ultimatum on 9 January: all prison property, except bibles and prayerbooks, would be subject to destruction because some prisoners were still not getting political treatment. They were being treated as criminals, as he had been so treated in Maryborough.

Knowing well his destructive powers, the authorities had all vulnerable items removed from the cells immediately. They intended the spy-holes to remain where they were: in the doors. Fleming and his friends set to work destroying the spy-holes and, with 'a trenching tool', cutting other holes in the dividing walls between the cells and using these holes to establish communications between the prisoners.

What was this 'trenching tool'? The bone of a ham that had been sent in to the prisoners. And so an announcement was circulated amongst them that 'Samson has started an offensive with the jaw-bone of an ass'; Fleming was soon in irons. They were so narrow that they cut into his flesh and he endured this terrible torture for a week. The visiting justices, to their credit, protested. He was then given larger irons and, to nobody's credit except his own in Irish history, he was in these for six weeks.

By 17 January the political prisoners were manacled and denied all exercise. And once again Fleming was, for four days, in the dilemma of attending to the call of nature in his cell while denied the sanitary pot which he had smashed – it was not replaced. His reaction to the unhygienic state of the cell was to insist on having the sanitary inspector called in. And, as a result, he was removed to a clean cell.

Fleming used his handcuffs to wreak damage, from almost impossible positions, on any vulnerable prison property. At 9.30 one night he was found trying to take the floor apart. His hands were again fastened behind his back. About 3 o'clock next morning, again weakened by this long struggle, he fainted. Because of the hole in the wall a prisoner in an adjoining cell was able to notice this. He reported it, but through that long, terrible night, no help came. It was 7 a.m. before a warder came to Fleming's aid.

His privations were reaching their peak again: weakness from the brutalities to which he was almost constantly subjected, hunger strike, denial of exercise except for a brief period one day a week – and the date of his release 'postponed' for six months.

No promise was given by the prisoners in return for permission to exercise – they would never break a promise freely given to get any concession. And so they felt free, when returning from exercise, to engage in such protests as tearing the crown badges from warders' caps.

If more of the prisoners were in hospital perhaps their 'fighting forces' would be reduced and the warders' lives made easier. So the jail authorities thought, and some prisoners were encouraged to remain over-long in hospital, to achieve the desired thinning-out. The republicans disapproved of this and there was the interesting situation of the prison doctor reporting daily to Fleming, as commandant of the prisoners, on hospital prisoners' condition.

It was in this atmosphere that plans for escape began to go ahead – plans which succeeded and which form a separate chapter. Volunteer headquarters arranged the priority in which the prisoners would go over the wall when the great day came. Piaras Béaslaí was ordered to go first, Fleming next. That was how they went and eighteen others followed them out. The escape was the culmination of one of the most tenacious struggles ever told, the story of Padraic Fleming's fight for political rights against the many and powerful resources of an empire.

Fleming did not wish to set down his own jail story. He did not wish to have it published in case it savoured of vainglory. But he obeyed the orders of his superiors, dictated his notes to a priest, checked the manuscript written by the priest, and so this remarkable record remains as part of our history.

Chapter 7

Recollections of jail riots and hunger strikes – grim times in Mountjoy, Dundalk and Belfast jails

by Fionán Lynch

In June 1917 all of us in penal servitude in Britain for our part in the Rising of 1916 were released under the general amnesty and, after a short time at home, many of us were thrown into the political arena, for the historic East Clare by-election campaign was being fought. Éamon de Valera, the Sinn Féin candidate, had been released from Pentonville with the rest of us from Lewes, Pentonville and other British jails. His opponent, Paddy Lynch, KC, of the Irish Parliamentary Party, was soundly beaten at the polls on 23 June. Nineteen years later Lynch was appointed attorney-general by de Valera.

Tom Ashe and myself were sent to Killaloe to look after Sinn Féin interests in that area during the campaign. We were joined there by Gearóid O'Sullivan who afterwards became adjutant-general of the Volunteers during the Black and Tan period and retained that rank in the National Army. Ashe was much sought after as a fine public speaker in both Irish and English, and also because of the fame of his great fight at Ashbourne during Easter Week 1916. He and I had been close friends since long before the Rising. We were both members of the Keating branch of the Gaelic League and we were both national teachers – he in Lusk, County Dublin, and I in a city school. Ashe usually came to the city on Saturdays and we would have a little session in the Ship Hotel, Abbey Street, then owned by Alderman Davin, an old Fenian whose daughter is the wife of Frank Aiken – Chief-of-Staff of the anti-Treaty forces at the end of the Civil War and Minister for External Affairs in successive Fianna Fáil governments.

Our company in 'the Ship' nearly always included Gearóid O'Sullivan, Diarmuid O'Hegarty, afterwards secretary to the government and later chairman of the Board of Works; Piaras Béaslaí, the well-known writer; Con Collins, a post office official; and Seán MacDermott, one of the seven who signed the 1916 Proclamation of the Republic and who was executed after the Rising – of which he was one of the main architects. On many occasions we were joined by Arthur Griffith and some of his friends and, indeed, many others who included 'Páidín' O'Keeffe, later assistant clerk of the senate and Cathal Paor, afterwards a circuit court judge.

During our time in penal servitude Tom Ashe and myself had one visit – his sister Nora and my sister Eileen travelled over together to see us in Lewes. Eileen afterwards became Mrs Moran, mother of Dónal Ó Moráin, founder of Gael Linn; both she and Nora Ashe were teachers. Shortly after the East Clare by-election I went to the Oireachtas in Waterford. It was attended by a large number of ex-prisoners. After the Oireachtas Tom Ashe, Gearóid O'Sullivan and myself were in the same railway carriage with others, on our way home, when we read a newspaper account of the courts martial, in Cork, of the three Brennan brothers from Meelick, County Clare, and of another Clareman named O'Loughlin. They were the first Volunteer prisoners who refused to recognise the British courts, and I expressed my strong approval of their attitude in the circumstances then prevailing – to me, it was the proper course to be followed, especially by those of us who had been sentenced immediately after the Rising. No man was obliged to adopt that attitude of defiance, however, and a number of very good men did not believe in it at all. The Brennans afterwards fought with distinction in the 1920–1921 period, and all three held high rank in the National Army. Mick, the youngest, finished his army career as chief-of-staff.

During my time in Kerry after the amnesty, I was often in the company of Austin Stack. We addressed meetings in many parts of the county and were both in Volunteer uniform at Casement's Fort (formerly known as McKenna's Fort, Killourane, near Ardfert, County Kerry, where Roger Casement landed from a German submarine on Good Friday 1916, and was arrested some hours later) for the first anniversary of Casement's execution. Tom Ashe gave the oration that day, and I led a recital of the Rosary in Irish. After the ceremony at the fort had ended, he and I were driven back to Tralee by Tom Slattery of Rock Street, in his pony-trap and entertained by him at his home. Tom had been interned in various British jails, the last being Frongoch after the Rising – and, though by no means a young man then, he was still an outspoken and uncompromising opponent of British rule in Ireland. A couple of years later he became my father-in-law. In November 1920 his premises at 10–11 Rock Street, as well as other Tralee business premises and the County Hall, were burned to the ground by the British, as reprisals for attacks on crown forces on November Eve.

A few days after the Casement anniversary I was arrested at home in Kilmakern, Caherciveen, brought to Cork for court martial and detained in the military barracks. Austin Stack, arrested in Dublin about the same time, was also brought to Cork for trial. We were charged with making seditious speeches in various parts of Kerry, and with wearing Volunteer uniform at the Casement anniversary ceremonies. We discussed the attitude adopted by the Brennans at their trial and decided to follow their good example. We had the opportunity to do so at our own trial when we were both allowed to speak in our defence, as it were, and we used it to hurl defiance at the court and British rule in Ireland. Though warned several times that we were not doing ourselves any good, we were actually allowed to finish the most seditious speeches we ever made!

After sentence was pronounced we were sent to Cork jail for a few days. Amongst the characters who were there with us was Ned Keane, proprietor of the *Kilkenny People* and a native of Listowel. He had been arrested because of some seditious articles in his paper. To him is attributed that wonderful witticism: 'God be with the days when the cost of living was trippence a pint.'

We were soon transferred to Mountjoy jail where we met the Brennans and a number of other men who, like ourselves, had been sentenced for Volunteer or political activities. We were all being treated as criminals, as indeed were some British conscientious objectors (to serving in the war) who were also in Mountjoy at the time. Some of these were working in the wood-yard with us and one of them, when asked by Stack if he really was in conscience opposed to fighting for his own country, replied: 'My dear fellow, necessity is the mother of conversion!'

Tom Ashe, at that time, was awaiting trial for seditious speeches he had made at various places but especially because of a speech at Ballinalee, County Longford. He was held in another sector of the jail and we had no communication with him until later. On instructions from Mick Collins, Tom recognised the court and was defended by counsel – this was in the vain hope that he might escape sentence and so be available as a public speaker when required throughout the country. He was tried and sentenced and then he joined us one day while we were at exercise in the prison square, walking around in single file and supposed to be maintaining silence. I stepped out of my place in the file, pretended to be tying a shoe-lace, and then I moved in beside Tom and shook hands with him. Whilst warders shouted at us, I told him that we had decided to adopt the Lewes tactics (the wrecking of prison property) with a view to forcing the issue of political treatment, and that if these failed we should start a hunger strike on 1 October.

Tom said he would fall in with anything we had decided, but he was undoubtedly fey about the hunger strike. He seemed to have a premonition that he would not live to see the end of it. When I mentioned hunger strike he said: 'Fin, that's the last word for me.' I laughed it off, saying he was about the heftiest man amongst us. He did likewise and added that, of course, he would go all the way with us. In fact, the hunger strike had to start at once, for we had already smashed up our cells after which the warders removed everything from them, so that we were left without bedding or anything else. Our clothes and even our shoes had been forcibly taken from us.

After a few days of the hunger strike the authorities decided to forcibly feed us.

Amid the grimness of it all some vestige of humour lingered in Mountjoy. A number of the tradesmen warders who were not normally required for cell or disciplinary duties were brought in to reinforce the others during the hunger strike. Amongst them was a very decent Kerryman, a shoemaker warder named John Daly from near Caherciveen; and a Dublin man called Hickey, the tailor warder, who was also very friendly to us. After four or five days on hunger strike some young prisoners from Dublin, who had become weak, were removed to the prison hospital, and John Daly was chaffing Hickey about how much better the Kerrymen were standing up to the hardship than the Dublin lads. 'Wisha, and why wouldn't they,' retorted Hickey, 'for what were they ever used to in Kerry but the hunger!'

I was the last person to speak to Ashe. It was when he was being carried down to be forcibly fed – we resisted the warders all the time in everything they attempted to do, and so we had to be carried bodily from our cells to the place where the doctor and hospital warders had the forcible-feeding apparatus ready for us. Our arms and legs were then strapped to a high chair after which our mouths were forced open by means of a wooden spoon so that the doctor could insert the stomach tube. I had already been forcibly fed that day when I saw Tom being carried past my cell, and I called out through the broken spy-hole in my door (broken in accordance with the Lewes tactics): 'Stick it, Tom, boy.' And he replied: 'I'll stick it, Fin.' Those words were to make big headlines subsequently when the Dublin evening newspapers reported the inquest on Ashe.

I saw Tom being carried back after the fatal forcible feeding and it was obvious that he was very ill indeed. He was quite blue and appeared to be unconscious. It was not until the next morning, however, that I heard in a whisper from John Daly that Tom had died in the Mater Hospital. I passed the word to Stack, and eventually the rest of the prisoners were told the tragic news. In anger, and in sorrow also for our dead comrade, we determined that nothing short of the acceptance by the authorities of our full demands would cause us to give up the hunger strike, even though the demands were extreme for those times and had been made initially as a basis for compromise. Now we were unanimous that we would not allow them to be whittled down the slightest bit.

The forcible feeding continued for a few more days. Then, late on the night before Ashe's funeral, Larry O'Neill, Lord Mayor of Dublin, came in and told us that, following his intervention, the government had given in. Our demands had been conceded in full.

There is no doubt in my mind that the propaganda which emanated from the inquest on Tom Ashe, with the huge coverage it was given in newspapers at home and overseas, constituted the greatest single contribution to the Sinn Féin cause since the Rising. I believe I am now (1965) the sole survivor of those who had a major part in that inquest. Of four of us who were selected from the prisoners to give evidence, Austin Stack, Joe McDonagh and Phil McMahon are long since dead. The counsel for the next of kin, Tim Healy, KC, and Joseph Dixon, BL, and the solicitor, Éamonn Duggan, are dead; so is the counsel for the crown, Sergeant Hanna, KC, and Mr Wynne, who instructed Hanna. In later years I became very friendly with Henry Hanna, then a judge of our High Court, and also with the man who had conducted the crown prosecution of Stack and myself at the Cork court martial – Jasper Wolfe, solicitor, Skibbereen, who was for many years a very popular Dáil representative for Cork.

Shortly after the Ashe inquest all of us in Mountjoy were transferred to Dundalk jail, and on our arrival there the British tried to break their agreement with Lord Mayor O'Neill by withdrawing our political status. So we went on hunger strike again. This time they did not attempt to forcibly feed us. Instead, after about a week, we were released under what used to be called the Cat and Mouse Act. That was towards the end of November 1917.

I took part in by-election campaigns in south Armagh and Offaly in the early months of 1918, and spent short periods also in Waterford and Donegal organising the Volunteers. While I was in Donegal, P.C. O'Mahony, later secretary of the Kerry County Council, was setting up Sinn Féin branches in Kerry, and a very capable organiser he was.

In May 1918 I was arrested again – this time in Dublin – and I was taken to Pearse Street (then Great Brunswick Street) DMP barracks and later to the Bridewell; there I was soon joined by Stack, and next day we were taken to Belfast jail to complete the sentences which had been passed on us in Cork in the previous August. Practically all the prisoners who had been released under the Cat and Mouse Act were rearrested about this time and brought to Belfast jail – an operation that coincided with the sudden discovery by the British of the 'German Plot', their excuse for the arrest of scores of prominent Sinn Féiners whom they interned in Britain without trial.

Immediately on our arrival in Belfast we started to give trouble, for the jail authorities were denying us the political treatment which had been agreed before we ended the Mountjoy hunger strike. We made the nights horrible by shouting and 'singing' into the small hours, to the great annoyance of the Orange and Tory element who lived near the jail. We used the customary Lewes tactics which meant breaking the spy-holes in our cell doors and generally doing as much damage as possible to prison property. Eventually the RIC were brought in to help the warders overpower us. My memory is not quite clear as to how long this particular row continued, but I know we were in handcuffs for a number of days and nights, until political treatment was restored and all was quiet again – for a time.

Our numbers in Belfast were being constantly added to as more prisoners were brought in. At one stage all four future Kerry MPs (all to be returned unopposed in the general election of December 1918) were in the jail. They were Austin Stack (West Kerry), Piaras Béaslaí (East Kerry), Jim Crowley (North Kerry) and myself for South Kerry. Stack and I were in Belfast jail when the election took place and, as far as I can remember, the news of my election was the first intimation I had that I was a candidate – there was great amusement amongst the prisoners when we got letters, signed by David Lloyd George, inviting us to take our seats for the opening of parliament at Westminster!

The Brennans and a number of other Claremen were in Belfast jail then, and at some stage Ernest Blythe joined us, as also did Gerry Boland, formerly Minister for Justice. Amongst other prominent prisoners there at the time were three Listowel men – Jim Crowley, Jack McKenna, who was then chairman of the Kerry County Council, and another fine sincere Irishman, Dr Michael O'Connor, who remained a dear friend of mine until his death in 1951. Some of the prisoners were serving short sentences – a number from various parts of the country had been brought in following the reading of a Sinn Féin proclamation on 15 August 1918; I don't remember now what the proclamation was about, but apparently an order went out to have it read outside every church after last Mass on 15 August, and I know that Jim Crowley read it in Listowel and thus came to find himself in Belfast jail.

The most significant thing that I remember about Belfast jail, between the end of June and the great row towards Christmas 1918, concerns the bout we had of the influenza that was sweeping through the world and killing millions. Warders and prisoners were stricken down. Our cell doors were left open, night and day, so that the prisoners who were able to move about could help those who were incapable of doing anything for themselves. Sinn Féin propaganda was highly efficient then, and I think the British government were much concerned about the publicity that would follow the death of any of us. Anyhow, they called on the assistance of all doctors available in Belfast and these included a number of Catholics – to be a Catholic in Belfast then, as now, was almost synonymous with being a nationalist. The doctors were most attentive to us, and they prescribed large doses of brandy for those who were ill. Whether it was due to the medicinal properties of brandy administered in generous measure or not, there is no denying the fact that, whilst the flu was killing off people by the million all over the world, not a single prisoner died of it in Belfast jail – our only casualty was one poor man who became insane.

Sometime in November 1918, John Doran, a six-footer from County Down, was brought into the jail. Awaiting trial by court martial, he was kept apart from the rest of us. We learned that, after his trial, he would be sent to Derry jail as a convicted criminal. This we determined to prevent. So while we were all at Mass on the Sunday before Christmas, Stack passed word to him to join up with us after Mass and then come with us to our wing of the prison. Doran succeeded in joining us, after which a number of us formed up around him and returned with him to our quarters. There he was immediately installed in the attic above the topmost cells, and a mattress and blankets were pushed up to him through a trap-door. When the governor of the jail told Stack that Doran must be given up because he was a prisoner of the military, he was told firmly that there would be serious trouble if an attempt was made to take Doran away by force.

We then took complete control of our part of the jail. Warders were allowed into the ground floor only; the stairs to the upper flights of cells were barred to them. After this situation had continued for some days we got word that the military were coming to take Doran by force. We determined on making it as difficult as possible for the soldiers to get into our quarters. So we decided to demolish a section of the stairway that led to the upper floors and to deal similarly with the railings outside the top-floor cells.

Prior to these events we had been mixing freely during the daytime and we arranged all kinds of sports and athletic contests amongst ourselves. We were allowed to have a fifty-six pound weight for weight-throwing and this 'half-hundred' was soon to be brought into service for quite another purpose. Amongst our number was a hefty young Kerry blacksmith who was easily the best of us at throwing the weight. His name was Tadhg Brosnan and he hailed from Castlegregory. To him was assigned the leading part in the destruction of the stairs and railings, and for this purpose he decided to use the weight.

He slung it by strong towels which he had bound together and pushed through the loop on top of the weight, and it was an unforgettable sight to see him swing that 'half-hundred' as though it were no more than a light sledgehammer.

After Brosnan had wrecked the stairway, he then proceeded to break free six or seven of the main posts of the railings. A number of us grabbed these and gave them a big pull and push that sent them, railings and all, hurtling to the ground below, smashing through the floor and wrecking gas and water pipes, to the accompaniment of shouts of triumph. The destruction of the railings made the narrow thirty-inch passage-way outside our cells a terrifying strip along which to walk, and attackers could approach us only at their peril and in single file. If one should fall over, the prospect was grim, for there was a sheer drop of fifty or sixty feet into the tangled mass of wreckage below.

Whilst the demolition of the stairway and railings was in progress Doran and a number of other six-footers were ordered to the attic to destroy the roof. This they accomplished most effectively by using broom handles to push out the slates along the entire wing. As one can imagine, the place was a shambles after it had been given the complete treatment, and we were effectively cut off from the jail authorities and their forces.

The military, in fact, did come to where our wing joined the circle, and though they trained machine guns on our quarters they did not open fire. In Belfast, as in nearly all jails I have known, the wings were approached from the circle.

Being cut off from all other parts of the jail we could not get our food rations, but there was little danger of our being starved into an early submission by the authorities, as all of us had stocks from the Christmas parcels sent in by our friends.

Of course this made for a somewhat unusual diet. While we had plenty of sweet cake of many kinds, for instance, and such odd items of prison fare as cold turkey, beef and ham, we had no plain ordinary bread! There was a scheme of rationing arranged, and usually five or six of us messed together in a cell. Austin Stack, Ernest Blythe, the three Brennans and myself ate in one cell. I remember that on Christmas Eve, then a strict fast day, the only food we had left in our mess was the carcass of a turkey, a little ham and some sweet cake. Blythe was absent when we started our midday meal but, shortly after we had begun, he arrived, rubbing his hands in pleasurable anticipation. When he saw us all 'wiring' into the grub, he stopped short and, pretending to be shocked, observed, 'It's no great advantage to be a Protestant amongst you lot on a fast day.'

After all the time that had elapsed since then, I can't remember now just how long this particular situation lasted in Belfast. Anyhow I was in so many similar rackets that I can easily become confused as to the sequence of the different events. It was Larry O'Neill, Lord Mayor of Dublin, who again came to the rescue. This time he was assisted by Most Rev. Dr MacRory, Bishop of Down and Connor, and later Cardinal-Archbishop of Armagh. They arranged an honourable settlement with the British on our behalf. Doran was to be left with us and we were all moved into a new wing of the jail.

I have often felt that, in the records of those times of strife, nothing like proper tribute has been paid to the memory of Larry O'Neill. He was a most kindly man and was unremitting in his efforts to get better conditions for the Sinn Féin prisoners of the British. As far as I can remember, he did not himself belong to Sinn Féin.

How our next row with the jail authorities came about, I can't recollect now. Suffice to say that it needed only the slightest excuse for us to create trouble in jail, for in doing so we were also creating the elements of some of the strongest propaganda against British rule in Ireland. Our people on the outside, with the invaluable use they made of propaganda, and the support they were given by sections of the national press and especially by some of the provincial newspapers, spread that propaganda to almost every quarter of the globe. Articles from the Irish papers were copied by the Press of America, New Zealand, Australia and elsewhere. And, without doubt, this publicity was the cause of very great embarrassment to the British government.

Whilst I can't remember our excuse for starting the final row in Belfast jail, I do, however, remember the day and date on which it began. It was after Mass on Sunday morning 19 January 1919. Tadhg Brosnan, the Kerry blacksmith, had plenty of brain as well as brawn, and it was he who showed us how easy it was to tear our cell doors off their hinges. The ponderous doors were made largely of iron. We had only to insert the prison prayer book midway between the two hinges of an open door, then smartly swing the door shut and it flew off the hinges. It was as simple as that. Soon after Mass on 19 January not a cell door remained on its hinges.

As the warders and police came along to deal with us for this latest destruction of prison property and the disruption of their measures for our safe keeping, they could not reach us in our cells. We had barred them out. This we did most effectively by using our plank beds to keep the unhinged doors wedged firmly in position, thus making an impenetrable barrier. The plank bed was slightly more than half the length of the cell, so that by taking out the middle plank (the bed consisted of three planks) putting it against the end of the bed and forcing it down against the door until it was quite tight, we were able to jam the door securely in position. To get into our cells the authorities used pick-axes on the walls on both sides of the doors. Eventually, they broke through and gained entry to the different cells. They burst in on us, manacled us and marched us off to yet another wing of the jail. For my own part, I know my arms were manacled behind my back for almost twenty-four hours. For several weeks afterwards we were handcuffed night and day except at meals – or so the authorities thought! Again it was Tadhg Brosnan who passed the word that by straining the handcuffs and hitting them sharply against the round surface of the hot-water pipes which passed through our cells, the handcuffs would snap open. This operation required skill, and I gave my wrists some painful knocks against the water pipe before I succeeded in getting the knack of the operation. Each night after ten o'clock, when the warders had made the last round of the cells, we removed our handcuffs. We put them on again before breakfast was brought round in the morning.

During the period that this row lasted, from 19 January until the day when eleven of us were picked out and transferred to Strangeways jail, Manchester, at the end of April 1919, we were allowed out of our cells only to go to the toilet and then only one at a time. We were locked up for more than three months. It should be stressed, however, that a number of the warders were friendly towards us, and though I have forgotten the names of most of the friendly men, I well remember 'Shaugh' or O'Shaughnessy as being the best of them all in this respect. Some of the RIC were on duty in the jail every night during those months, and even amongst 'the force' we were not without a few friends. I got to know one of them, a first cousin of my own, when he got 'Shaugh' to open my cell one night and came in with a letter from my mother. On half-a-dozen nights or so afterwards, throughout that period of turmoil in the jail, he came into my cell again. 'Shaugh' was the only warder he would trust, so it was only when 'Shaugh' was on duty that we had a chat. I gathered from my cousin that he was anxious to help our cause in any way he could, and after I was released and back in Dublin eventually, I told Collins about him. Before long he was attached to Mick's intelligence staff and working for us from inside the RIC. This man was Matt McCarthy, a native of Tarmons, Waterville. Mick Collins thought very highly of him and later chose him to act on the committee which he set up to organise the Garda Síochána. He was the first commandant of the depot and chief superintendent in Wexford and Mullingar.

Throughout this final upheaval in Belfast jail we maintained communications by shouting to each other through the broken spy-holes of the cell doors, and by singing – rather raucously, I fear, for we didn't have much musical talent amongst us. As if t'were only yesterday, I can remember the voice of Paddy McCarthy from Newmarket, County Cork, raised in song at the crack of dawn; he was a gay soul with the lightest heart amongst us, and his voice was the first to be heard in the morning. He fell fighting bravely in the town of Millstreet, in a gun battle with Black and Tans.

One morning towards the end of April 1919, without any warning, eleven of us who were still held in Belfast were picked out to be sent to Strangeways jail in Manchester. We were in bed when the news of the transfer reached us, and when the warders and police came in and ordered us to dress we refused to do so. They had to put on our clothes forcibly and then, after they had handcuffed us also, they had to carry each one of us bodily down the stairs and out to a waiting military lorry. We were dumped into the lorry like so many sacks of potatoes and driven to the docks. On our arrival there they had to lift us out, one by one, and carry us bodily into the Fleetwood boat. Our cross-channel escort was a young British 2nd lieutenant and a squad of military, with an RIC sergeant and some half-a-dozen constables. When we arrived on the British side, following an hour or so stuck on a sandbank near Fleetwood, we were immediately put on a train for Manchester, and by that stage we had got on chatting terms with members of the escort. On our arrival at Strangeways we were paraded before the governor, who had a list of our names in his hand. 'When I call your name,' he told us, 'you will take one step forward.' The first to be called was Patrick McCarthy. Nobody moved. The governor, having looked at us in amazement, repeated his order. Again he called Paddy McCarthy's name. Again nobody moved. The governor then turned to the RIC sergeant and asked him if he could identify us. 'No, sir,' said the sergeant. And then, without waiting to be asked, the 2nd lieutenant observed: 'Well I'm sure I cawn't!'

We were told to get into the vacant cells near us, which order we obeyed with a grin. As was our custom, I got into the cell next to Austin Stack. After about an hour the governor returned to our prison block and said loudly, so we could all hear him, that he had been in touch with the Home Office and that he 'wanted to speak to either Austin Stack or Finian Lynch'. I shouted to Austin that he ought to go and talk to him. Austin's cell was then opened and he accompanied the governor to his office. He was back in about a quarter of an hour and told us that full political rights had been restored. Our cells were thrown open all day, and soon we were even taking Irish lessons. From then until my release, on 19 August 1919, when I had finished my eighteen months' sentence, I had as much of 'the life of Reilly' as one can have in jail.

I can't now recall the names of the entire eleven in Strangeways, but, in addition to Paddy McCarthy, Austin Stack and myself, there were also John Doran and Nelius Connolly from Skibbereen. Neilus was afterwards a commandant in the fight against the British, and he fought in the National Army during the Civil War.

About three months after our arrival in Strangeways, the original eleven of us were joined by Piaras Béaslaí and D.P. Walsh – as far as I can remember, they were the only prisoners to join us there. At that time Manchester had a big Irish population, and a number of the city grocery establishments were owned by Irishmen. I remember particularly the O'Connor brothers who came from near Killarney. They had a thriving business in Manchester; and also Liam McMahon, a Clareman, who was in the grocery business there. These men were the very soul of generosity and they saw to it that we lacked nothing that they could provide. I am sure we were a source of envy to the British warders when they saw us with 'lashings' of good Irish creamery butter and all sorts of delicacies that were then very scarce and much beyond the pockets of warders.

We had free association all day, and every day, in addition to the Irish classes, we also held lectures and generally did much as we liked. We were avid readers of the newspapers and books of every kind, and, as there was little or no restriction on our having visitors, all of us at various times had visits from our Dublin and Manchester friends.

Elsewhere in this book, Piaras Béaslaí tells about my code message to Austin Stack after I was released from Strangeways, and of the subsequent escape of all the remaining prisoners. So I shall not repeat any of that story, except one incident that I especially look back on with a chuckle.

On the day of my release, I was met at the gates of the prison by Paddy O'Donoghue, a native of Barraduff, Killarney. 'I have an order for you from Mick Collins,' he told me. 'You are to stay the night with me. We have a job to do.' I said: 'Right, Paddy,' and off we went to his place in Greenhayes, a suburb of Manchester, where he had a greengrocer's shop. Mick Collins had been Paddy's best man on his marriage to Violet Gore, a Dublin girl whom I knew well in the movement and who used to sing at all our rebel concerts before her marriage. O'Donoghue, later sentenced to penal servitude for life because of his IRA activities in Britain, was not released until the Treaty had been signed. He was subsequently a prominent member of the licensed trade in Dublin and a founder of the Shelbourne Park Greyhound Racing Company of which he was managing director.

I stayed with the O'Donoghues on the night of my release, and next morning Paddy and myself went back to view Strangeways from the outside. I pointed out to him a section of the prison walls on which there were no downward spikes on the inside. This was a stretch fifty or sixty yards long, and I have no idea why it was left without spikes. All along the rest of the outer walls there were slanting spikes about a yard long, extending outwards and downwards, to make escape over these stretches of the walls impossible.

On our arrival at that section of the walls which was free of the spikes, Paddy took out a foot-rule and measured three or four of the bricks. Nonchalantly, he sang out the figures to me and I entered them in a notebook. We then counted the bricks from top to bottom of the wall and calculated the total height of the wall. Whilst we were thus occupied dozens of people passed by. Most of them took no notice of us whatsoever, but we did hear one man observe to another: 'Jolly old Board of Works, what!'

When I look back on that incident and the chances we took (one of the prison warders might easily have happened along, recognised me and realised that we were up to something) I have to smile to myself. I returned to Dublin that evening and reported to Mick Collins on the result of our inspection of the prison walls. He passed me on to Rory O'Connor who gave orders for the making of the rope ladder that was eventually used to get the prisoners over the wall, and who also made the general arrangements for the escape. The escape took place eight or nine weeks after my release, and all six of our men who were still held in the prison got away successfully.

Chapter 8

Journal of the big Belfast jail riot

by Austin Stack

*Fionán Lynch's account of the riots and other events which took place
in Crumlin Road jail, Belfast, between May 1918 and April 1919,
written forty-seven years afterwards, is corroborated by Austin
Stack, the prisoners' commandant and leader of the revolt within
the jail, in a day-by-day diary which he kept at the time. Fionán's
recollections and Austin's chronicle of the struggle to win political
treatment for republican prisoners are complementary documents.
A verbatim transcript from the diary follows* – Editor.

About Saturday 29 November got message to see John Doran,
prisoner, awaiting trial in D wing.

On Sunday sat next Doran at Mass and chatted with him.
From what he told me I believed the authorities would try
to treat him as a criminal when tried. I told Doran this and
suggested getting him to my own wing in prison after his trial
and before sentence.

Doran tried on 21 December.

Sunday 22 December I sat next Doran at Mass and told
him to turn into B wing as he left the chapel. Several of our
men went out with him and got him into B wing safely.

Kept cell doors closed and prevented search. I was sent for by governor who began interview by saying: 'I believe you captured a prisoner this morning.' I said 'Yes.' Told him Doran should be a political prisoner; instanced the case of Derrig, Kettrick and Murray who had been taken away from Belfast prison and treated as criminals although the governor had recommended them for political treatment. I offered to give up Doran if I got a guarantee that he would be sent with us after sentence. I offered anyway to produce him to the military for purpose of having sentence promulgated. The governor pointed out seriousness of situation and which I admitted. I told him we were prepared to lose lives to establish the principle that we were the judges as to who were or were not political prisoners. On his saying he would have to report the matter to the board the interview closed.

I refused Deputy Chief Warder Willis, who wished to see Doran for purposes of 'check'.

We put on guards all day and all night.

Monday 23 guards on. Put up barricades on Monday night. About midnight governor held up by guards and explained that he only wished to see warder in kitchen to which place he was escorted by our guard. He then retired.

Tuesday 24. Interview with Fr MacCauley. He suggested an armistice – coming from the governor so as to allow the warders to do their duty for the present. I agreed to this provided I got twelve hours' notice before military or police were brought in. The chaplain saw governor again and returned saying this was agreed to. Our guards were taken off then. This was about midday and one barricade was taken down temporarily. Doran came out after dinner and exercised with us in yard. The cell next mine, i.e. C.3/12, fitted up for Doran.

Wednesday (Christmas Day). Doran messed with Blythe, Lynch, MacMahon and Hoolan in my cell. All passed off well. The boys held dance and concert Christmas Night, announced as 'victory ball'.

Thursday 26. Uneventful.

Friday 27. Got notice through Fr MacCauley of withdrawal of governor's undertaking. I enquired whether this meant the stipulated twelve hours' notice and was told it was. It was then 1.30 p.m. Attack might open any time after 1.30 a.m. tomorrow.

After dinner men went on to A.2 and A.3 and sang and cheered and afterwards ascended the roof of the laundry and planted the tricolour on the chimney. Large crowds attracted and gathered in Crumlin Road. The prisoners sang and cheered for about one and a half hours. The mob outside the prison then began to throw stones. The vice-commandant signalled to men to come off the roof, which they did.

Barricades re-erected and strengthened, also new barricade on stairs in B wing. Part of stairs cut away. Guards on all night.

Saturday 28. Breakfast had to be brought up by means of improvised lift owing to condition of stairs. About 11.30 a.m. heard that commissioner of police was in the prison and that police were to lock us up. Ordered all doors to be sprung off hinges at once. This was done. All men in yard and laundry and men belonging to A.1 ward brought on to B.2 and B.3. Some of the hospital patients with us. The others were cut off. They arrived outside B gate but could not gain admittance.

Chaplain comes on scene and administers General Absolution. All the men then join in a great cheer when I have said: 'Now, boys, we're ready.'

All hands set to work at once to throw down iron railings on B.2 and B.3. As parts of railings fall on ground floor with heavy noise from time to time, great cheers arise from the prisoners. A few men were sent up into the attic to attend to the roof and we heard slates fall in fine style. In less than half an hour the whole place was a scene of wreckage. The fallen railings with wire netting are lying along the whole ground floor (which the railings have broken through) and on the stairway and form a regular masterpiece of defence work. The landings B.2 and B.3 are now only narrow ledges and dangerous for any attacking party.

Soon after midday or perhaps before, approached by Fr MacCauley who informs me that the military have come to the prison with machine guns and he suggests we might now reconsider our position, having done so much. (I took it he meant giving up Doran.) I said, 'let them come.' I felt very sorry for him, he looked so anxious.

The military and police now take up positions in the circle on ground floor and around B wing outside our barricades. There seems to be a lot of military in C wing.

Expecting attack all day and during the Saturday night. None comes, however. About 11 p.m. we have supper. Prior to this men prevented from cooking. Food supply consists of Christmas parcels and must be conserved.

About midnight concert held at end window of B.3. During concert we hear general election results from the men in hospital, who shout across to us. First news was Dillon's smashing defeat in East Mayo. Great demonstration. We get most of the results and they put us in better form than ever.

Sunday morning 29. We hear Mass on ledges of corridors behind barricades.

Interview with Fr MacCauley at B.1 gate, and later with Fr Mageegan.

Men on guard all the time behind barricades. Military and police on duty at other side of same.

It being evidently the intention now to starve us out, we call in all the food. Every man gives up his parcels and everything else in the way of eatables in his possession. We also put in a water supply lest the water should be cut off. The food is rationed: two small meals per man per day. Concert about midnight as usual.

Half the men ordered to bed. Others remain on duty for several hours. Those who have rested then take turns on guard.

Monday 30. Gas and water cut off. (The heating had been discontinued from the beginning.) Interview with Fr MacCauley. He comes up into B.2 and sees all the men.

Attack not come so far. It looks as if they hope to exhaust us soon, but we have food enough to do us by rationing for three or four days more at least.

Guards as usual and resting by turns.

I had told the priest we would burn everything burnable in the place if gas and water not restored. They are restored very soon after. Concert, etc. at midnight.

Tuesday 31. Fr MacCauley arrives with lord mayor of Belfast, Sir J.J. Johnson. Priest goes upstairs while I discuss matters with lord mayor. I offered to give up Doran if an assurance is given that he will be given political treatment. I refuse to accept promise that the case will receive best consideration of chief secretary.

About 6 p.m. Most Rev. Dr MacRory and the lord mayor of Dublin arrive with Fr MacCauley soon after. We have a long discussion. The lord mayor of Dublin is prepared to give a promise that Doran will be made a political prisoner after sentence. He hands me Mr Shortt's letter which says 'he will consider any representations made to me regarding his (Doran's) case' if we surrender. The lord mayor pledges himself that underlining the chief secretary's statement there is an unofficial undertaking. I express myself satisfied with this and raise the points that we must not be punished and must get back to our former status. Doors open all day and night, etc. Dr MacRory and the lord mayor go away to see if they can 'phone Mr Shortt about this. The lord mayor also assured me that we are to be removed to internment camp (at Oldcastle probably).

They return later. The authorities will only consent to giving us the pre-influenza conditions. I demur but Dr MacRory tells me of probable bloodshed in Belfast if matter is not arranged tonight. I call the officers and members of parliament together. We agree to accept terms pending removal to internment camp.

All officers, etc. then meet bishop and lord mayor and we inform them of our agreement. The question arises of a possible effort to punish me for wrecking of prison, and lord mayor can give no definite undertaking. Dr MacRory and himself go away again to settle this with Mr Shortt.

About 9 o'clock they returned with Mr Chippendale (Acting Governor) and Col Eoin Lewis, Chief Inspector of prison. It is agreed there is to be no attempt to punish us and that Doran be handed over by me at 10.30 o'clock tonight. They want all of us to evacuate B wing tonight but I refuse saying: 'We will see the New Year in, in our present quarters.'

Doran handed over at 10.30 p.m. to acting governor. In answer to a question he (Chippendale) tells me we are to go to Mass next day in the ordinary manner. He wants to have no noise tonight. I tell him we will have our usual concert.

I send men to take down barricade on B.2 to enable us to go to chapel in the morning, but the acting governor prevents the work being done.

Wednesday, New Year's Day 1919. Chief warder about 7 o'clock wants barricade removed by our men. I tell him that I sent men to do this on previous night and the acting governor had ordered them away and insulted them, that the men would do the work only at the time I appointed for them and would take no bullying from the governor, deputy governor or anybody else.

We hear Mass in corridors behind barricades.

Interview with Fr MacCauley after Mass. He is much upset about the occurrence. He thinks it will smash the settlement. I tell him we don't care.

About 9 o'clock I ask chief warder to let me know hour fixed for our moving to new quarters. He cannot answer. Dr MacRory and lord mayor of Dublin visit prison again about 10 a.m. today. They seem to think we have broken through the arrangement. I explained and they are satisfied. Apparently they were not told about the men being stopped from removing barricades last night nor that I had asked chief warder to fix hour for evacuation. They leave to make arrangements.

Bishop and lord mayor come again soon with acting governor, and we are to march out at once into A.1 to have dinner pending preparation of C wing this evening. Our guards are now withdrawn. We line up and march in single file along narrow landing around the circle (the barricades previously removed by volunteers into A.1) where a few words are spoken by Ernie Blythe, Fr MacCauley and myself. Dr MacRory also addressed the men. Cheers are given for Dr MacRory and lord mayor, and the men are dismissed. British military officers were interested spectators of the scene.

Ameliorations were suspended on the morning of 21 January 1919, for alleged 'general disorder' on the previous night. We were kept in solitary confinement from that date until 29 April when removal to Manchester took place.

About 6.30 a.m. on 29 April 1919 the Belfast Governor, Captain Barrowes, entered my cell and said: 'Well, it has come at last. You are to be removed for internment. The military will be here at 7.30 to take you off.' I said I wanted a guarantee that we were going to an internment camp. He replied that he could not give that and I then told him I would resist being taken away. He left to inform the other men but he does not appear to have repeated his falsehood about our being interned.

Half an hour or so later two warders and three police came into my cell and I was thrown down and handcuffed. In my weak state of health after fourteen weeks' confinement I was able to offer but a feeble resistance, and at 7.30 I was carried down stairs and out into A wing yard and put into a military lorry in which there were a number of soldiers and police. Then I heard for the first time that we were to be put on board a ship but I did not learn its destination. We were driven to the Fleetwood steamer's dock and put on board a vessel. In the cabin with me were Fionán Lynch, John Doran, Paddy McCarthy, Patrick Gaffney, Seamus Duggan, Seamus P. Cassidy, Con Connolly, Michael Keating and Seamus Mulcahy Lyons – ten in all.

This left thirteen behind us in Belfast for release on grounds of ill-health. It was 9 p.m. or so before the steamer got under way, and we had a few songs from time to time. The voyage was very slow; much delay took place entering Fleetwood. The boat got on the mud for an hour or so and had to be taken off by a tug. We landed about 9 a.m. and were put on board a train for Manchester, where we arrived at 11 o'clock. (Not a bite of food or sup to drink had been offered us since leaving Belfast prison fifteen or sixteen hours previously.)

A black maria conveyed us from Victoria Station to the prison, where we were ordered into the 'reception'. (After a while the governor came along and got papers from military officer.) The name of Patrick McCarthy was called out but none of us responded. I heard the military officer saying he did not know who was who amongst us, and apparently the police did not know all of us. I believe I was known, however, for the chaplain seemed to take me as the leader when he came to see me not long after, but this is anticipation. When they found we were not going to answer names we were put into 'reception' cells. A kind of dinner was served to us then. It was there the chaplain came to see me in a quarter of an hour or so. He asked me to facilitate matters, that everything would be all right, and I told him I should know first how we were to be treated. He left me then and the governor came along in about half an hour. He enquired whether I was Stack. I admitted I was as I wished to learn how we stood. He looked and spoke like a decent man and we discussed matters for some time. He said he had no definite instructions about us and, at his request, I told him the terms we had enjoyed at Belfast prior to 21 January. He promised to give us the same conditions pending arrival of instructions, and I agreed to let the men give their names, etc. This was done and we were conducted to C.1, a wing to ourselves. I was located in No. 33. After a while we went out and exercised.

Chapter 9

Bobby Byrnes of Limerick was among the first to fall — his rescue a Pyrrhic victory

by Bill Kelly

Although Bobby Byrnes felt tired and weak, in his narrow cot in public ward one of the Limerick Union Hospital, there was tension mounting within him. Like the other patients in the ward he would be having visitors soon. Unlike those calling on the other patients, however, his visitors would be men who would snatch him from the custody of the RIC. That it would be no easy job, he knew well, for at his bedside were armed members of that force, placed there to prevent what the Limerick Brigade of the IRA were about to attempt. To ease the nervous tension that was building up while he waited for the rescue to commence, Byrnes cast his mind back over three weeks of hunger strike in Limerick jail and thought about the beatings, the solitary confinement, the many indignities and the other methods used by the authorities to break the spirit of resistance of the republican prisoners who were demanding political status. It was the hunger strike which had sapped his strength.

A former telegraphist in the Limerick Post Office, Byrnes was only twenty-eight years of age, and had been in every way a normal active athletic young man. He was dismissed from his job because he had attended the funeral of a Volunteer. Now, as the minutes ticked by, he tried hard to be calm, to conserve what remained of his energies for the break for freedom he was about to make. Inside the alcove which cut his bed from the view of the other patients sat two RIC men, Constables O'Brien and Spillane. Three other members of the RIC, Sergeant J.F. Goulden of Ballyneety, Constable J. Tierney of Kilteely, and Constable J. Fitzpatrick of Clarina, as well as Warder John Mahoney of Limerick jail, were also on duty in the ward.

Just before Christmas 1918, Byrnes, of Townwall Cottage, Limerick, was elected adjutant of the 2nd Battalion, Limerick Brigade, and he brought all his energies and the disciplined mind of a civil servant to bear on filling the position successfully. He was known to the RIC as a 'Sinn Féiner' and, consequently, a 'troublemaker'. Soon a squad of the force swooped upon him at his home.

Byrnes was charged with being in possession of a revolver and ammunition, and his colleagues believed that these had been planted on him. On 13 January 1919 a British court martial sentenced him to twelve months with hard labour. When serving the sentence he would not accept the treatment prescribed for criminals. He had committed no crime but had been jailed for serving his country and working for her independence, and, as the senior officer amongst the prisoners in Limerick jail, he led their fight for political status. A policy of disobedience led to reprisals being taken against the prisoners. Their boots and clothing were removed. They were beaten up.

Their leaders were handcuffed day and night in the cells, they were put on bread and water and kept in solitary confinement. At last, their patience exhausted, the prisoners rioted and, led by Byrnes, they wrecked the cells and smashed up the fittings. By sheer force of numbers they were overpowered following intervention by reinforcements of baton-swinging men of the RIC. After that the treatment worsened. Bruised, barefooted and without clothing, they were left in their wrecked cells, exposed to the cold and damp of winter. Byrnes decided that only one course remained to them: they would go on hunger strike until political status was accorded them.

After three weeks on hunger strike Byrnes was in poor shape and the authorities were worried. They did not attempt forcible feeding, for they remembered the worldwide adverse publicity which followed the death of Thomas Ashe as the result of forcible feeding in Mountjoy jail, Dublin, in September 1917. Their concern now was solely on account of the danger of damaging publicity and had nothing to do with the condition of Byrnes. And so they removed him from the jail to Limerick Union Hospital and placed him in the general ward where he was guarded night and day by six armed RIC men and a prison warder.

The armed guard in the hospital was arranged without the consent of the Chairman of the Board of Guardians, Austin Brennan. Shortly before the British removed Byrnes from jail to the hospital they wrote to the Board of Guardians and requested that he be received and kept in the hospital under armed guard. Brennan summoned a meeting of the board and advised Ned Dundon, the Master of the Union Hospital, to refuse permission. The British, however, influenced two members of the board to give a written consent and Brennan, having returned to Limerick following a business trip, found himself faced with a *fait accompli*. Byrnes had already been whisked from the jail to the hospital and the armed guard installed.

The Limerick IRA wanted their adjutant out and they knew it would be a blow to British prestige in Ireland if he was rescued from the RIC. Commandant Peadar Dunne called a battalion council meeting in Hogan's, next door to Matt Boland's shop in Gerald Griffin Street. Around the table with him were Captain Paddy Doyle, Captain Dave Dundon, Captain Michael Hartney, Captain Tommy McInerney and others. A rescue plan was agreed. It was simple, but split-second timing was essential to its success. On Sunday 6 April, 1919, some twenty-four IRA men would enter the general ward as visitors, and towards the end of the visiting hour – as three o'clock approached – they would overpower the guard and take Byrnes out. A car would be waiting in the courtyard to get him away. All but one of the rescue party would be unarmed. In addition to the twenty-four IRA men in the ward, a covering party of about fifteen would be on duty in the hospital corridors and grounds. None of the senior officers of the brigade or battalion would take part in the rescue, but they ensured that the assault party was carefully chosen and rehearsed so that every man knew what was expected of him and was prepared to spring into action the minute a blast on a whistle gave the signal.

As March blustered into April, Section Leader Mick 'Batty' Stack of E Company, 2nd Battalion, who was in charge of the operation, and Section Leader Jack Gallagher of D Company, 2nd Battalion, finalised the preparations. Over and over again the men of the rescue party were briefed and rehearsed in their task. Then came a hitch. No motor car was available to take Byrnes away. Cars were few and so were drivers in those days, and Captain Tommy McInerney, the battalion driver, had to leave Limerick city hurriedly and unexpectedly to drive Dan Breen and Seán Hogan from north Tipperary, through a cordon of British military which was closing in on them, to a place of safety in west Limerick. (With Seamus Robinson and Seán Treacy, Breen and Hogan were badly wanted by the British.) Alternative transport had to be arranged for the escape of Byrnes, and a carriage known in the Ireland of those days as a 'mourning coach' was got from a local undertaker. In the coach was Nurse Mary Giltenan who had clothes and a disguise for Byrnes.

Sunday 6 April was a 'pet' day and there was warm sunshine in Limerick as visitors stood about, chatting and waiting for the gates of the hospital to be opened. Amongst them were the IRA men, taut but determined, all of them unarmed with the exception of their leader, Mick Stack.

In his cot in the ward Byrnes tried desperately to remain calm and to give no outward sign that might alert Constables Martin O'Brien and Spillane who sat on either side of him. From vantage points in the ward Sergeant Goulden and Constables Tierney, Fitzpatrick and Clarke scrutinised the visitors. Their training and experience in the RIC, which was a basic part of the political intelligence system of the British government in Ireland, fitted them to assess the visitors, classify them and mentally place them in the appropriate category. There was always danger when those damned 'Shinners' were involved.

Singly and in pairs the men of the rescue party drifted into the ward and casually observed the location of Byrnes' bed as they mingled with the other visitors who had called on various patients. Mick Stack checked his dispositions. A nod from Gallagher confirmed that everything was in order.

The fifteen men mobilised for duty outside the ward were in their positions in the corridors and grounds. The driver shook up his reins as the horse drew the mourning coach through the main gate and around to the entrance. Inside the coach Mary Giltenan arranged and rearranged the clothes, unable to keep her hands still or her professional mind from considering the possible treatment which Adjutant Byrnes might have need of.

Nearer and nearer to three moved the hands of the clock. Inside the ward the pitch of conversation had risen as visitors sought to cram into the few remaining minutes the things that had been left unsaid during most of the hour.

The policemen were observed to have sharpened their watch. They had orders to shoot if a rescue was attempted, and general orders had been issued to the force that prisoners were to be shot in such circumstances.

Byrnes gathered his reserves for the effort that was now required of him. Paddy Dawson looked at his watch calmly, gave a quick glance around to check that the men were ready, then whipped out his whistle and blew a shrill blast.

The policemen drew their guns, startled visitors sprang to their feet, bewildered by the alien sound, and the men of the rescue party sprang into action – there were six from each of the four companies, and they included Tim Buckley, Jim Downey, 'Soaker' Ryan, Dinny Maher, 'Lefty' Egan, 'Corky' Ryan, Michael Clancy, Tarry Enright, Michael Danford, Billy Wallace, Mick Walters and Joe Saunders. Their plan was to overpower the RIC men and tie them up, but that was easier said than done. The RIC were armed and, with the exception of Stack, the IRA men were not. A volley of shots boomed out in the ward, and panic-stricken visitors, men and women, stampeded for the door. All was bedlam.

Although they had been on the alert for trouble, the police were nevertheless surprised by the ferocity of this onslaught by unarmed men. The IRA knew what they had to do. So did the police, for that matter. Constable Martin O'Brien was already firing. Constable Spillane had his revolver out also and, as Bobby Byrnes tried to heave himself out of bed, the burly RIC man hurled himself bodily on top of him. Curses and confused orders were shouted above the din of combat as IRA and RIC, locked in struggling groups, rolled about the floor. Mick Stack kept his head. His pistol cracked and the burly Spillane, who was throttling the weakened prisoner on the bed, collapsed, his spine shattered by a .38 bullet. Again Stack fired. This time at Constable O'Brien, and the eighteen-stone policeman crumpled in an ungainly heap on the floor, his life ebbing rapidly.

Byrnes struggled from under the wounded Spillane and staggered towards the door. A bullet whizzed past Dinny Maher's head, grazed his forehead, smashed against a plaster statue of the Child of Prague and shattered it to atoms. Maher wrested a gun from Constable Fitzpatrick. Tierney, obviously having decided that discretion was the better part of valour, was about to hand over his weapon when a blow from Michael Danford caught him on the back of the head and he toppled unconscious to the floor. Spillane, helpless from his maiming wound, groaned on the bed which had lately held his prisoner.

The short sharp struggle had ended. The RIC were overpowered and the attackers faded away. Brian Crowe had ensured that the alarm would not be given readily, for he had cut the telephone wires with a pliers that had been provided by Stack.

An overcoat wrapped about him, Bobby Byrnes staggered down the stairs and out to the lodge, supported by two of his comrades. They made their way to the front of the hospital where the coach should have been waiting to take Bobby to Bensons' house, near the Jesuit church in the Crescent. With sinking hearts they found it was not there. The driver, by mistake, had driven it to the mortuary at the back of the hospital and was waiting there in an agony of suspense, convinced that the operation had failed.

With Byrnes leaning heavily on the shoulders of two of his comrades, the three had covered only some of the distance to Hassett's Cross, which is about 300 yards from the hospital, when his escort noticed a trail of blood on the ground. It was only then they realised that Byrnes had been shot. Just above his heart was a bullet hole almost the size of a halfpenny, and it testified to the zeal of Constable Spillane who did not intend that the prisoner should escape.

The clop clop of hooves aroused Thady Kelly, one of the escort, from the slough of despair into which he had slumped after seeing the dreadful wound on Byrnes' breast. Kelly was the only man, apart from Mick Stack, who knew that Byrnes was to be taken to Bensons', but, with the adjutant so badly wounded that plan had to be abandoned. The hoofbeats drew nearer, and then Kelly saw John Ryan of Knocklisheen and his daughter Nancy, in a pony and trap. Without delay the wounded Byrnes was put in the trap, Ryan whipped up his pony, and as fast as the gallant little animal could gallop, the wounded adjutant was rushed to the Ryan home.

Close by was the home of Michael Brennan, the well-known Clare IRA leader. Messengers were sent at once for a doctor and a priest. Both arrived in a short time. But it was already too late. The RIC man's bullet had done its job. At 8.30 p.m. on Passion Sunday, 6 April 1919, at Knocklisheen, three miles from the scene of the rescue, Bobby Byrnes breathed his last. He had been taken from the enemy but it was a Pyrrhic victory. Apart from Dinny Maher who had been grazed by a bullet, none of the other IRA men was wounded. Constable Martin O'Brien was dead and Constable Spillane seriously wounded. Sergeant Goulden, Constables Tierney, Fitzpatrick and Clarke and Warder Mahoney suffered only minor bruises.

Chapter 10

Daring rescue of Seán Hogan at Knocklong Station

by Desmond Ryan

The daring rescue of Seán Hogan from an RIC escort of a sergeant and three constables on a train at Knocklong railway station, took place on 13 May 1919. Hogan, with Seán Treacy, Dan Breen and Seamus Robinson, were much sought after by the British following an ambush at Soloheadbeg, near Tipperary town, in which two RIC constables were killed, on 21 January 1919. A reward of £1,000 was offered by the British for information leading to their capture.

Seán Hogan had fallen into the hands of the RIC on the morning of 12 May and was being held in their Thurles barrack. His captors were not at first aware of his identity but they established it later. When the news of the arrest reached the other three wanted men they resolved to rescue Hogan at all costs. – Editor

When Treacy learned that Hogan was in Thurles he knew at once that Hogan would be taken to Cork, the usual destination for all men arrested under DORA (Defence of the Realm Act) in Munster, and he knew, too, that Hogan would be removed there by train. An attempt at rescue en route was at once decided upon. Emly was first discussed as being suitable as it was near the borders of Cork, Limerick and Tipperary, with the RIC barrack a mile from the station, and no military garrison nearby. Moreover, Treacy, Robinson and Breen had the trusted Galtee Battalion at hand, if the need arose. The plans were several times, of necessity, changed; eventually, Emly was dropped in favour of Knocklong at the last minute, and adjustments in detail were necessary.

Having satisfied themselves that an attack on the barracks at Thurles was impossible, they cycled by a circuitous route to Maloney's of Lackelly, near Emly, arriving in the early hours of 13 May. Mai Maloney was impressed with the extreme agitation of Seán Treacy. He was, she declared, 'nearly off his head thinking'. And when he asked a question aloud, it was about trains and timetables, about this station and that station. In those tense small hours of 13 May, around the breakfast table, the Knocklong rescue was planned. As the three men sat there it was very evident that they had reached a decision. Knocklong it was to be. The countryside there was quiet and deserted on one side of the station, and the two nearest barracks were at least three miles away.

Seán Treacy was disturbed when he could not discover definitely whether Hogan would be moved or not. He asked Mai Maloney to go to Thurles and make inquiries. Before she left, the final rescue plans had been fixed. An idea of summoning men from the Tipperary Town Battalion, some seven miles away, had been abandoned. Nor would it have been possible to summon them. Four messengers only were available. In Lackelly, Mai Maloney, who had gone to Thurles; Jerry Callaghan, who left for Galbally with an urgent message for

Éamonn O'Brien from Treacy; Joe Taylor and Bill Fitzpatrick. Seán Treacy instructed Fitzpatrick to inform David Bourke, who was in charge of the area, to tell Thomas Shanahan of the Knocklong Coal Store to be on the look-out for code telegrams, which would be sent to him. These telegrams would deal with Hogan's movements and should be brought to Treacy at Knocklong station. Hogan would be referred to as 'the greyhound'.

Unfortunately, David Bourke had been unable to get in touch with Shanahan who was, therefore, very bewildered when he received a telegram in the early afternoon. This telegram had been dispatched from Thurles at 1.45 p.m. and read 'Greyhound still in Thurles. Michael O'Connell.' The 9.15 a.m. train from Dublin had reached Knocklong at 1.29 p.m. and left three minutes later. The three men met this train at Emly. Seeing that Hogan was not on board, they returned to Maloney's and prepared to meet the next train at Knocklong, which was due there about 8 p.m. On their return to Lackelly, Jerry Callaghan was sent, as before mentioned, with a short dispatch to Éamonn O'Brien informing him, to quote the actual words of the message: 'Will operate in Knocklong, 7 p.m. Meet Maloney's, Lackelly, and bring help.' Éamonn O'Brien knew at once what this short dispatch meant, and what Treacy wanted him for. He knew that Hogan had been arrested and guessed that it was a last desperate attempt to save Hogan from the hangman. The result of any trial of Hogan was a foregone conclusion, and Éamonn O'Brien understood quite well that Treacy, Robinson and Breen would stop at nothing, not even this desperate venture of intercepting the train and snatching their young comrade from his well-armed guards. Nor was Éamonn O'Brien a man to count the cost. He and his brother John Joe had two revolvers between them, but he knew quite well that he had no arms to give the men whom he immediately summoned: Jim Scanlon, Edward Foley and Seán Lynch. He told his brother: 'I'll be away this evening. If anything happens and I don't come back, keep an eye on my wife and child.' But when John Joe heard what dangerous work was afoot, he at once said that he, too, was coming to share the risks.

The five Galbally men set out for Maloney's at Lackelly, where they met Treacy, Breen and Robinson. Treacy came to the point at once and explained the revised plan. Four of the Galbally men, John Joe O'Brien, Foley, Lynch and Scanlon, were to cycle to Emly, board the train, find out if Hogan was on board, and signal to Treacy, O'Brien and the others at Knocklong station. Word had been sent to Thurles that a local Volunteer was to watch and board any train by which Hogan might travel, and to wave a white handkerchief from the window as a signal that Hogan was on the train. This man, 'Goorty' MacCarthy, did, in fact, travel on the train. His presence aroused no suspicion but he had, perhaps, little opportunity to give his signal as things moved much too fast. It is very probable, however, that it was he who gave Seán Hogan the first inkling that something was in the air. Hogan was unable to shake off the vigilance of the RIC escort. Several times he asked to be taken down the corridor, but he was always under strict guard. He noticed a man, vaguely familiar in appearance, who persisted in hanging round the corridor and who edged near him as if to whisper. The incident set him thinking as he sat in the carriage. He knew that Treacy, Robinson and Breen were capable of the most reckless and determined efforts to save him, and in some way this hovering figure was a message of hope. Hogan was seated with his back to the engine, still handcuffed, between Sergeant Wallace and Constable Enright, both of whom were armed with revolvers. Opposite him were Constables Reilly and Ring, both armed with loaded carbines. He looked past Wallace into the corridor through the sliding door of the carriage ...

Already the party at Maloney's in Lackelly had broken up. The four Galbally men had set out for Emly. Robinson and Breen cycled straight into Knocklong. Treacy and O'Brien went down to Knocklong station by the chapel, and arrived about 7.45 p.m. They still had some twenty minutes to spare. As David Bourke's message had failed to reach Thomas Shanahan, he was still a bewildered man. O'Connell's telegram about the greyhound was in his pocket, and, by a coincidence, it might very well have concerned his own private business. He had not connected it with Seán Treacy or Volunteer affairs. The day before he had sent a greyhound bitch to Mr Twamley, of Rathcoole, County Kildare, by the morning train, and wired to Twamley that it had been sent. The telegram from Thurles puzzled him, but he connected it naturally enough with the previous day's business. After some discussion with the stationmaster, Thomas Canty, he wired to Michael O'Connell to send back the greyhound; and then, still a worried man, he went across the road from the coal store for a drink. Shortly afterwards Treacy and O'Brien arrived in Knocklong. Treacy had expected that a messenger would meet him at the station. He sent Éamonn O'Brien in search of Shanahan, and gave him a close description of the man as O'Brien did not know him. O'Brien was directed to the public house where he looked round and at once saw a man who resembled the description that Treacy had so minutely given. He called the man aside and asked him his name. He was Thomas Shanahan, who looked very relieved when O'Brien next asked him whether he had any message. Shanahan knew then that the telegram was a code and that he could stop worrying about his greyhound in Kildare. He handed O'Brien the telegram which read: 'Greyhound in Thurles still.' As O'Brien hastened back to Treacy, he thought that there would be no rescue that evening. Treacy heard the message without comment and without giving any sign of his feelings. He decided to wait for the Galbally men who were coming on the train from Emly.

At that moment there was a warning of the grave risks the rescue party were taking. As a rule, the evening trains from Cork and Dublin arrived simultaneously at Knocklong, and very often there were RIC and military on both. The Dublin-bound train came in first. Treacy and O'Brien stepped back into the shadow of the platform shelter. There was a party of armed soldiers in one compartment of the train, and in another some Galbally RIC men, who descended and made their way out of the station. The train moved out towards Dublin. Treacy and O'Brien stepped out on to the platform, much relieved. They wanted no sideshows until Hogan was rescued, if indeed he ever was rescued. Seán Treacy, as a much-wanted man, could afford no risk of recognition until he had done the work upon which he was staking his life. Éamonn O'Brien was glad that he had escaped the eyes of the Galbally RIC men, who knew enough about him to keep a constant watch on his movements. Away down the line came the welcome sight of the Cork-bound train, and the whirl of smoke from its funnel as it swept rapidly in under the bridge. Just then, Thomas Shanahan came through the door and handed a second telegram to Éamonn O'Brien, which he was never to read. He found it in his pocket the following day and tore it into small pieces. But Shanahan had read it, and the code was plain enough this time, although there was a new signature to the message, which ran: 'Sending Wednesday evening by 6.30. Bridget Fitzpatrick.' The time for codes was past, however. There was to be a very full quarter of an hour at Knocklong station.

As the train stopped, and before it quite came to a standstill, John Joe O'Brien, who was standing at the window of the carriage, opened the door and jumped onto the platform without waiting to use the footboard of the train. Behind him, as he jumped, another of the Galbally men pointed to a compartment near the engine. John Joe said quickly to his brother: 'They are there. Hogan's on the train.' Seán Treacy had half-turned towards the station exit as the train stopped. He thought the evening's work was over. As Éamonn O'Brien turned and told him what John Joe's message was, Seán Treacy took off his glasses, placed them in the case, shoved the case in his side pocket, with the words: 'Is that so? Come on then!' Treacy was first into the corridor, his revolver drawn, with Éamonn O'Brien close behind him, his revolver ready too.

The two men passed down the corridor, the startled passengers gaping at them as they went. They threw back the sliding door of the carriage where Seán Hogan was sitting, with a sharp cry of command: 'Hands up! Come on, Seán, out!'

The challenge took the RIC by surprise, and for a moment it appeared that the rescue would be a bloodless one. Sergeant Wallace and the three constables half rose, half raised their hands. Then Seán Hogan felt the cold muzzle of Enright's revolver on his neck as the constable crouched behind him suddenly, using Hogan as a shield. Treacy and O'Brien promptly opened fire with their revolvers. Enright clutched

Seán Hogan's shoulder tightly and fell back dead, with a bullet through his heart. Afterwards, Treacy and O'Brien could scarcely remember why they fired, but they agreed that they would not have done so if Enright had not menaced Hogan. They resented the RIC evidence at the inquest later, and the ban on any questions which might have shown that the Knocklong rescuers had repeatedly asked Wallace and the rest of the guard to surrender or that there had not been any intention of shooting, except in a fair fight. That Treacy and O'Brien should fire in these circumstances was very understandable, in view of an order that all prisoners were to be shot in case of an attempted rescue. O'Brien himself, in describing the opening shots, said that the action of Treacy and himself had been spontaneous. 'We certainly,' he said, with emphasis and feeling to the writer, 'would never have fired if Enright had not made a move to attack Hogan.' As will be seen, too, in their subsequent prolonged duel with the determined Wallace, they made repeated appeals to him to surrender. Hogan wrenched himself free, and crashed his manacled hands in the face of his nearest captor. Treacy and Sergeant Wallace were locked in a death-grip. Enright's body thudded on the floor as Hogan hurled himself at Ring. Reilly had leaped on O'Brien's back after the first shots were fired, and now these two men wrestled fiercely together. The other Galbally men rushed in – unarmed, with the exception of a dagger and a small revolver, both ineffective and futile weapons as it proved – Jim Scanlon, John Joe O'Brien, Seán Lynch and Edward Foley. They wrenched Reilly's carbine from his grasp, crashed it on his head and he collapsed apparently unconscious on the floor. Even at the height of the struggle, Seán Treacy was determined that Hogan, handcuffed though he was, should escape. Lynch was ordered to take Hogan away. At first, even if Hogan had been willing to go, it would have been impossible because the struggle between Treacy and Wallace barred the exit as they hurtled to and fro, from carriage to corridor. Finally, Hogan and Lynch got into the corridor, but they did not descend onto the platform until the fight was over.

Fierce and thorough as the Knocklong fight was, it was a comparatively short one. The actual rescue in all lasted under fifteen minutes, between the arrival of the train at 8.13 to its departure at 8.27, according to the statement of the stationmaster subsequently. The tussle between Treacy and Wallace, the central episode of it all, was finished in less than five minutes, although, to the participants, every second was packed with effort and danger. Seán Treacy remained cool and silent, not a word escaping from him in the heat of it all, except his appeals to Wallace to surrender. He admired Wallace's courage, but his own was unbreakable as the two wrestled stubbornly for life and death. Panic reigned in the neighbourhood of the compartment, crowded with struggling men. Ring, dazed by the blow that Hogan had dealt him, and the reports of the revolvers ringing out in the narrow space of the carriage, jumped, or was thrown, out of the window. Wallace was deaf to every appeal; his great physical strength defied the combined onslaught of Treacy and O'Brien. Ever after, they spoke with deep respect of his courageous and stubborn stand. Wallace and Treacy battled for the possession of the sergeant's revolver, a short Webley. Seán's own weapon had fallen from his hand and was lost in the scurry of the struggling mass, hurtling and heaving together, cramped and constricted.

Treacy gripped the sergeant's hand tightly; he stuck his thumb between the trigger and cap and held on. None of the others could help him very much. John Joe O'Brien drew his revolver, a small .32, and fired at Wallace point blank, but the weapon misfired. He asked Jim Scanlon to give him Reilly's carbine which Scanlon was vainly trying to use as a bludgeon, hampered by the proximity of his companions.

With the carbine John Joe O'Brien would have opened fire and finished the fight, and thus averted an approaching danger that was soon to threaten disaster to the rescue. But Jim Scanlon, who had come unarmed into the fight, obstinately refused to surrender the carbine.

At last, seizing a favourable opportunity, Éamonn O'Brien closed with Wallace from behind and shouted at him for the last time to give up the struggle. Wallace was twisting his revolver towards Treacy's head; O'Brien tried to throw the sergeant to the floor, but Wallace, with a powerful effort, shook himself free. A shot rang out and a sharp pain seared Treacy's throat. For a moment Seán believed that he was dying. With a violent concentration of all his will and strength, he wrenched the gun from his enemy's hand and fired twice.

In that last stand against Treacy and O'Brien, Wallace's resistance had at last snapped, and now he collapsed on the floor, unconscious and fatally wounded. As the party turned to leave the train a carbine cracked sharply twice outside on the platform and O'Brien and Scanlon were wounded, although not seriously. Wallace had already wounded Treacy, who was feeling himself grow weaker and weaker, though no word of this escaped him. 'I thought I was a dead man,' he told Brian Shanahan afterwards. 'I had to hold my head up with both hands, but I knew I could walk, and I could jump off a ditch.'

It was Constable Reilly who was firing the carbine. According to his own story later, he had lain senseless on the floor – or shamming insensibility, as Jim Scanlon always contended. At all events, Reilly recovered either his senses or his nerve towards the end of the struggle and noticed Ring's carbine, which he knew was loaded, under one of the seats. He secured it and wormed his way out unnoticed while the last stage of the fight raged.

His own story was that Wallace and two men were in the corridor struggling, and the sergeant was on the point of collapse. Reilly gave one look round the carriage, empty except for Enright lying on the floor, dashed onto the platform and fired through the window at the two men, and saw blood immediately on the face of the man who was holding Wallace from behind. He saw no more of the two men who then, according to his story, disappeared. But he certainly became very busy with his carbine.

The *Tipperary Star* report of the rescue somewhat acidly commented that Reilly 'when he recovered from the staggering jab he had received in the affray, dashed out firing shots like a man entirely out of his senses. The stationmaster, among others, had a narrow shave from random bullets.'

At this critical moment the reports of the revolver and rifle fire brought Dan Breen and Seamus Robinson hurrying down the crowded platform thronged with excited passengers. The last phase of the Knocklong rescue was a fast and furious exchange of shots between Reilly and Breen. Just as Reilly had fired into the carriage, Breen rushed up and distracted his attention by a fierce and determined fusillade of revolver shots. Reilly fell back, still firing his rifle, and turned his attention to other targets.

Breen had saved a very ugly situation, because his comrades were half exhausted, some wounded – Treacy, as we have seen, almost fatally – and they had lost nearly all their weapons in the struggle. Breen himself, however, was shot through one of his lungs and right arm. His revolver dropped from his hand. Dizzy with pain, he picked up his revolver with his left hand and stood his ground. Robinson and Breen had been on guard outside the station and both had been misled by a message sent out to them earlier that Hogan was not on the train, that is, when O'Brien had read the first telegram: 'Greyhound in Thurles still'. Robinson had also been surprised by the suddenness with which the fight started. During the discussion of the plans he had more than once impressed upon the party not to open fire without orders, and, as he heard the revolver and rifle fire as he entered the station, he first feared that a premature shot had ruined the rescue.

Panic still reigned, and it was some minutes before Robinson could discover the actual position. He saw, however, that the worst had not happened. He prepared to intervene as soon as he could with effect. A thought flashed into his mind, a curious oversight in the plans … there had been no provision against any attempt to start the train. Robinson hurried quickly to a spot where he could keep his eye and his gun on the engine driver. The next minute he saw Treacy, Breen and Hogan, and knew the rescue had indeed succeeded.

Hogan had been snatched from an armed guard and death, but at a heavy cost. It was the merest chance that Seán Treacy left the station alive. Dan Breen was semi-delirious with pain, and on the edge of collapse from loss of blood. He had a vague memory of being helped from the station into the roadway by an Irish soldier in khaki who had previously cheered for the Irish Republic while the fight raged.

The rescuers hurried from the scene. Seán Hogan was taken

into a neighbouring shop and his handcuffs broken with the aid of a butcher's cleaver and a heavy weight. At the first blow the handcuffs flew open, and Hogan hurried forward to rejoin the others. Seamus Robinson was the last to leave the station.

The party pressed on quickly to Michael Shanahan's near Knocklong, where Dr Hennessy of Ballylanders (later a member of the Dáil) attended to Breen and Treacy. Breen's condition was so serious that morphia was administered at once, and both the doctor and a priest, who arrived soon afterwards, were certain that he would not survive his wounds. Treacy, on the other hand, kept on his feet, remained cool and silent, and apparently had recovered from the shock of the encounter. Breen and Treacy were soon afterwards removed to Clancy's of Cush. In the meantime, Volunteer guards had been posted at all approaches to the house, and preparations pushed forward to place the rescuers beyond pursuit.

Treacy and Breen had been driven from Shanahan's to Clancy's in a pony and trap. They arrived early in the morning and stayed there a day. Treacy had already met David Clancy with Liam Manahan at Ballylanders in 1916. Clancy was a first lieutenant in the local Volunteer company. His brother, Patrick, was in jail at the time; he was later O/C of the North Cork flying column, a vice-commandant, and took part in many engagements in the Black and Tan war. Patrick Clancy was shot dead at Derrygallon, three miles from Kanturk, County Cork, on 16 August 1920.

Dr Fitzgerald, of Mortalstown, Kilfinane, was summoned to Clancy's soon after the two men arrived. He found Breen lying in a deep and drugged sleep. Seán Treacy was walking about, very calm and self-possessed. When the doctor examined him, Treacy merely complained of a loose upper tooth, caused by a blow during the struggle. Dr Fitzgerald removed it with a forceps, and Treacy said no more.

Ever after the doctor judged Treacy by that request. He had had the narrowest of escapes, said Dr Fitzgerald, and it was the merest luck that he ever left Knocklong alive after the throat wound inflicted on him, because the slightest deviation of the bullet to the right or left would have been fatal. The big blood vessels had just been missed. In its way, the wound was serious enough; it was very near the jugular vein and carotid arteries.

'Seán Treacy,' said Dr Fitzgerald to the writer, 'was not complaining about the big and painful wound in his throat. Most men, myself included, would not have bothered about anything else. Yet all that worried Treacy was that loosened tooth. Treacy was the coolest man there, far cooler than I was. That was Seán Treacy!'

Until the removal of the Knocklong party, the Kilfinane Volunteers remained actively on guard with their scouts vigilant, while Seán Finn (Commandant, West Limerick Brigade, killed in action in March 1921) completed the arrangements to remove Treacy, Robinson, Breen and Hogan as quickly as possible. Between eleven o'clock and midnight two cars arrived at Clancy's in the charge of Garrett McAuliffe. Breen, still very weak and semiconscious, was carried to one car which was left in darkness; and Seán Hogan accompanied Breen. The first car went ahead with lights full on, as a pilot car, or decoy. The cars rushed along at a high speed right through the town of Kilmallock where the bodies of Wallace and Enright had already been brought to the local barracks for an inquest, and eventually reached their destination safely, Keane's of west Limerick, between Newcastle West and Drumcollogher.

During the summer of 1919 the Big Four (Treacy, Breen,

Robinson and Hogan) spent a wandering life in the south. In west Limerick they stayed in turn with the Longs, Sheehans, Keanes, Duffys and Kennedys, then with friends in Kerry, Clare and north Tipperary. Among their friends in Kerry were Mattie O'Connor's and J.T. O'Connor's, Meenleitrim, and Hickey's of Ballinathair. Seán Treacy spent some of the time on an island off the Clare coast with Seán Carroll and Joe Herbert of Castleconnell. Among their friends in north Tipperary were Frank McGrath, Brigade Commandant of the area and a prominent GAA man, and 'Widger' Meagher, also a famous athlete.

A week after the Knocklong rescue Seán Treacy and Hogan arrived at Michael Dore's, Ballystin House, Shanagolden, west Limerick. By order of Seán Finn, Brigade Commandant, west Limerick area, Dore later led them to Tom Wallace's, Washpool, Kildimo, County Limerick. From there they left for Ringmoylan, about a mile from the village of Pallaskenry, where they crossed the Shannon with Breen and Robinson.

Chapter 11

Escape from Strangeways jail, Manchester

by Piaras Béaslaí

Having escaped with nineteen other prisoners from Mountjoy jail, Dublin, on 29 March 1919, I was recaptured in May in what was then the village of Finglas, County Dublin, and again imprisoned in Mountjoy. As an 'escapist' I was regarded as being a dangerous man and kept apart from the other political prisoners – with one exception. For some reason D.P. Walsh of Fethard, County Tipperary, who had been arrested a short time previously, was allowed to exercise with me every day. Except for him I had no companion this second time in Mountjoy, no one else with whom to exchange a word other than the warders – some of whom were in touch with Michael Staines, and, through him, with Michael Collins. Through friendly warders I had contacts with the outside world.

It has been observed by jailers that a prisoner who had once escaped and been recaptured is likely to attempt another escape. In my own case, from the day of my recapture I began to plan another escape. I was in communication with Michael Collins. A number of letters passed between us in which various plans were outlined for consideration; and also between us and Robert Barton who had escaped from Mountjoy jail on 16 March 1919. Plan after plan was considered and rejected. At last a daring, indeed a desperate, plan would have been attempted were it not for my being unexpectedly transferred to Birmingham jail.

Before the transfer I had been taken to Dublin Castle, tried by court martial and sentenced to two years' imprisonment. At the same sitting of the court martial D.P. Walsh had been sentenced to eighteen months. He and I were in the same boat, in every sense, from Kingstown (now Dún Laoghaire) to Holyhead – he en route to Leeds jail and I on my way to Birmingham. I was the only Irish political prisoner in Birmingham, though a number of the 'German Plot' men had been interned there in the previous year.

I had an empty ward in the prison hospital all to myself, and a file which I had managed to conceal could be used to cut through a single window-bar (as Robert Barton had done in Mountjoy). I could then get out, climb along a wall and drop into the street. Having considered this project I decided against it. I did not know Birmingham or anybody in it, I had no money, and, as the attempt must be made in the small hours of the morning, my recapture was almost inevitable. Later I was transferred to an ordinary cell and an attempt was made to treat me as a criminal. This I resisted, and ultimately the prison authorities abandoned it.

Early in August I was sent to Strangeways jail, Manchester, where other Irish political prisoners were held. With many others, these men had been imprisoned in Belfast jail originally and whilst held there they carried on a prolonged revolt against the jail authorities who denied them political status. At length, on 29 April 1919, they were transferred to Strangeways and all their privileges as political prisoners were restored to them. Their leader throughout this period was Austin Stack and, at the time of my arrival in Strangeways, they numbered eleven. At the same time D.P. Walsh was transferred from Leeds to Manchester. Like me, he had had to fight for his rights as a political prisoner.

Part of the trouble in Belfast jail had its origin in an attempt to treat a political prisoner, John Doran of Loughinisland, County Down, as a criminal. Austin Stack ordered the other political prisoners to take him into their wing of the jail and keep him there in open defiance of the authorities, a campaign that ended in triumph for the prisoners after months of resistance and suffering. Doran was one of the group that ultimately escaped from Strangeways.

Directly I arrived in Strangeways' jail I began to consider methods of escape, and it seemed to me that the plan which had worked successfully in Mountjoy (to scale the jail wall in broad daylight by means of a rope ladder thrown over by friends outside) could be adapted to Strangeways. It was true that the situation outside the walls was vastly different: the difference between the canal bank at Drumcondra, Dublin, and a street in a hostile British city. But I persisted in being hopeful.

The yard in which we exercised during the day was surrounded by the jail buildings; but at five o'clock in the evening, before we were locked up for the night, we were allowed out to exercise in another yard that was enclosed by a ring of high railings. Outside the railings stood a wall some forty feet high and downwards from the top of the wall extended a row of iron spikes, each spike about three feet long. It looked as if this was the outer wall of the jail, and it was obviously impossible to get over it because of the spikes. I noticed in the distance, however, a section of the wall that had no spikes. This section was barely visible from the ring where we exercised. I found out that it was in front of the hospital for women prisoners, from which point an escape was not considered to be likely. If we were to make an attempt to cross the wall, that surely was the place for us to make it, and there was nothing but a six-foot railing between us and it. But what was on the other side of the wall? It was a question that agitated me for some time.

I mentioned my ideas to Austin Stack who became keenly interested, and to Fionán Lynch who was due to be released soon, as his sentence was almost served. Fionán undertook to reconnoitre the outside of the jail immediately that he was released, with view to locating the spiked and the unspiked sections of the wall and mapping them in relation to the city streets. We arranged a code in which the escape was to be referred to as the 'examination'.

Within a couple of days of Fionán's release we had a letter from him in the course of which his prospects of securing a certain professional appointment were mentioned. 'I have studied the syllabus,' he wrote, 'and I think the examination can be passed quite easily.' Obviously, the prison official who censored the letter saw no harm in this 'innocent' message.

Fionán had made contact with Paddy O'Donoghue (later managing director of Shelbourne Park Greyhound Racing Track, Dublin) and Liam MacMahon of Manchester, both of whom were working in close association with Michael Collins. They had been considering a plan of rescue which involved the use of explosives, and they abandoned it in favour of my plan. They had already found a means of secret communication with Austin Stack.

There were no friendly warders to assist us as in Mountjoy but messages were sent to us in code (as in Fionán's letter) and baked in cakes or buried in butter and jam – Mrs Paddy O'Donoghue managed that part of the job. We sent out verbal messages by Seamus Mulcahy Lyons and Seamus Duggan, two prisoners who were released after their sentences had been served.

On other occasions we arranged for visits by O'Donoghue or MacMahon and, whilst shaking hands with them, contrived to slip them messages written on pieces of rolled-up paper. The other prisoners were not yet taken into our confidence concerning the escape project, as Stack and I thought it better to keep the plans to ourselves until they had been perfected. Michael Collins was keenly interested in the enterprise and I received a number of letters from him about it. These he sent through the ordinary post and they contained information about affairs in Ireland, veiled in code. The letters were boldly signed 'Michael Collins', a name which then meant nothing to the prison censor.

Our friends put the operation in train by sending us a map of the outside of the prison, and it got through to us baked in a cake. For our part we endeavoured to enlighten them as to the layout and other features of that section of the prison where we were confined. At length we learned that immediately outside the section of wall without spikes was a small side-street off a main thoroughfare and that opposite that proposed point of escape was a piece of unenclosed waste land which suited our purpose admirably. It was decided to get on with the job.

Michael Collins brought the project before the general headquarters of the IRA in Dublin, and Rory O'Connor was sent over to examine the plans on the spot. In the code used for communications between the rescuers and ourselves Collins now became known as 'Angela' and Paddy O'Donoghue as 'Maud'. And so it happened that Austin Stack received a postcard from a convent school and signed 'Your loving cousin, Maud'. This contained the seemingly innocent information: 'We are all busy preparing for the examination. Professor Rory has arrived. He is a very nice man. I hope I shall pass.' No doubt the prison censor considered this message to be quite charming and innocent. A few days later Collins arrived and, under a false name, paid a visit to Stack. Despite the presence of a warder throughout the visit, he contrived to give Stack a pretty good idea of the situation in Ireland and mentioned also that he was now living at his old address in Mountjoy Street, Dublin, as the G-men (detectives of the political branch of the G-Division of the Dublin Metropolitan Police) were afraid to interfere with him. At the time the dense ignorance of Englishmen of the prison-warder class, of Irish affairs, made it easy to defeat their censorship on such occasions.

By now the overall plans for our escape had begun to take definite shape, and Mulcahy Lyons and Duggan were able to take out elaborate details of them to our friends outside. In addition to Stack and myself there were Seán Doran of Loughinisland, County Down; D.P. Walsh of Fethard, County Tipperary; Paddy McCarthy of Freemount, County Cork; and Con Connolly of Clonakilty, County Cork. Six in all. The others had completed their sentences and been released.

In the daytime we took our exercise in the closed-in yard, two warders in charge of us, and we had our meals in our separate cells; but we were allowed to have our evening meal together, and we got out again at five o'clock for a half-hour's additional exercise during which we were enclosed within the railings in the yard by the spiked wall. By that time all the non-political prisoners had been locked up, most of the warders had gone off duty for the evening, and only one of them remained in charge of us. We decided that this warder should be overpowered, tied and gagged the moment he had unlocked the door of the ward to let us into the yard after supper. Then we would climb over the railings, run to the wall at the point where the spikes ended and throw over a stone as a signal to our collaborators on the outside. They would then fling over a rope by means of which we could pull a rope ladder over the wall which was twice as high as that of Mountjoy. The greatest risk was incurred by our outside collaborators who had to 'hold up' the street for the purpose of our rescue.

One problem that worried us was how the last man over the wall could slide down the rope on the outside when nobody remained inside to hold down the rope ladder. Our only hope was that it would be possible to tie the end of the rope ladder to a railings outside the women prisoners' hospital, but we were not certain that this could be done. We urged that our collaborators should bring a patent-ladder and place it against the wall, but in the beginning they did not realise how very important this was, as no such ladder was needed for the Mountjoy escape.

The escape was fixed for Saturday 11 October at 5 p.m. (following one postponement). Five days before that date Stack and I were informed that a visitor, a Mr O'Brien, wished to see us. We were escorted into the visiting room and found that 'Mr O'Brien' was one of our IRA colleagues, J.J. Walsh, himself an escaped prisoner and a 'wanted' man. He knew nothing of our plans to get out and had come merely to pay us a friendly visit, as his business had taken him to Manchester.

Having chatted with us for some time he turned to the warder and threw all of us into consternation by facetiously enquiring of him: 'Have these fellows tried to get over the wall yet?' On the spur of the moment Stack sought to avert suspicion by telling the exact truth as though it was a huge joke. 'We're going over the top on Saturday,' he said. We learned afterwards that this passage was reported to the governor, and in the following days there were indications that the jail authorities suspected us of having some plot in train. One of our problems was to find plausible pretexts for sending out to friends those of our belongings which we could not take with us when escaping and did not wish to leave behind. Stack and I had sent out our books and other property by Mulcahy Lyons and Duggan, but the other four prisoners, not having learned of the plot until later, had to resort to various ruses to send the articles they valued into safe keeping outside the jail.

Saturday 11 October found us in a state of tense excitement. Just after dinner Doran received a visit from O'Donoghue who slipped him a note for Stack. It was stated in the note that there was a danger the escape would have to be postponed again; that if at three o'clock we heard three whistles outside the wall we were to react by singing and shouting loudly and to consider the arrangements as being off for the present. At three o'clock the whistle told us that we would not be going over the wall that day and, as instructed, we signalled that the message had been received. Paddy McCarthy began to sing and shout wildly in a manner that the warders regarded as being characteristic of a 'mad Irishman'.

We remained in a state of suspense until next day when a note in code got through to us from O'Donoghue. It was hidden in a pot of jam and it explained that the escape had been postponed because Christy O'Malley and Owen Cullen from Dublin had not arrived with the patent-ladder. They had reached Manchester all right, but because of some misdirection they failed to find the correct place of rendezvous. The abandonment of this first attempt was providential because it would certainly have failed as our friends outside had not provided a patent-ladder. They believed that they could throw a rope over the wall and that we could then haul over the rope ladder as was done in the Mountjoy escape; had they depended solely on this method, without having a patent-ladder at hand, the attempt would have ended in fiasco.

We were left for several days without further news from our collaborators on the outside, and in that time our position had become difficult. The plans were now known to all six of us, and we had torn sheets and blankets into strips for the purpose of tying up the warder. The strips were hidden under our plank beds, and we lived in hourly fear of their being discovered.

At length we got word that the date of the escape had been re-fixed for Saturday 25 October. Handcuffs to secure the warder had been obtained from an Irish policeman in Manchester, and they had been sent in together with a dummy pistol to intimidate anybody who might attempt to prevent the escape. These items came concealed in butter. It was arranged that Doran, Connolly and McCarthy would spring on the warder and tie him up as soon as he had unlocked the door to the yard. Stack would run out and give the signal by throwing stones over the wall. My task was to rig bedboards over the railings of our enclosure so that Connolly, Doran and McCarthy could each clear it with a rapid bound; and, to delay pursuit in case of an alarm, D.P. Walsh was to hammer wooden plugs into the keyholes of all the doors leading into the yard.

The postponement of the attempt on 11 October was probably useful in that the delay may have allayed the suspicions of the authorities and caused them to relax their vigilance.

When the appointed time came, on 25 October, our part in the plan worked admirably. The warder was overpowered without difficulty. He was a stranger and we were glad, for it would have been unpleasant to rough-handle one of the men with whom we had become friendly. He was secured by the handcuffs, gagged and thrust into a cell, the doors of which, as in all cells in British jails, locked automatically when closed. While Connolly, Doran and McCarthy were securing the warder, Stack, Walsh and I dashed out to perform our allotted tasks. Quickly the signal was given, the rails were cleared, and in a few moments all six of us were at the appointed place inside the wall. This was in broad daylight, and, as many of the jail windows overlooked the spot where we assembled, it was extraordinary that nobody saw us and raised the alarm.

With beating hearts we fixed our eyes on the top of the wall. In a matter of seconds a rope, with a weight attached, soared over our side of the wall but it came down only a few feet and dangled high above our heads. The rope was pulled back and thrown again with no better result. With mounting anxiety we awaited the outcome of the third effort. It succeeded in getting the rope a few feet nearer to us, but still hopelessly beyond our reach. Despair fell upon us. We had burned our boats and now the attempted escape looked like ending in a ludicrous fiasco. Our friends could not get the rope down to us and nothing appeared to be happening outside. The minutes that passed seemed like so many hours, for we were in constant danger of discovery. Then we saw reason to hope once more. A head and shoulders appeared above the wall. They belonged to Peadar

Clancy, and he had come up by the patent-ladder. That ladder had been brought on a cart through the streets of Manchester by a man who posed as a window cleaner, and only for it all was lost. At once grasping the situation, Peadar crawled along the wall to the rope and lowered it down to us. Then we pulled down the rope and with it came the rope ladder.

Austin Stack was the first to go and he got over safely. I was climbing after him and D. P. Walsh was following me. Just as I had got my arm over the wall the fourth prisoner in line impetuously sprang on the rope ladder. There was only one man holding the rope on the outside and the combined weight of three prisoners was too much for him. To avoid being pulled up he had to let the rope slip a few feet and, in the process, it caught my arm and pinned it to the top of the wall. I could not move and I suffered awful agony. Worse still, none of those below could pass me on the rope ladder. In an urgent whisper I explained the situation to them and they had to get down off the rope ladder so that I could release my arm. To all of us this seemed to take ages and, of course, it did involve serious loss of time.

More than twenty men were posted outside the jail and they were holding up all persons who attempted to pass along the street. Nobody offered resistance. The hold-up men were mostly Liverpool and Manchester Irish. Rory O'Connor and Peadar Clancy were in charge of the rescue, and they had with them two other Dublin men, Owen Cullen and Christy O'Malley. There were twelve men from Liverpool and they included Stephen Lanigan and the veteran Neil Kerr and his son Tom. Paddy O'Donoghue was there from Manchester, with James Murphy, Dick Hurley, William Concannon, Joe O'Sullivan, 'Jock' and James MacGallogly, Matt Lawless and Paddy O'Meara.

Stack and I cut the skin of our hands to pieces when sliding down the rope. The last two prisoners came down the patent-ladder. When we reached the street we ran across to the waste land where Paddy O'Donoghue was waiting. Afterwards, I vaguely retained the impression of an almost deserted street with a man standing in the middle of it. He was in shirt sleeves, wearing an apron, and was the man who had brought the patent-ladder. O'Donoghue directed us down a side-street at the end of which a young man named George Lodge had a taxi waiting. Lodge, another of the Manchester Irishmen, later took Stack and me to his home in a city suburb. D.P. Walsh travelled with us as far as Piccadilly where the taxi driver was paid off. The driver, who had been engaged by O'Donoghue, was in complete ignorance of the nature of the work on which he was employed. Lodge told us to walk on while he was paying him, so as to avoid attracting attention. We walked on to such effect that we lost Lodge and were wandering about in the crowds for about ten minutes before we found him again. Stack and I then went with him by tram to his house in a remote suburb. We left Walsh in the care of some of the rescuers who took him in a different direction to ours.

The other three prisoners were provided with bicycles but, having missed their guides in the excitement of the occasion, they got themselves lost in the streets of Manchester. All three were country lads with no knowledge of city ways. An adventure that befell two of them would be considered a most improbable coincidence if read in a work of fiction. Lodge, who later came to live in Dublin, was not long in Manchester at the time and was little known there. For that reason his home was regarded as being a safe hiding place for Stack and myself. Little more than an hour after our arrival at his place there was a knock on the door. He sent us upstairs before he opened the door. A strange girl stood outside. She first asked him if he was Irish and then if he was a Sinn Féiner. Naturally, under the circumstances, he was greatly startled by the second question, and, of course, he denied all sympathy with Sinn Féin. The girl then said she had a very urgent message which she wished to deliver to some trustworthy Sinn Féiner.

Lodge was non-plussed. This might be a trap, and with two prisoners hidden upstairs he could take no risk. On the other hand the message might be genuine and really important and urgent. What should he do? That was the question. Then he had a brainwave. He gave the girl the address of the president of the Irish Self-Determination League which, he said, had appeared in the latest issue of *The Catholic Herald*, and he read out the address to her from *The Herald*, pretending not to know the man. The president was Liam MacMahon, and Lodge knew he was sending her to the right quarters without giving anything away. But, nevertheless, he remained uneasy following her departure.

The explanation of the incident was astonishing. At the time when the girl was talking to Lodge, two others of the escaped prisoners, Doran and MacCarthy, were in the street outside. Having got themselves lost in Manchester they took refuge in a religious institution and whilst there they met this girl. She was Irish and they confided in her the story of their escape from Strangeways. She agreed to help them. Of all possible houses in Manchester, with its huge population, the first place to which she brought them for refuge was the very house in which Austin Stack and I were hiding, although she did not know Lodge. It was an amazing coincidence.

All the prisoners who had got lost were soon traced and

housed in safe places of refuge, pending the return of all of us to Ireland.

After we had stayed a week in Lodge's house we were visited by Michael Collins who was accompanied by Liam MacMahon and Neil Kerr. Three days later MacMahon and Lodge travelled with us by train to Liverpool. We travelled openly, without any attempt at disguise, but we played cards all the way to avoid getting into conversation with other passengers. We gave the impression of being a carefree holiday party. At Liverpool we were handed over to Neil Kerr and Lanigan and they conveyed us to the house of Mrs MacCarthy, the same Mrs MacCarthy who had hidden de Valera following his escape from Lincoln jail. A few nights later we were smuggled from Liverpool across to Dublin in the fo'castle of a B & I steamer. Stack and I crossed first and Ned Kavanagh, a sailor, smuggled us into a couple of bunks – his own and that of a comrade. The other sailors showed no curiosity whatever, for they were accustomed to such smuggling. At six o'clock in the morning we arrived at Sir John Rogerson's Quay, Dublin, where the trustworthy Joe O'Reilly awaited us with a motor car.

The escape was an exciting and surprising achievement, and our share in it was the smallest part of the exploit. The daring of the rescuers who, in a Manchester street in broad daylight, held up all traffic and carried out their task with such efficiency, cool courage and military precision that all prisoners and rescuers were enabled to get safely away, is part of the saga of Ireland.

I was never recaptured though I had some narrow escapes, notably on the night before 'Bloody Sunday'. Neither was Austin Stack recaptured. Paddy McCarthy, a north Cork man, was killed in action against the Black and Tans. And a year later

Seán Doran was recaptured and brought back to Strangeways where he was held until the Truce. About the same time D.P. Walsh, having been arrested and tried on another charge in Glasgow where he was buying guns for Michael Collins, was subsequently identified and also brought back to Strangeways. He, too, remained there until after the Truce.

Chapter 12

Rescue of Frank Carty from Sligo jail

by Bill Kelly

The British armed forces, both military and police, owned or controlled almost all the motor transport that was permitted to use the roads of southern Ireland in 1920. In the darkness of a June night in that year two motor cars were driven cautiously along a road above Sligo cemetery. They did not belong to the crown forces, but there were five armed men in each. In fact, the British would have given a lot to be in control of those two cars and the men in them. They were men of the Sligo Brigade IRA and they had come in from the north and the south of the brigade area in response to a summons from Billy Pilkington, their brigadier.

Men who had been summoned included Jack Brennan and Mick O'Hara of Cloonacool; Mick McLoughlin, Harry Brehony and Frank O'Beirne of Collooney; Harry Conry and Jimmy Devins of the 2nd (Grange) Battalion.

Other IRA men had urgent business in Sligo that same night. The Sligo Town Battalion was mobilised and its commandant, Jim Keaveney, was busy. One of his captains, Tom Scanlon, was checking the dispositions of his men. Quartermaster Charlie Dolan was there, and so was pint-sized Dominic McHugh, the

Battalion Adjutant, whose heart and courage and efficiency made all men overlook his lack of inches. McHugh, too, had work to do. From the Ballymote Battalion had come Thady McGowan and Alex McCabe, and Peadar Glynn of the Sligo (1st) Battalion had, perhaps, been busier than most during the previous few days.

Alex McCabe had not come direct from Ballymote. He had been lying low in Summerhill College following a hunger strike in Mountjoy jail and a spell in St Vincent's Hospital. The IRA prisoners in Mountjoy had gone on hunger strike to gain the rights of political prisoners. After the strike had continued for some weeks the British, fearing for the health of the hunger strikers, sent McCabe, Barney O'Driscoll and Christy Lacey to St Vincents for medical treatment. A fortnight later Michael Collins had word sent to them that, immediately they were discharged from the hospital they would be rearrested under the Cat and Mouse Act. So the three IRA men discharged themselves from hospital, and Linda Kearns drove McCabe back to his native Sligo where he took refuge in Summerhill College.

O'Driscoll and Lacey headed homewards also, but Lacey was unfortunate. Shortly afterwards his hide-out was raided and he was shot dead 'while attempting to escape' – or so the enemy reported. McCabe had been in the college a few days when a recognition signal heralded the approach of Peadar Glynn. A short exchange of greetings, the message from Pilkington was passed on and the pair set off for Sligo town.

In many other parts of the brigade area men were carrying orders from Brigadier Pilkington for the mobilisation of certain of his active service men. He had decided that Frank Carty, his Vice-Brigadier, had already been long enough a prisoner in

Sligo jail. Carty had been inside for some months and this was how he came to be there. Like many other British ex-officers at the time, Major Percival of Temple House had arms. The IRA needed arms badly and so, one night in February, a party led by Jim Hunt and Frank Carty entered the Percival home, a few miles outside Sligo, and acquired the Percival guns and ammunition. Mrs Percival was a problem and she had to be tied to a chair during the process of acquisition. Later she deposed that Carty was the man who had tied her. In fact, Carty was not the man, but, after a police swoop had dragnetted twenty men suspected of having taken part in the business, he was lodged in Sligo jail and accused of this violence to the lady.

Brigadier Pilkington wanted him out and laid plans carefully. Sligo was held by strong forces of the enemy. Across the river, about 200 yards from Cranmore where stood the jail, was the military barracks. There were also two police barracks in the town and their combined RIC and Black and Tan garrisons were at full strength. Breaking into the jail would be the easy part of the job. Getting Carty away safely might be difficult. If the enemy were alerted there would be a gun fight such as Sligo had never seen before. For the Town Battalion had, on Pilkington's direction, thrown a ring of barricades and outposts around the jail and covered all the approaches from the barracks. Their orders were to hold off the enemy.

Earlier, men of the Sligo Town Battalion had put ladders in position near the jail, to be used by the men scaling the jail wall. At zero hour the telephone wires would be cut and, while the assault party went into action to release Frank Carty, the ring of IRA men would cover the withdrawal.

The armed party of ten which had come in by the road above the cemetery joined a small body of waiting men and all moved off cautiously through fields above the town. No smoking was permitted. Each man kept close to the man in front of him. They covered ground rapidly, the swish of the dew-wet grass against their boots being the only sound to break the silence of the pitch-black night. Here and there pinpoints of light stabbed the darkness that enveloped the sleeping huddle of the town and warned the column of men that not everybody slept and that, above all, the enemy might be on the alert.

As the men made their way across the fields and approached the town the wind freshened from the bay and the slight tang of the sea tasted fresh and clean. Soon the great hulk of the jail wall loomed high in the darkness and the column halted as its leader held a whispered consultation with a shadowy figure which had materialised as though from nowhere. It was the brigadier. In a quiet voice which carried down the line, he detailed their duties to the men from the country companies who had volunteered for the dangerous tasks inside the walls. It was essential that the men who went in should not be local men, in case of recognition by warders or others of the prison staff. There had been no lack of volunteers.

'There is a ladder here on the outside,' Pilkington told them. 'You will climb that and you will find a rope ladder in position on the inside.' To two of the party he said: 'You will take up positions in the main hall and make sure that the patrol man doesn't ring the alarm bell.'

Of the men present, each had a part to play and he knew it to the last detail. Pilkington had seen to that. The signal was then given for the operation to commence. Massive iron gates, taken from Kilgallon's, a big house within a quarter-mile of the jail, were put in position across the avenue leading to the jail. Twenty men with crowbars, sledgehammers and a pickaxe moved through the darkness to positions outside the wicket gate in the main avenue. Another twenty or more occupied the outpost positions. The telephone wires leading to the jail and to the military and police barracks were cut.

The scaling-ladder squeaked as it was raised and placed firmly in position against the weather-beaten stone of the 32-foot-high wall of the jail. Rapidly, thirteen men climbed the ladder which was held securely by two men on the ground. As each man arrived on top of the wall he immediately started down the rope ladder into the jail courtyard. Alex McCabe was the contact man between the parties.

Harry Conry went over first. The others followed. In the yard they paused for a minute, on the alert for the slightest sound which would indicate that their entry had been detected. Nothing stirred. Not a thing was heard save the soft whistle of the wind around the jail walls.

In his cell Frank Carty waited tensely. Throughout the week messages had been brought into him by Warder O'Connor who was one of the brigade contacts inside the wall. In the dimly lit hall sat Chief Warder Hooke, armed but at ease. How could he suspect that desperate men were about to shatter his illusions of the security of Sligo jail? In his house, separated from the cell block by an open yard, Governor Reid slept soundly. In the yard beneath the shadow of the wall thirteen men waited breathlessly, each waiting second an hour of suspense.

Thirteen hands gripped gun butts. In mounting tension thirteen men lived an eternity as they waited for a significant sound. At last it came. The sound of the ponderous, assured footsteps of the night patrolman on his rounds. Nearer and nearer came the sound, and now the waiting men could hear the patrolman whistling tunelessly under his breath, his thoughts, no doubt, on his meal-break which was due shortly. This was a vital moment. A blunder now and the entire carefully laid rescue plan could be ruined. If the patrolman heard a sibilant breath, if he even suspected anything untoward, his whistle would alarm the entire jail and Carty would remain inside, the men in the yard would be trapped, and blood would be spilled in the inevitable gunfight between the IRA and the enemy. Nerves were stretched to breaking point as the patrolman approached. Two figures sneaked silently along in the darkness, so unobtrusively that the waiting men were not sure if they had imagined the movements. Still, not a sound was heard other than that made by the patrolman. Suddenly the plod of his footsteps ceased and the tuneless whistle died in his throat as a rough hand closed firmly over his mouth. Terror and consternation gripped him, for he had no doubt that he was in deadly peril. Something was pressed hard into his ribs, and he nodded his head vigorously in acquiescence when a low voice enjoined him to remain silent if he valued his life.

The patrolman was only doing a job. He looked forward to a quiet life and a pension on retirement. He had no wish to be a dead hero for Britain and so he remained alive. Trussed up with his own belt, he was gagged with a piece of cloth and left sitting on the ground, his back resting against the wall. But he was alive and witness to part of the strangest happening of his prison career.

The men outside the jail wall waited, their eyes straining to probe the darkness, their ears attuned to the slightest sound. Captain Jim Keaveney had one bad moment. Checking the positions of the men, he happened upon a small figure muffled up in cap and coat. Some young fellow from the town, no doubt, whose curiosity had got the better of his good sense.

So Jim thought, and he gruffly ordered: 'Get home out of here, quickly, my lad, and forget you saw anything!' A stuttering incoherence was his first warning that he had been guilty of a *faux pas*. For the muffled figure drew itself up to its full height of five feet nothing, and Adjutant Dominic McHugh spluttered his indignation to Jim whose embarrassment, when he discovered his error, was mercifully hidden in the darkness of the night.

Inside the walls the climactic moment of the rescue was at hand. Pilkington, who never raised his voice, never lost his temper, never swore, never permitted a man in his company to swear, was leading the operation personally. Having marked off five of his men, he tapped them on the shoulders as a signal to get going. They skirted the archway with its faint glow of light and vanished into the darkness near the governor's house. Seconds later two men moved into positions, their task to maintain communications. Four others crossed the yard in single file, five paces between each man. Quietly but purposefully they headed for the hall where Warder Hooke drowsed in his high chair. Before the warder knew what was happening, Pilkington had poked a pistol into his ribs. Within arm's reach of Hooke was the switch which could set off the brazen clamour of the alarm. But he made no movement towards it. In a flash two men pounced on him and he was bound and gagged and relieved of his keys.

Harry Conry, later to become one of Michael Collins' intelligence officers, signalled a contact man who doubled across the yard to the governor's house, regardless of the noise he made. When he got inside the house he made straight for the governor's room and saw grey-haired Governor Reid sitting up in bed, his hair tousled and his eyes filled with sleepy astonishment following a rude awakening from slumberland. Reid was being menaced by five armed men. Defiant, but with an undertone of fear or uncertainty, he said to them: 'Even if I had the keys, I'm blowed if I'd give them to you. The governor doesn't keep keys …' The voice tailed off, interrupted by the metallic click of a safety catch being released. 'The keys or else …' The keys changed ownership. There was a murmur of voices and a curt order directing two men to secure the governor. The other three men, with Pilkington in the lead, dashed full pelt across the yard to the cell block. It was the work of but a moment for one of them to unlock the door to the corridor. In another moment Pilkington had raced down the corridor and turned a key in the lock of Frank Carty's cell. The vice-brigadier, dressed for the street, followed him through the corridor and out into the fresh air of the courtyard.

Fourteen men crowded at the foot of the rope ladder in the courtyard. Speed was more essential than ever then, for surely the alarm must be raised any second. None of the men inside the yard could even know for certain whether enemy forces on patrol in the town had not been inadvertently alerted through some action by members of the rescue party. Even now military and police might be converging on Cranmore.

Brigadier Pilkington decided that escape over the wall by means of the rope ladder would be dangerously slow. Everything had gone well for him. Now he must not risk any of his men being shot or captured as they dangled more or less helplessly from the wall. There was no time to look for the keys to the gate. Pilkington nodded. One of the men, his mouth almost dry with tension, managed to whistle. His shrill note had scarcely ended when the night silence was shattered by the crash of sledgehammers and crowbars on the sturdy wicket gate, as the twenty men on the outside worked with a will to demolish the barrier between Frank Carty and the others of his rescue party and the completion of their mission. The din was deafening. It seemed as though the whole town of Sligo must be awakened and the military in the barracks across the river startled into action. The fourteen men inside the jail checked their weapons.

With a crash like thunder the gate collapsed and Frank Carty and the thirteen others dashed through the gap. As soon as he saw them emerge, Jim Keaveney sped from outpost to outpost, ordering the stand-to parties to dismiss at once. The men from the country companies doubled across the sodden fields and were then driven to their homes in cars which had all lights switched out. The men of the Sligo Town Battalion slipped home and into bed. Frank Carty was whisked out of town. Through all this activity the jail personnel, the police and the military remained silent and inactive.

It was after one o'clock in the morning. Kilgallon's gates still blocked the avenue to the jail. All was peaceful in Sligo town. Nobody noticed two young men who were making their way to Rosehill on the outskirts – Peadar Glynn was escorting Alex McCabe to where Alex was to spend the night, or what remained of it. They were pleased with themselves, rejoicing in the parts that they had played in the rescue of Frank Carty, and proud of their brigade which had got him out of jail. They were in high good humour when, having reached Rosehill, they sat drinking coffee with their hostess, Mrs Connolly. Each recounted his experiences since they had last met. That was some time ago, and much had happened in the meantime, for while Peadar Glynn had been active in Dublin where he was studying and in Sligo where he was attached to the Town

Battalion, Alex had been in jail, in hospital and on the run. An hour passed pleasantly, and then Glynn decided he had better head for home. It was after curfew hour and his home was in the same street as the military barracks.

He made his way carefully into town and through the streets. As he rounded the last corner for home he saw British forces swinging into action at long last, in reaction to the rescue. Glynn chuckled as he waited in the shadows whilst a lorry load of troops roared away. Then he slipped in through the doorway. Next morning he roared with laughter when he learned that the lorry, driven at breakneck speed towards the jail, had crashed head-on into Kilgallon's gates which still barricaded the entrance. The smash, in which several British soldiers were injured, caused the only casualties in the rescue of Frank Carty.

Chapter 13

Escape of three leaders from Kilmainham jail was aided by British soldier

by Simon Donnelly

On Thursday 10 February 1921, I was arrested in Dame Street, Dublin, and brought to Dublin Castle to be questioned by British intelligence officers. Following the preliminary interrogation I was taken to the guardroom of the Castle and detained there until Friday 11 February when I was summoned before the notorious Captain Hardy.

Hardy was infamous as a bully and for his brutal methods of attempting to force information from prisoners. He tried his usual methods on me, warning me that I was suspected of being implicated in the shooting of British intelligence officers on 'Bloody Sunday' (21 November 1920) and giving me a pretty fair idea of what I and other prisoners were to expect if evidence could be found connecting us with that operation.

From the Castle I was sent under heavy escort to Kilmainham jail, and there I soon recognised a number of my comrades who were awaiting trial on various charges. The identity of one of the prisoners puzzled me. I was sure that I knew him and yet I could not place him at first. He was known as 'Stewart' and I could not recollect having met anybody of that name in the Dublin Brigade. I quickly learned, however, that he was none other than Ernie O'Malley, without doubt one of the bravest and most resourceful soldiers who had fought for Irish independence. He had grown a heavy moustache and generally altered his appearance. Also, his face was much disfigured as a result of a beating-up he was given by intelligence officers in the Castle.

Our men had to be careful of fellow prisoners of whose identity they were not certain, because it was usual for the British to 'plant' spies amongst us, who were supposed to be prisoners, in the hope that we would unwittingly betray ourselves to them. Once my comrades were sure that I was the man I represented myself to be, they took me into their confidence and told me that they were working on plans for an almost immediate escape. Among the prisoners in Kilmainham at that time were Captain Paddy Moran, NCO Frank Flood, Volunteers Thomas Bryan, Pat Doyle, Thomas Whelan and Bernard Ryan, all of whom were executed on 14 March 1921, Frank Teeling, who had been wounded and captured on 'Bloody Sunday', and Ernie O'Malley. So many of us were charged with murder – for the British did not recognise us as prisoners of war although a state of war was in existence – that we used to talk about our part of the jail as 'Murderers' Gallery'.

'Murderers' Gallery', incidentally, was in an old and long disused part of the jail which had been reopened to cope with the increasing number of prisoners held in Kilmainham since the commencement of the War of Independence. Fortunately for us, as it transpired later, this old wing had never been fitted with modern lock-and-key systems, and the old bolt-and-padlock method was still being used there. As well, the older peephole, four inches square, was also retained there, although the modern portion of the jail had been fitted with the new-sized peephole, an inch and a half square. These two factors were to prove invaluable to us when the time came to attempt our break-out from the jail.

The Irish Republican Army was never known to shirk coming to the rescue of comrades in danger, so we were full of confidence that our people on the outside were doing everything in their power to rescue us from the clutches of the enemy. For some time prior to my arrest the prisoners in Kilmainham had been kept in touch with plans that were under consideration to effect a rescue; with the aid of two friendly soldiers communications had been established with the IRA on the outside. Immediately that my identity had been established to the satisfaction of my comrades, I was brought up-to-date with these plans and learned that, with luck, the escape would be attempted on the following night, Sunday 13 February.

Difficulties and dangers had to be overcome by our deliverers. With curfew in force, any of them found loitering near the jail after nightfall would have to fight his way through enemy forces and, if captured, would probably be shot out of hand; of course, the rescue could not be attempted in day time.

Kilmainham was no easy place to penetrate at any time, with its high surrounding walls, barbed-wire entanglements, machine guns mounted at every strategic position, and its heavy guard of soldiers. At first the IRA had almost despaired of rescuing any of us, but the news from inside the jail that two friendly soldiers had been found who were willing to help brought a ray of hope. The first plan, quickly abandoned as impracticable, had been to drug the guards.

Eventually, it was a shipyard worker who suggested the plan which was adopted and he also provided the implement which was successfully used to set us free. This man used a bolt-cutter in the course of his work, and he assured the O/C of the Dublin Brigade IRA that it would be just as simple to cut a jail bolt as any mere 'civilian' bolt. The type of bolt-cutter used then was an implement as long as a pair of garden shears; there were obvious difficulties in the way of smuggling a pair into Kilmainham. Also, the tool had to be procured first, and it could only be got by breaking into the Dublin dockyards, not an easy thing to do with curfew in operation and the military and Auxiliaries combing the streets of Dublin for 'rebels'. A cutter was obtained, however, and the next problem was to get the big unwieldy implement into the jail. One of our soldier friends undertook to try. As he had himself to run the gauntlet of the sentries, it was necessary to reduce the size of the cutter by sawing away the wooden handles, so that he could bring it in concealed under his uniform without its being detected. Minus its handles the cutter did not have the necessary leverage to cut bolts, so detachable handles of tubular steel had to be provided also, to replace the original wooden ones. There was a right and a wrong way to fit the handles; if they were fitted the wrong way the instrument was not workable. Accordingly, the soldier had to be given demonstrations in the correct way to fit them. After the demonstrations he assured the O/C that he was ready to carry out his part of the job as planned. In fact, he succeeded in smuggling into the jail not only the cutter and the handles but a number of revolvers also.

An alternative plan for our rescue, made in case the one

involving the use of the bolt-cutter should fail, provided that a rescue party, with a rope ladder and a rope tied to it, should take up positions close to the jail wall near a certain rarely used gate. Following an agreed signal they would throw the rope over the wall and we would haul the rope ladder over to our side.

We were not sure whether the bolt-cutter would work, and we were not counting upon more than one or two of us making the escape if the rope ladder alternative had to be employed. Our principal concern was to save the life of Frank Teeling who had been sentenced to death. Ernie O'Malley's escape was essential also, for if his real identity was established he could expect from the British the same brand of treatment which they had given to Dick McKee, Peadar Clancy and Conor Clune in Dublin Castle on 'Bloody Sunday'. The fate of the rest of us had not yet been decided.

No general jail-break was intended, therefore, so that the chances of Teeling and O'Malley getting out might be all the better, for the greater the number who tried to break through the greater was the risk of detection by the jail guards. For my own part, I merely tagged along with Teeling and O'Malley, intending to take my chance of getting away only when I was sure that they were safe.

Members of 'F' Company of the 4th Battalion of the Dublin Brigade, who had been detailed for the rescue operation, had to leave their homes every night during the period in which the agreed signal might be received from us. They had first to get outside the city boundary in order to avoid enemy curfew patrols along the city approaches to Kilmainham, and then make their way stealthily back by the railway lines, so as to be near the jail gate when needed.

Meanwhile our revolvers were concealed amongst a lot of old lumber and boxes in an unoccupied cell convenient to our own cell. We had decided that, when making the break, we would go through a disused gate that led on to a side-road. Two circumstances aided us considerably when the escape was attempted. Our cell doors were, as I have mentioned, fitted with the old-type bolts, padlocks and peepholes. The warders rarely troubled to use the padlocks; they merely pushed home the bolts. A prisoner could slip his hand out through the peephole and ease back the bolt from its socket. This we were able to do without difficulty. Also, evidently confident that the thirty-foot wall which surrounded the jail could not be scaled, the authorities seldom locked the door leading out of the yard from the jail building, and so it was possible for us to get from our cells to the gate in the outer wall through which we hoped to escape.

Our plans having being perfected, we sent word to our friends waiting outside the walls that we were on our way. The rescuers, as they approached the gate, came upon some soldiers with their girlfriends loitering on the side-road outside the wall, and for the purpose of ensuring that no alarm could be passed to the guards, the soldiers and their girls had to be 'arrested' and removed to a place of safety, a development which interfered with the plans which had been originally prepared by our friends and which, in the event, could have jeopardised our escape.

Meanwhile, armed with our revolvers and the bolt-cutter, we reached the gate and were actually in sight of the rescue party when, to our dismay, we found that the cutter would not work. The make-shift handles had been wrongly fitted and so they did not give sufficient leverage for cutting through the stout iron bolt.

We whispered urgently to our friends outside to throw over the rope to which was attached the rope ladder. Over it came. But another disappointment awaited us. When we commenced to haul over the rope we could make no headway; the harder we pulled the more securely did the rope seem to fasten on top of the wall. It transpired that it had sunk into a joint in the masonry, and the more we pulled the more firmly it got locked. With one terrific pull we got the rope loose – only to find that it had broken.

Baffled and dispirited we had to say a sad goodbye to our friends outside, not knowing whether we would ever see them again, and return to our cells in 'Murderers' Gallery'. In our disappointment over the failure we were inclined to think that the soldier who had provided us with the cutter was not playing straight with us, and we doubted whether the implement could ever be of any use to us for jail-breaking. The soldier, however, was sincere in his sympathy with us, and in his wish to help us. He had either misunderstood or forgotten his instructions, and gone the wrong way about fitting the tubular handles to the bolt-cutter. He was so ashamed of the muddle he had made that he went to the O/C again without delay and told him he was sure that none of us trusted him any longer, and that the O/C himself must think he was double-crossing. The O/C took him very kindly; he realised what had happened and patiently demonstrated again how the handles should be fitted in order to get the correct leverage. The soldier then said that if we would make another attempt he would, himself, cut the bolt for us to prove his sincerity.

Prior to the formulation of the escape plans, prisoners had been grumbling about the dirty condition of the prison. The complaints had ceased, however, since the urgent problem of the escape had come under serious consideration. To our great consternation, on Monday morning, 14 February, we learned that the jail authorities had decided to clean out the place immediately, including the disused cell in which our weapons and the bolt-cutter were hidden. Discovery of these would kill our last chance of escape. Something had to be done quickly to save the situation, so we established a precedent for IRA prisoners in enemy hands by volunteering to do fatigue duty and clear up the cells ourselves. The authorities fell for the ruse and so we were able to prevent the discovery of our weapons. We had reason to believe, however, that our jailers must suspect that some escape plan had been tried and had failed, for the newspapers of that morning carried a vague story of an escape. The arrest of the soldiers and their girlfriends had probably given rise to suspicions and rumours. Security measures would probably be tightened up at any minute. Having weighed up the situation, we decided that we must make another attempt to get away about 6.30 p.m. the same night, and we sent word to this effect to our collaborators outside. The position of Teeling was desperate – he was to be executed in a few days. Should 'Stewart' be recognised as Ernie O'Malley, his fate would be the same, I was facing a murder charge, but even at that the position of Ernie and myself was nothing like so urgent or desperate as that of Teeling.

When the time had come for the break to be made, O'Malley and Teeling began to make their way down to the gate, a trying ordeal, for all the while they ran the risk of being observed by a sentry and bayoneted or shot. I remained behind for a few minutes, talking to a soldier named Roper who was on duty that night. He told me he was due for discharge from the army the following week and was happy to be going home. I encouraged him to talk and did all I could to hold his attention while Teeling and O'Malley were slipping away towards the gate. When I considered that they must have reached it, I also managed to slip away quietly. On my way I passed Paddy Moran's cell. It was open and I tried to persuade him to accompany us. He was also awaiting trial in connection with the shootings on 'Bloody Sunday' but, having a clear-cut alibi, he was so sure of acquittal that he absolutely refused to leave and said that any attempt by him to get away would be interpreted by the British as an admission of his guilt. Paddy Moran was to pay with his life for this decision.

When I realised I could not bring Paddy with me I began the hazardous journey across the yard in the wake of my two companions. Crossing the yard was a nerve-racking ordeal, for the place was covered with a substance called breeze and every time I set foot on a loose bit of breeze it crunched under my boot with a sound that seemed to me as loud and sharp as a rifle shot. So, every second I was tensed for a sentry's challenge and what must follow it. When at length I reached the gate I found that, this time, the bolt-cutter had done its work. Teeling and our soldier friend had cut the bolt with it. The soldier had gone to the gate with Teeling and O'Malley and shared the hazard with them.

But the way to freedom was still barred: we had yet to manage the tedious and critical task of working back the rusted bolt from its socket. We greased the bolt with some butter which we had saved from our rations, and, following some minutes of hard work and extreme anxiety, we eventually succeeded in easing it back. Slowly we opened the gate while keeping a sharp eye out for soldiers who might be hanging about on the side-road; but there were none, and so the way to freedom was open before us. Our soldier friend slipped back into the jail.

We had had our revolvers at the ready all the time we were working on the gate, for had we been discovered then we intended to fight it out with our jailers; in such an eventuality, our soldier friend had intended to fight with us. Thanks to our comrades on the outside, however, we met with no opposition. As on the occasion of our first attempt, they had made sure that there would be no alarm given from the outside: they had again 'arrested' some soldiers and girls whom they found in the vicinity of the gate. For some extraordinary reason no change in the lax security measures had followed the 'arrests' made on the night of our first attempt.

So we three prisoners walked casually out of Kilmainham. Down a back-road we went and hid our revolvers in the garden of a private house. We passed close by another enemy stronghold, Richmond barracks, and walked along the banks of the canal. Then we got something of a fright. As we were about to cross a canal bridge an enemy armoured car drove up. We flung ourselves flat on the grass and only just in time, for a searchlight flashed out from the car. Luckily, it missed us, as we were then unarmed we would have been entirely at the mercy of the enemy had we been discovered.

After a few minutes the armoured car passed on its way. We picked ourselves up from the grass and boarded a tram for the city. O'Malley had borrowed the tram-fare from Desmond Fitzgerald before we set out on our escape bid. At different points along the tram route one of us got off the tram, and each of us in his own way set out to rejoin his unit.

Chapter 14

The rescue of Frank Carty from Derry jail

by Bill Kelly

The walls of Derry jail are stout and high – about five feet wide and over forty feet high. Well guarded, the jail stands in Bishop Street but is no longer used as a jail. No man had ever escaped from it since it was first opened for business, on 16 August 1824, until Brigadier Frank Carty of the Sligo No. 4 Brigade broke out in the curfew hours before the dawn of Tuesday 15 February 1921. In the process he managed somehow to squeeze himself through an aperture of about twenty inches by twelve inches, swing his fifteen-stone bulk over a sagging rope and climb the rope to the top of the jail wall despite an injured wrist. After which he scrambled down a rope ladder on the outside, into the backyard of loyalist George Moore in Harding Street. Then he scaled two yard walls and walked out to freedom through the door of a vacant house.

The escape, one of the most daring of the War of Independence, was effected only just before Carty was due to face a court martial in Derry. It happened, too, on the day after Warder James Lynch from Boyle, who was serving in the jail, had news that his brother, a Black and Tan, had been shot dead in an ambush at Balbriggan. Added to the fact that Carty was a badly wanted man awaiting court martial, the shooting of Lynch caused a tightening of security measures in the jail, so that in the circumstances Frank Carty's escape astonished his jailers and vastly encouraged the small band of IRA who were carrying on the fight against overwhelming odds in the north of the country.

Frank Carty, three years older than the century, had joined the Volunteers in 1914 and was appointed vice-brigadier of the Sligo Brigade in 1918. Six feet tall and weighing fifteen stone, without an ounce of fat, he was an aggressive, active commander. He had been rescued from Sligo jail in June 1920. After that rescue Carty commanded a flying column for about five months. His luck ran out in November of the same year when, in Vesey's house in Moylough, Tubbercurry, he and two others were surrounded by Black and Tans and, following a desperate resistance in which he was wounded in the wrist, he was overpowered and carried off to the maximum security jail in Derry. There he was held throughout the winter. He was not cut off from information about what was happening outside, however, for even in Derry jail the IRA had friends amongst the warders, almost all of whom bought their cigarettes and newspapers in a little tobacconist shop in Bishop Street, opposite the main gate. The owner of the shop was an IRA sympathiser and his place became an important unofficial post office; messages left there by IRA men were passed on and a number of them were slipped to Carty inside the escape-proof fortress.

Charlie McGuinness knew the place well. A native of the Pennyburn area of Derry, he spent a lot of his time at sea. His father was captain of the collier *Carricklee* on board which Charlie made many trips to smuggle in arms for the IRA; but routine trips between Derry and Glasgow bored the younger McGuinness and he sought adventure with the IRA in Donegal. Charlie was a swashbuckler to the manner born. Slightly over middle height and sturdily built, he walked with a swagger and, on shore, he invariably wore a black trench coat and a black trilby hat. It seemed as though it was his intention to display himself, to trail his coat, as it were, and provoke the RIC and Black and Tans into some action against him. A dangerous way to go about in those perilous times. There was something about Charlie's dark features which, though pleasant looking, warned that he was not a man to be trifled with. In fact, he didn't know the meaning of fear. When he heard that Carty, whom he had met on his inshore forays, was in Derry jail, he decided to get him out. Single-handed, he would rescue him. No IRA unit ever knew anything about his rescue plan.

Towards the end of January he sent in word to Carty, through a friendly warder, that he would make the attempt about 4.30 on the morning of Saturday 12 February. As a first step he had a hacksaw smuggled in to him, then a message that it was essential for him to be in the hospital block at the back of the jail yard, abutting on Harding Street, at the time of the attempt. Carty's wound had healed, though the wrist still troubled him and was stiff; but it was not bad enough to warrant the prison doctor having him transferred to the hospital. So Carty worked the old army dodge of a pain in the back. It took days and nights of acting before he finally convinced the doctor that he was a hospital case.

McGuinness, having got word that Carty was in the right place, sent him the final details of his plan. Carty was to saw through the bars of his cell window in the hospital; McGuinness would himself gain entry into the backyard of one of the little houses in Harding Street, scale the wall and throw a rope ladder to the prisoner.

Hour after hour, ever on the alert for a footfall which would herald the approach of an enemy, Carty sawed painfully through the bars. As many an Irish felon had done before him, he filled the gaps in the bars with a mixture of soap and dust, and then waited impatiently for the early morning of Saturday 12 February. He already knew that he was due to face a court martial on the following Tuesday. His position, therefore, was doubly precarious because at any time the doctor might realise the truth about his histrionic performances and send him back to a cell in the jail.

At four o'clock on Saturday morning, while the city was enveloped in darkness and enemy troops patrolled its streets, Charlie McGuinness crouched by a wall guarding the hospital block. Wound about his arm was a coiled rope to which a hook was attached. His first cast missed the top of the wall and the steel hook crashed to the ground with a noise that sounded to him like thunder in the stillness of the early morning. Tensely he waited. One minute … two … three … No alarm. He tried again. This time the hook gripped. Agile as a monkey the sailor started to swarm up the rope. He had climbed only a few feet, however, when the coping stone which held the hook gave way. Stone, hook and rope plunged to the ground, the stone missing him by inches. It was enough for that morning. Regretfully, he called it a day and melted into the pre-dawn darkness.

Long after McGuinness had gone Frank Carty stood by his cell window in the hospital, ready, at the signal, to push the sawn-through bars aside. It was only when the dawn reddened the sky that he turned dejectedly and went back to his cot. McGuinness, however, had not given up the attempt. He had merely postponed it. Within hours of that first failure, a friendly warder had smuggled in a present to Frank Carty – a ball of twine. With it went instructions on how it was to be used and when. Following a signal from outside, at 4.30 on Tuesday morning 15 February, Carty, holding the loose end of the twine in one hand, was to throw the ball over the wall and then haul up a rope ladder. It was as simple as that and the rest should be just as easy.

The half-dozen little houses that were huddled under the grim wall of the jail in Harding Street might have been so many tombs for all the signs of life they showed that Tuesday morning, but just as the Guildhall clock, less than half a mile away, boomed the half-hour after four, Charlie McGuinness was very much alive. Climbing over wall after wall, through the backyards of houses in Harding Street, he finally arrived in the backyard opposite Carty's hospital cell and anxiously awaited the signal which would show that Frank was alert and waiting. In a matter of minutes the soft bounce of the ball of twine eased his mind. In a flash he had an end of the twine reefed around the rope ladder.

A tug on the twine signalled to Carty to haul away. Almost immediately the rope ladder seemed to creep up the wall of the jail, as in a performance of the Indian rope trick. The ladder caught once but McGuinness shook it free. Then came near disaster. The ladder again: it fouled as it reached the top of the wall, and, in the darkness below, McGuinness could sense rather than see Frank Carty's frantic efforts to release it – efforts that could result in breaking the twine and ending the rescue attempt once more. With controlled haste McGuinness drew the ladder down and Carty, fortunately, having realised what was happening, slacked the twine. The sailor then cut the ladder free. In its stead he fastened a rope to the twine, and at the knot he tied a note which explained that as the ladder would continue to foul it could not be used and that, consequently, Carty must swarm over the rope to clear the fifteen-foot gap between his cell window and the wall. This time the haulage operation was successful and Carty fastened the rope to a sound window-bar. Then he forced his great bulk through the space that opened after he had pushed aside the sawn-through bars. With desperate energy he managed to lever himself painfully along the rope. His wounded wrist was of little use in this operation during which the rope sagged so much under his weight that he had to haul himself almost perpendicularly up the last few feet to the top of the wall.

Somehow he made it. Seconds later the hefty brigadier was scrambling down the rope ladder into the yard at the back of Moore's house. Whispered greetings were exchanged by the pair, and then they were both climbing the backyard walls of the street of houses until they arrived outside the unoccupied end house. Having entered this house by the back door, they slipped out through the front into Harding Street, hugged the shadows as they made their way across Abercorn Street, and through a maze of back streets out of the Orange quarter towards the Strand and comparative safety. Alert for the booming cannon which would signal the discovery of the escape, they hurried along and fortunately succeeded in avoiding the enemy patrols. Still the cannon did not boom. They were under cover when the escape was discovered and the alarm was sounded at seven o'clock.

They remained under cover throughout the next few days

during which Derry was like an upturned hornets' nest as the RIC and military, fiercely prodded by their authorities, swarmed into the suspect nationalist districts and even into isolated nationalist homes in the Orange sectors of the city, as they frantically sought their man. But Frank Carty was hidden well, although, in all truth, Derry at that time did not offer much variety in hiding places, for the only people to be trusted with important matters were those who were actually in the IRA movement. Carty was important. Incidentally, he never divulged his hiding places of the few nerve-racking days that immediately followed his escape. Neither did Charlie McGuinness. But the searches were still being made in Derry when the *Carricklee* left the Foyle for Glasgow with Carty aboard – thanks to the aid of her Swedish mate.

So far as the British were concerned, Frank Carty, the only man ever to escape from Derry jail, had vanished off the face of the earth. They were baffled and well they might be.

What Derry had lost by the defection of one Frank Carty, Glasgow gained. Frank Somers, a new citizen of no mean city, did not advertise his presence on Caledonian soil but immediately got in touch with the Glasgow Brigade of the IRA and made known his identity as Frank Carty to some of its officers. The news that he was in Glasgow was sent to IRA headquarters in Dublin, and, following receipt of instructions from headquarters, Carty spent the latter part of February, the entire month of March and part of April in lecturing and training the Glasgow IRA men.

In the search for Carty the British Special Branch in Scotland was not idle and, as in England, its task was much easier than in southern Ireland. The Irish quarters in Glasgow became suspect and were kept under surveillance. Scottish detectives of the Special Branch examined their dossiers on suspected IRA men and they were no less zealous in organising raids than were their colleagues in Ireland. It was through sheer bad luck, however, that Frank Somers was eventually captured during a raid in the east end of Glasgow late in April. At first his captors had no idea that he was Frank Carty, the badly wanted jail-breaker who had twice escaped from their clutches.

The Glasgow IRA knew that it would be only a matter of time before Carty's real identity was discovered by the British, and so they set about making plans to rescue him for the third time. There was no hope of getting him over the walls, they believed; the jail was in the heart of the city and the warders were tough and loyal. So they decided they would attempt to take him from his escort in the streets of Glasgow as the Fenians had rescued Kelly and Deasy in Manchester in 1867. The difficulties were similar and the penalties for any of the rescuers who might be captured were the same as those which faced the Manchester Fenians. Nevertheless, several dozen men volunteered for the job of rescuing Carty from a prison van in broad daylight in the heart of Glasgow, as he was being conveyed between the court and the jail.

Carty-Somers was scheduled to be taken from the jail to the sheriff's court on the forenoon of 4 May. He would be conveyed in a black maria, escorted by three armed detectives and two unarmed policemen in addition to the driver.

An IRA council of war was held. Ambush plans were laid. On the return journey the black maria would be attacked almost at the jail gates, when the members of the escort were likely to be relaxed in a sense of greater security. As the rescue party had no means of knowing how long the court proceedings would last, their positions must be occupied the moment Carty-Somers was taken into the court and they must remain loitering in the busy streets of Glasgow centre until the attack began. Three parties of men were involved and contact must be maintained between all three. There would be difficulty in remaining unobtrusive. To add to the problems, the prison-van's journey between the court and the jail would take no more than five minutes at the most. There was need for split-second timing.

The men were briefed, their stations allotted and signals agreed. Scouts were posted to warn when the black maria had left the courthouse. It must be held up, the escort overpowered, the keys taken and the prisoner released – all within a matter of a few minutes.

Carty-Somers appeared in the dock shortly after midday and the proceedings were brief and formal. Police enquiries had not yet been completed. The Bailie remanded him in custody for forty-eight hours. Within minutes of the remand he was hustled to the black maria.

As the handcuffed prisoner entered the van the chain of IRA scouts moved into action. The escort, led by Detective-Inspector Robert Johnston, was taking no chances. Carty-Somers, in a small front compartment, was guarded by Detective-Inspector McDonald and Detective-Sergeant George Stirton. Johnston sat beside the driver. The two unarmed constables were in the back with another prisoner.

The van was driven from St Andrew's Square, through High Street, and it arrived without incident at Rottenrow, 200 yards from the Drygate entrance to the jail. Suddenly, at a street corner, six armed men attacked it from the rear. Six attacked also from the right-hand side and three or four more from the front. The van stopped. The driver said afterwards that his brakes had jammed. Inspector Johnston jumped to his feet and drew his pistol. Before he could use it he fell dead, shot through the heart. Sergeant Stirton leaped out of the van and ordered the driver to go like hell while he attempted to cover his retreat. Constable McDonald was firing also. From a peaceful, busy place the centre of Glasgow had suddenly erupted into bedlam.

The flat splat of the automatics, the whiplike crack of the revolvers and the screams of the people as they scattered helter skelter for shelter brought crowds surging from nearby streets to see what was the matter. Those trying to escape from the scene of the shooting met the incoming crowds and confusion and panic spread through the streets. A stray shot shattered the lock of the black maria and jammed it; now, even if the attack was successful, Carty-Somers could not be got out.

Stirton stood on the roadway, his pistol blazing defiance until he staggered under the impact of a bullet which hit him in the arm.

Police whistles were shrilling and then, as inexplicably as she had stopped, the black maria shot forward again. Stirton still stood his ground, one injured arm useless, his empty pistol in his good hand. He was then an easy target if murder was the object of the attack. But the attackers were no murder gang; as soon as the black maria had got going again it was obvious to all of them that the rescue attempt was a failure, and, at a signal, they dispersed rapidly. Momentarily, Detective-Sergeant Stirton found himself alone on the street. Then came the crowds and police reinforcements. The attackers had vanished and could not be identified. Carty-Somers was back in jail – soon to be identified as Frank Carty. Sentenced to ten years' penal servitude, Carty was transferred to Mountjoy jail in Dublin. There he remained until after the Treaty was signed in December 1921. The Glasgow Special Branch men had not been inactive in the meantime. They cast their nets far and wide through the city and came up with a catch of twenty-four prisoners who were charged with having attacked the black maria. Included were six women and a priest, Father McRory. None was convicted. All were acquitted after a short hearing.

Chapter 15

Heavily guarded, wounded prisoner rescued from Monaghan County Hospital

by Donal O'Kelly

The rescue of Commandant Matt Fitzpatrick from Monaghan County Hospital is a classic example of a brilliantly conceived and executed plan, carried out under the nose of a strong enemy garrison.

In the early part of 1921 north Monaghan was a centre of IRA activity along the newly created border. In districts such as this the IRA had to face many problems of a kind that were unknown to their fellow fighters in other parts of the country. If they wanted arms, as of course they did, they had in the main to fight for them at loyalist houses in many cases occupied by armed 'B' Specials of the Royal Ulster Constabulary. Thus, in the province of Ulster, raids for arms, which were almost a routine activity elsewhere in the country, became in many cases assaults upon enemy strong-points.

It was in one such raid that Commandant Matt Fitzpatrick, a young officer of exceptional popularity and of great character and soldierly ability, was severely wounded. He received a charge of shot in the left side and right forearm – his side being severely torn and his right wrist shattered. His comrades conveyed him by pony and trap to Joe Duffy's house in the mountainside near Newbliss, and from there, following the usual safety measures adopted in such cases, he was moved from time to time to other friendly houses in the vicinity. One day Matt was visited by a member of his own Wattlebridge Company and it is believed that, all unwittingly of course, it was this visit which led to the discovery of his whereabouts by the enemy. Matt's visitor had come by cycle and on the way back to Clones he met a party of RIC and Black and Tans. Cleverly enough, the police did not molest him, although he was suspected of IRA activities. Instead, they followed the tracks of his bicycle back along the muddy roads and by this method, after raiding several houses along the way, they eventually found their severely wounded quarry. Matt was arrested and taken to the County Hospital in Monaghan where he was placed under armed guard. This guard, consisting of two NCOs and six men, placed one sentry in the prisoner's ward and one in the ground-floor corridor near the improvised guardroom. An armed RIC sergeant was placed as a 'patient' in the next bed.

Word of the arrest reached the IRA nearly as soon as it was made. Captain Jim MacConnon of Threemilehouse learned of it from the conversation of two British secret service men, who he overheard in a barber's shop in Monaghan while he was being shaved. Jim hastened with the information to Dr F.C. Ward, Monaghan, who was then a brigade staff officer. There was no certainty as to how soon the prisoner would be brought to Belfast jail and, in the light of his record in the IRA, it was believed that, once there, nothing would save him from the hangman's rope. The only hope, therefore, lay in immediate rescue. Dan Hogan, O/C, and other available members of the brigade staff immediately were informed of the facts, and a conference was held at H. Farmer's house at Cornasoo. At this conference the possibility of rescue was discussed and it was decided that detailed rescue plans should be worked out. It soon became evident that the difficulties were enormous and that only the most meticulous planning and split-second timing could bring off the job successfully. The presence of an armed guard and the armed policeman in the bed beside Fitzpatrick was bad enough, but, in addition to this, there was a garrison consisting of a company of military and some sixty RIC and Black and Tans in the town. There were many civilian patients in the hospital, some of them seriously ill, who must be disturbed as little as possible. If the job was to be done at all it must be done swiftly and in silence; the guard must be taken completely by surprise and the prisoner rescued before people knew what was happening.

Detailed plans of the approaches, the lay-out, position of guard and times of changing guard were submitted by Dr Ward to Dan Hogan, who decided to take command himself, choosing as his associates Jim MacConnon, Pat Kierans, Phil Marrin, John MacCarville, James Flynn, Seamus O'Donoghue, Joe MacCarville, Frank Tummin, Pat Mulligan, Joe Shannon, Paddy McCarron, Jimmy Winters and Pat Monahan. At a further conference between Hogan, Dr Ward and members of the flying column, arrangements were made for the requisitioning and placing of transport and for the alerting of the different companies for road blocking.

Paddy McCarthy, Town Surveyor, Monaghan, furnished to Dr Ward a plan of the hospital and its approaches together with a report setting out the day and the hour when the guard was due to be changed. It had been ascertained that the guard did a forty-eight hour tour of duty, and it was decided that 2 a.m. on the second night of duty would be the hour most likely to find the guard at the lowest pitch of vigilance. Paddy McCarthy had also arranged with a friendly member of the staff to leave a door unlocked but, lest there be any hitch here, duplicate keys were prepared. A stretcher was provided for the removal of the wounded man and on Jimmy Winters was placed the all-important task of disconnecting the telephone immediately the rescue party entered the grounds. The attempt was finally fixed for 2 a.m. on the morning of 30 March.

On the evening of 29 March the rescue party assembled at Cornasoo, with three commandeered cars driven by John McKenna of Newbliss, James Nolan and a garage worker named Stephen who was a native of Donegal. Dan Hogan once again repeated his orders, the Rosary was recited and the party moved out. The curfew hour for cars was then 8 p.m. Two of the cars, with their drivers in charge, were stationed some distance from the hospital and left facing in the direction of Tyholland and Clontibret crossroads. The men took off their boots and, as silently as possible, manoeuvred the third car into a position of readiness outside the hospital, with John McKenna at the wheel. On a perimeter outside the town of Monaghan parties stood ready to block the roads at selected points after the rescue party had passed through. The laying of roadblocks earlier was prohibited lest their presence might alert the enemy.

The stealthy approach of the party through the hospital grounds passed unnoticed and the hospital door was unlocked as had been arranged. In the corridor the sentry drowsed, his rifle beside him. One of the party grabbed the rifle and Dan Hogan overpowered the sentry, but not before the latter had been able to utter a shout of warning. In the guardroom some of the men off duty were asleep but one, who was sitting on his bed at the time, was alerted by the sentry's warning cry, and, seconds later, when Paddy McCarron appeared in the doorway he was halted by a rifle bullet which wounded him in the arm. Pat Monahan then fired both barrels of his shotgun high over the heads of the guard, blinding them with mortar and plaster which fell from the ceiling. The guardroom was rushed in the confusion which followed and the guard surrendered.

The report of rifle and shotgun fire in the dead of night destroyed all further hope of surprise, and the wonder is that the British forces outside the hospital were not alerted. The RIC man in the bed beside Matt Fitzpatrick jumped up, drew his gun and covered the prostrate prisoner; while the sentry in the ward, evidently a resolute man, opened fire through the door. Fitzpatrick said to the RIC sergeant: 'Are you going to shoot a wounded prisoner?' In reply the sergeant, from what motive we do not know, threw his revolver onto an adjoining bed and went back to his own. Whatever his motive may have been, by not shooting Fitzpatrick there and then he undoubtedly saved his own life. Had he killed Fitzpatrick the men on the rescue job would have given him short shrift. The problem of the remaining sentry had still to be solved, and very quickly at that. Dan Hogan tied the hands of the disarmed prisoners in the guardroom behind their backs and forced them to precede him into the ward, shouting as they went, 'Don't shoot.' Confronted with this situation, the sentry, a brave man, could only follow his comrades' example and surrender, which he did.

MacConnon and Kierans, with all haste, then placed the prisoner on a stretcher and started off for the car whither the wounded McCarron, having had first-aid applied, had already gone. Before he was carried out Matt Fitzpatrick told Dan Hogan of the RIC sergeant's action and where he had thrown his gun. Hogan collected the gun, at the same time telling the sergeant he would not be injured. Other members of the party collected the arms and equipment of the military guard – eight rifles, ammunition, a .45 revolver and some bandoliers. They then reassured the civilian patients and the staff of the hospital and quietly took their departure. They retired along their pre-arranged route, leaving MacConnon, Kierans, Mulligan and Shannon to make their way, along the railway line, to Three-milehouse.

So ended an entirely successful action. It had taken less than fifteen minutes, there were no casualties on either side (except for McCarron's flesh wound in the arm), the rescued prisoner got clean away and a valuable addition was made to the Monaghan Brigade's slender store of offensive weapons. So effective were the security measures taken that the first news the enemy garrison received of the affair was when the sad, dispirited and unarmed members of the guard made their way to the barracks to tell their story, as best they could, to their infuriated superiors.

Chapter 16

Daring rescue of Seán MacSwiney and two other IRA officers from Spike Island

by Florence O'Donoghue

In the thirty-six years during which Spike was used as a convict prison there is no record of a successful escape from it. In 1920 and 1921 the island was once again used as a prison for Irishmen, though most of them were internees rather than convicts and they were not confined in the dreadful underground cells. Three of them, Seán MacSwiney (a brother of Terence MacSwiney), Tom Malone and Con Twomey, made a successful break from it on 29 April 1921.

Cork No. 1 Brigade had a line of communication to the prisoners and, when early in 1921 there was a possibility that some important prisoners would be executed, it was decided to try to take Seán MacSwiney and some others off the island. A moat surrounded the fortifications and prison buildings on the island. Outside the moat, on the south-east side of the island, some efforts were being made to construct a golf course with prisoner labour.

MacSwiney and a number of his comrades volunteered for this work in the hope of being rescued. Normally, three prisoners were so engaged under the eye of an armed sentry. The prisoners themselves had to estimate the date on which the men to be taken off would be on this duty, and the brigade had to arrange that a motor boat would come as close as possible to the island on that day at the right time. No boat could hang around without arousing suspicion and there was only one possible time, between 10 and 11 o'clock in the morning. Transport had also to be available on the mainland at the nearest point on the Ringaskiddy side, to get the rescued men away.

Cobh Company was one of the best in the brigade. Headquarters had no hesitation in entrusting the job to them. Denny Barry went to Cobh on 19 April and asked Michael Burke, the Company Captain, to come to brigade headquarters in the city. At Master's restaurant in Marlboro Street he met Dan Donovan and other brigade officers, and a plan of action was settled on. Fr Callanan, chaplain to the prisoners on Spike, had brought out word that the date was Saturday 29 April. That morning a motor launch flying the Union Jack put out from Cobh. In it were Michael Burke, George O'Reilly, Frank Barry and Andrew Butterley. It was owned by a master mariner, skipper Ned O'Regan, who later presented it to Michael Burke.

The launch had never been handled by any of the four Volunteers previously, and its steering, being wheel type, was unfamiliar to them. There was a slight mishap at the start. They collided with a military launch carrying a party of British soldiers plying between Spike and Cobh, but no serious damage was done. They steered out of the harbour and moved in towards the point on Spike where the prisoners should be at work. Yes, there they were! But the position was not exactly as anticipated. In addition to the three prisoners and the armed sentry, there was another man in a white sweater on the scene, apparently an NCO or instructor, giving directions about the work to be carried out.

The launch moved into position and its occupants pretended to commence fishing. Nothing happened. The prisoners made no move to attack the sentry and his companion. The men in the boat could see no reason for the delay unless it was the presence of the man in the white sweater. Boat and prisoners were in full view of each other. As the Volunteers in the launch waited tensely a new anxiety loomed up. A British cruiser steamed into the channel on their side of the island and anchored less than a mile away.

Michael Burke had decided that for some reason the prisoners were unable to carry out their part of the plan and had given the order to move when he saw the three prisoners close with the sentry and the other man. The sentry's rifle was wrested from him. Both men were quickly knocked out, dragged off the golf course and dropped over an embankment. The prisoners raced towards the boat, bringing the sentry's rifle and ammunition with them.

Michael jumped ashore with ropes for tying up the soldiers, but was assured by the prisoners that tying up was not necessary – they had been knocked out. The three escaping Volunteers waded to the boat. They were dragged in and got to lie down out of sight. The boat turned for Paddy's Block, the nearest point on the mainland. The engine, which had been kept idling, was found to have lost power. It barely moved the boat. The trouble was possibly seaweed picked up in the water intake pipe when the boat went inshore to take the prisoners on board. There was no way of remedying the defect quickly and half-a-mile of water lay between them and even a fair chance of evading pursuit.

Slowly, all too slowly, they crawled towards Paddy's Block, while they anxiously watched the island for any sign that the rescue had been observed. About 200 yards out from the shore they were astonished to see the sentry and his companion emerge from the bushes at the back of the embankment and run towards the fort. Shortly afterwards, while the boat was still a considerable distance from the mainland, they saw an armed party of troops rushing from the fort to the point at which the prisoners had been working. The troops began a search of the bushes evidently under the impression that the prisoners were still on the island. They did not appear to realise at first that the launch flying the Union Jack with four men visible on it, had taken them off. The few minutes' respite was invaluable.

At last, the launch reached the nearest point of land and was beached. The seven Volunteers spread out a little and began to run along under the old Martello tower and uphill towards Ringaskiddy where transport should be waiting. Jerome Crowley, Captain of Ballinhassig Company, and Seán Hyde were not far away, although they had not been able to bring their horse and trap as close to the landing place as they would have wished. There was no road or passage possible for a vehicle of any kind.

There was but one horse and trap and it could not take nine men. It was decided that Jerome Crowley, Seán Hyde and the three released prisoners should take the trap. They drove away through Ringaskiddy and thence on by-roads to Ballinhassig and safety. They took the sentry's rifle and ammunition with them.

Michael Burke and the three other Cobh Company men commandeered a rowing boat and rowed to a point between Raffeen and Monkstown. Barry and O'Reilly crossed the river by ferry from Monkstown to Rushbrooke. Burke and Butterley came to the city by train, Burke to report the success of the job at Miss Wallace's, St Augustine Street.

News of the escape of the prisoners must have been sent to the police on the mainland very quickly because the train on which Burke and Butterley travelled was held up at Glenbrook. All the passengers were ordered out, searched and interrogated. The stories put up by the two Volunteers stood the test and they were allowed to continue their journey. All four returned to Cobh. It is a tribute to the many people in the town who saw them leave at 9.30 a.m. in a boat which was captured by the British a little later, that none of them was subsequently arrested. The boat, minus its engine, was handed back to the owner after the Truce.

At a time when the British military strength around Cork harbour was at its maximum, one of their strongest fortresses had failed to hold its prisoners. The three Volunteer groups who were engaged – the prisoners, Cobh men and the Ballinhassig men – had combined to carry out a neat and successful operation.

Chapter 17

Captured armoured car driven into Mountjoy in an attempt to rescue Seán MacEoin

by Professor Michael Hayes, Colonel Joe Leonard and Lieut-General Seán MacEoin

Physical fighting against the British was of a rather different character in the country to what it was in Dublin. In the country, attacks on RIC barracks were first undertaken by men who assembled at night and who, after an attack on a barrack, resumed their ordinary civilian life. Later, small bodies of men in flying columns remained on full-time active service in the country, getting shelter and food from the country people, using assistance from local IRA men and civilians in their activities, and operating on the hit-and-run method. Leadership of these columns required certain qualities. The column leader had to be fearless, and as well as that he had to be resourceful, alert and responsible. In many cases, he had first to disarm members of the RIC or British military to provide his men with arms and ammunition. He had to keep in touch with units in adjoining counties and with GHQ in Dublin.

A time was reached when the RIC was unable to hold all its positions throughout the country and many of it barracks were evacuated. These barracks were promptly burned by local IRA units acting on orders from IRA headquarters in Dublin. A new problem then presented itself to the local IRA leader, because, as well as fighting, he had to take his share, sometimes a very important share, in the administration of justice in the area from which the constabulary had been withdrawn.

Seán MacEoin, a young blacksmith from Ballinalee, County Longford, was leader of the Longford flying column, and was also vice-brigadier and director of operations for Longford and a portion of Leitrim and Cavan. He had shown not only great courage, but also ingenuity, military knowledge and a capacity for taking responsibility. By 1921 he had many big exploits to his credit and had become a well-known figure. The British had warned him that they would shoot him on sight.

On 9 January he observed RIC, including Black and Tans, closing in on his headquarters in Miss Martin's cottage near Ballinalee. In order to avoid a fight in the cottage, MacEoin rushed out to meet the enemy, his blazing guns clearing a way though them. District Inspector McGrath of the RIC fell fatally wounded and MacEoin escaped. On 2 February MacEoin's column ambushed a British punitive party moving in lorries near Ballinalee. Two Auxiliaries and a district inspector of the RIC were killed in the fight, which had continued for almost an hour when the British surrendered. There were fifteen survivors, of whom eight were wounded. MacEoin released the unwounded prisoners and let them have one of the captured lorries to take their wounded comrades to hospital.

About a month later the British captured Commandant MacEoin. Though handcuffed he attempted to escape, but was shot at, wounded and recaptured. His captors beat him up with their rifle butts before taking him away.

While awaiting trial in prison he was elected a member of Dáil Éireann for Longford and Westmeath. On 14 June he was charged before a field general court martial in Dublin with having murdered District Inspector McGrath. Several Auxiliaries gave evidence that after the fighting in Ballinalee he had done his best for the British wounded and that he had, in fact, sent a doctor to attend them. The relatives of the dead DI made a plea that 'the man who spared and protected his prisoners shall be spared and protected himself when a prisoner'. But he was sentenced to be hanged and was lodged in Mountjoy jail, Dublin, with a special guard of Auxiliaries to watch over day him day and night.

The jail was an old building with a strong outer gate reached by a long passage from the main road and two inner gates, which, under prison rules, had always to be kept closed. The ordinary staff of the jail, all Irishmen, was augmented by Auxiliary police, and regular British military furnished the outer guards.

It will be readily understood that the loss of MacEoin was considered a very grievous one, and there was passionate anxiety that he should not suffer the supreme penalty; but the problem of effecting his rescue seemed impossible to solve.

Like the flying columns in the country, there had been formed in Dublin, in September 1919, a full-time active service unit called 'The Squad'. The men who belonged to it gave their whole time to active service. They operated in Dublin city and got co-operation not only from members of the IRA (Volunteer) organisation but also from many civilians, police, prison warders, civil servants and others. Conditions under which they operated were different from those in the country, with crowded streets instead of lonely places. Intimate knowledge of the city by-ways and the help of friendly civilians often brought men to safety when they had carried out a 'job'.

Michael Collins called 'The Squad' into play to attempt a rescue of Seán MacEoin. The attempt is described in the narrative that follows by Colonel Joseph Leonard who was a member of 'The Squad'.

Michael Hayes

LEONARD'S STORY — OUTSIDE MOUNTJOY

In May 1921 Collins conceived a plan to rescue Seán Mac-Eoin from Mountjoy jail. The plan was in three parts: (1) to capture and man a British armoured car for the purpose of gaining entrance to the jail; (2) having gained entrance, to get possession of MacEoin's body; (3) to make sure that it would be possible to come out of the jail again.

British military lorries drew meat rations for various barracks from the Dublin abattoir two or three times a day. The lorries were accompanied by an armoured car, a Rolls single-turret Whippet. Having in mind the use of an armoured car for the Mountjoy job, Collins instructed Charlie Dalton to take up his quarters in the abattoir superintendent's house and watch through the window the movements of the car. Charlie noticed that some days, on their first visit, which was at 6 a.m., the car crew would become restless, so that eventually the last soldier would get out to stretch his legs and, having locked the car, would ramble about the place. This led to the conclusion that it might be possible to capture the car. Collins took immediate action. In Jim Kirwan's public house he had a consultation with Emmet Dalton, myself and a Mountjoy warder who gave us full information about warders, the positions of military guards, meal times and relief times for police and Auxiliaries. Meantime, through another source, MacEoin was instructed to make some complaint or pretext every day to ensure that at 10 a.m. he would be with the governor in his office. The governor's office was outside of three obstructing gates, and the governor was usually alone in his office at ten o'clock in the morning, to interview prisoners. If we could get in at that time and find MacEoin in the office the rest would be easy.

The organisation of the parties was done by Paddy O'Daly. It was made the task of one group to capture the car, of another to man and drive it, and of a third to force an entrance through the main gate of Mountjoy after the car had been driven in. The last party was to reopen the gate and keep it open until the armoured car had come out again. I shall take these three parties in order.

One morning Charlie Dalton noticed that, on their early visit at 6 a.m., the soldiers were in a jaunty mood. He guessed that the last soldier would probably leave the car on their next visit. He made his report, returned to his watch-out post and the job was on.

The car with the same crew returned on its second journey, and the crew behaved as Charlie Dalton had guessed it would. The last Tommy got out and went for a stroll. IRA men wearing corporation uniform caps, who had been waiting about the abattoir, closed in at a pre-arranged signal and held up the Tommies, shooting some who resisted. They secured the keys of the car and, for the first time, a Rolls single-turret Whippet armoured car became the property of the IRA. Pat McCrea, a quiet and reliable man, had never seen the inside of a car like this in his life. But he got in calmly and stepped on the gas. He was accompanied by Tom Keogh, Bill Stapleton and Paddy McCaffrey as machine gunners, and went off down the North Circular Road. Emmet Dalton and myself were waiting for them, dressed and armed like British officers. Emmet was wearing his own British uniform and, having worn it for a long time when in the British army, he had all the appearance and manner of a British officer. He knew how to adopt the right tone when serving a Prisoner's Removal Order on the jail authorities. I had served for six months in Mountjoy and knew the prison well. Besides, Emmet's second uniform fitted me to perfection.

When he had picked us up McCrea drove to Mountjoy. Emmet Dalton, who was sitting outside as the officer usually did, waved an official-looking paper at the look-out warder. The gates opened wide and shut-to with a clang behind us. Two more iron gates were opened for us. McCrea used his head. He drove the car in one long sweep around by the main entrance and back through the two iron gates we had just entered, carelessly jamming both open and so leaving only the main gate to be negotiated in the getaway. Dalton and myself jumped smartly out of the car. We posted Tom Keogh, dressed in British dungarees and a Tommy's uniform cap, outside the main entrance door to cover our rear or give the alarm if necessary. Dalton and I entered the main door at 10.30 a.m. as the warders were coming on duty from their headquarters. One of them, Warder Kelly, had known me as a prisoner. He was so surprised at seeing me in a British uniform that he exclaimed, 'Oh cripes, look at Leonard', and then, clapping his hand over his mouth, he dashed back upstairs, knocking down all the warders who were descending. We were refused entrance to MacEoin's wing by the warder in charge and, as it was not possible for us to break down two massive iron gates and MacEoin's cell door as well, we continued on to the governor's office. The situation in the office at 10 o'clock should have been that there was only one warder on duty, but when we went in half an hour later we received a shock. Instead of finding Governor Charlie Munroe alone, there were seven of his staff present. And as we went in the office door slammed shut behind us. The governor received us nicely and all went well until he mentioned that he must ring up the Castle for confirmation of the order to remove MacEoin. I sprang for the telephone and smashed it, while Dalton, drawing his gun, held the staff at bay. We had begun tying up the staff, in the hope that we might secure the master keys, when a fusillade met our ears. It was now or never if we were to get out of the building. We forced the door open, goodbyes were said quickly and we left with all haste.

MacEoin was not in the governor's office. We had arrived half-an-hour late for that appointment through no fault of our own.

The plan for holding the main gate open was that Miss Áine Malone would approach with a parcel, have the wicket opened and that IRA men in several groups would then rush the gate. Miss Malone with her parcel arrived in good time, the wicket gate was opened and the main gate rushed. But a sentry on the roof, having seen the civilians rushing the gate, fired a shot which wounded one of our men and raised a general alarm. Tom Keogh, ever on the alert, shot this sentry dead from the courtyard with a Peter the Painter. The sentry's rifle fell down to the pavement. As Dalton and myself were rushing to the main door I spotted the rifle. Auxiliaries were on the roof with their rifles at the ready. A guard of regular soldiers turned out on the ground near the gate but were naturally confused at the sight of British uniforms. Acting the part of a British officer, I ordered them to retire and, on their refusal to obey, I took up the rifle, knelt down and threatened to fire. The soldiers, seeing an officer kneeling in the firing position, retired to their quarters; but, as the Auxiliary police were advancing from the other side, it was time to jump on the back of the Whippet and go, taking the rifle with us. We shouted to Pat McCrea to let her rip. Pat drove down that drive and onto the North Circular Road at a speed that was very satisfactory, seeing we were exposed to rather heavy fire from the jail. He had instructions to drive the Whippet to the Finglas Bridge area but, as the engine overheated badly on the way, he decided to abandon the car at Marino. Having stripped it of its guns and ammunition, he set it on fire and went back to his brother's shop to continue his daily work.

Dalton and I had no plan of action agreed upon and we transferred into a waiting taxi at the end of the street. We arrived in Howth and dismissed our taxi. It then dawned on me that my sister had good friends among the Sisters of Charity, so we decided to go and see them. We were very nicely received by a sympathetic sister who listened to our tale of woe. Having produced a lovely cup of tea and set out the best china, she went to see the Reverend Mother. A messenger was sent to Cassidy's public house on the Summit and he returned with two suits borrowed for the occasion. Our uniforms were packed away for dispatch and we emerged, less showy but feeling more comfortable and better pleased with ourselves. We returned to town by tram.

On arrival in Dublin we learnt that the British military authorities had confined all armoured cars to barracks, having got a scare at the loss of their baby Whippet.

Joseph Leonard

MacEOIN'S STORY — INSIDE MOUNTJOY

In May 1921 I received a dispatch from Michael Collins informing me that a new attempt would be made to rescue me from Mountjoy. The dispatch instructed me to contact Warder Breslin. Later on the same day I received information and instructions from Collins, also in dispatch. They were to the effect that an armoured car manned by men of the IRA would enter Mountjoy any time between 10 and 12 o'clock on the following morning and that I must take such steps as were necessary to be in the governor's office and remain there for that time. When I came in from exercise that evening I made contact with Breslin who informed me that everything was ready for action the next morning. On return to my cell I immediately sent for the Deputy Governor, Mr Meehan, and made a violent attack upon the conduct of (a) the warders, (b) the Auxiliaries, and (c) the Black and Tans who were in charge of C (1) wing and were our jailers. In accordance with the rules, I demanded an immediate interview with the governor and succeeded in arranging it for the following morning. Everything was working according to plan. Next morning at the appointed time I arrived in the governor's office escorted by an Auxiliary officer and a warder. I succeeded in remaining in the office with Governor Munroe until about 11.30 a.m. when I informed him that I had further complaints on behalf of many of the prisoners and would return to my cell and prepare notes for use next morning. This was simply a makeshift as I did not know what had happened to the rescue attempt.

When on my way out to exercise after lunch, Breslin contacted me again and told me the car had not been captured that day but the attempt would be made the following day and that the same plan must work. I then sent out a dispatch to Collins informing him that I would be in the governor's office on the following morning, accompanied by an Auxiliary officer armed with a revolver; that when our men arrived I thought that I could handle the Auxiliary. As arranged, I was again in the governor's office next morning and remained there for about the same time with the same result. Afterwards, on going out to exercise, I received a repetition of the same message from Breslin. For the third successive morning the interview was again arranged with the governor for 10 a.m. but, in the meantime, something had occurred which we had not foreseen.

The members of the Auxiliary and Black and Tan guard who were in charge of the wing were relieved and a new body of Auxiliaries and Tans took over the duty. The officer commanding the new party insisted that every prisoner in C (1) wing should be locked in his cell. This was done. Then the new party, accompanied by the officer commanding the old party, came and saw every prisoner. This was for the purpose of identification. Each prisoner was carefully scrutinised and notes taken of him by each member of the guard so that all guards would know and recognise the prisoners who were being handed over for the first time into their custody. It was then believed by the authorities that the warders could not be trusted and that prisoners might be enabled to exchange cells so that they would have wrong names and wrong cells. The identification exercise was intended to prevent this.

While this identification was going on I protested and claimed my interview with the governor. Meehan, the Deputy Governor, was present and explained to the commander that I had an interview arranged with the governor. The Auxiliary officer replied that my interview would be in time enough later and that his orders took precedence. While his scrutiny of the prisoners was taking place the armoured car arrived into Mountjoy and the first indication I had of its presence was the firing of shots. The Auxiliaries manned the inner gate of C (1) wing and a short time afterwards they returned and opened my cell door. They were very excited and proceeded to search every corner of the cell and my person. Before they had finished Breslin came into the cell and said to them, 'We are all safe', at the same time giving me the 'glad-eye'. From that wink I realised that the car had come and gone and that all those with it were safe. I bluffed the Auxiliaries a bit by saying, 'when you meet the armoured car down town you will have a hot time if I get much more abuse'. They then told me that they were aware of my line of communication and that they would be able to end it. I wished them luck in their efforts, satisfied that they could not have secured any information as to my method of communication.

When the excitement had died down I was blandly informed that the governor was ready to receive me, not in his usual office but in a cell at the end of C (1) wing. All interviews with the governor thereafter, while I was a prisoner in Mountjoy, were in this cell.

The capture of the armoured car and the attempt at rescue was a first-class effort. Had it been captured on either of the two first days for which the rescue was planned I would have been in the governor's room at the crucial time and would have had no trouble in accompanying Dalton, Leonard and McCrea out of Mountjoy.

Seán MacEoin

CONCLUSION

The reason for the failure is clear. The armoured car could be captured only, when, contrary to regulations, the soldiers had left it. Separated from the car they could be mastered; inside it they were impregnable. Unfortunately, on the morning when an opportunity arose to capture the car a new guard had come on duty in the prison. As General MacEoin points out, a more stringent and intelligent step had been taken about prisoners. It is clear that the exploit involved risk of death for the crew of the armoured car and, indeed, for MacEoin himself, but these things were all part of the day's work at that time.

Although the prisoner was not rescued the attempt was not without very valuable results from the point of view of the IRA. It was a great shock to public opinion in Britain to find that an armoured car could be captured from the regular British army, could be driven straight into a prison and that the raiders could escape unscathed in broad daylight in Dublin. Leonard's story is told with modesty but the nature of the exploit itself emerges clearly. There was great daring, resourcefulness and a fierce determination not to be stopped by any kind of danger. Above all, the incident showed well-directed organisation, good planning and considerable originality. It came after many other important actions and afforded added evidence to the

British that members of their administration in Ireland, apart altogether from the civilian population, were collaborating with the IRA. In fact, British administration in Ireland then showed symptoms of a complete breakdown. MacEoin's narrative indicates assistance on the part of members of the prison staff.

Answers by the chief secretary for Ireland in the House of Commons constantly repeated that 'outrages' in Ireland were the work of a small band of 'murderers'. Here, in the attempted rescue of MacEoin from Mountjoy, was proof positive of the existence of an armed force, widespread in its membership, well led, disciplined and daring.

The exploit, therefore, made its own substantial contribution to bring about the Truce on 11 July 1921, and the subsequent negotiations which resulted in the establishment of a sovereign Irish state. (MacEoin, who had been elected a member of Dáil Éireann while a prisoner in Mountjoy, was released in August following a threat that negotiations with the British would be discontinued unless he was freed at once. Thirty-seven other TDs who had been held by the British had already been released.)

Michael Hayes

Chapter 18

Two got out from Boyle military barracks and escaped execution

by Bill Kelly

It was Monday 21 May 1921. Chilled to the bone and drenched with the morning dew, two men lay stretched full length in the long grass by a bank of the Boyle river and strained their eyes through the dawn's early light. They were Pat Brennan, O/C 1st Battalion, North Roscommon Brigade IRA, and Pat Delahunty, Brigade I/O. Their gaze was fixed intently on the grey walls of the military barracks, and already they had kept vigil for some hours. Then, as the hands of Brennan's watch moved towards 6.30 they knew that the next few minutes would tell whether their carefully laid plans were successful. Brennan was the leader of a small party charged with the task of escorting Captain Jim Molloy to a place of safety if he succeeded in getting out of the barracks which was held by a strong detachment of the Bedfordshire Regiment. Some thirty yards behind Brennan and Delahunty, and near the road, was Batty Reid, the contact man between them and a rearguard of Luke Dempsey, Tom Derby and Tom Lohan. The men of the rearguard were under cover on the far side of the road and their function was to allow the other three through with Molloy and then cover the getaway in the event of pursuit by the enemy.

The IRA knew that this was probably Molloy's only chance of escape, as they had learned that he was to be taken to Dublin next day. Once in Dublin he faced almost certain death. He had been wounded and captured in a skirmish with Black and Tans in Ballymote, some weeks earlier.

The six IRA men were armed only with revolvers. Their part in the escape was based on the assumption that Molloy could get out of the barracks unnoticed. They would prevent his recapture in the event of an immediate hue-and-cry.

Almost on the stroke of 6.30 Brennan and Delahunty saw a man clamber out through a window in the wash-house, which was over the Boyle river, and wade into the river. Then, to their dismay, he moved upstream and away from them. Quietly but urgently they sought to attract his attention as he waded further away from them. Any unusual sound might alert the Bedfords, but Brennan had to take that risk. A low piercing whistle shrilled across the river. Molloy stopped wading at once and turned his head. A discreet signal from the river bank and he quickly changed direction. Minutes later he was being helped up the bank by Brennan and Delahunty.

Batty Reid got the signal that all was happening according to plan and he passed it on to Dempsey, Derby and Lohan. Positions were taken up by the rearguard to cover the getaway of Molloy, Brennan, Delahunty and Reid. It was then broad daylight and the four men slipped quickly through the Pleasure Ground and crossed the Carrick road. There the rearguard fell in behind them. There, too, Delahunty parted from them and returned home to breakfast. He lived less than 200 yards from the military barracks. As I/O it was imperative that he should avoid the risk of being identified with the IRA. The other six pushed on with all speed. They crossed the railway line at a level-crossing and skirted the reservoir, then crossed the Roscommon road. There the rearguard and Reid dispersed. Brennan and Molloy continued to Granny Bog where Molloy was handed over to the Ballineen Company for safe keeping and soon afterwards he was taken to Roche's house for a meal. Jim Molloy had escaped and got clean away from a closely guarded military barracks in one of the most heavily garrisoned towns in the west. In addition to the Bedfords in the military barracks in Main Street, there were the RIC, including Black and Tans, in the constabulary barracks, also in Main Street; and in the workhouse in Elphin Street there was a half-company of Auxiliaries.

There were about fifty prisoners held in the military barracks at the time of the escape. Most of them, including Molloy, were confined in an indoor miniature rifle range on the north side of the square. They included Commandant Peter Heslin of the Leitrim Brigade, the senior ranking prisoner; Brigade Quartermaster Martin Killilea of Doon, Boyle; Battalion Commandant James Feely and Battalion Adjutant Phil Murray. Four prisoners considered to be more dangerous than the others were kept in four cells at the north-west corner of the basement. The barred windows of their cells faced the barrack square at ground level. Those prisoners were Brigadier Michael Dockery and Adjutant Jack Clancy of the North Roscommon Brigade, and Commandant Jim Hunt and Dick McGough of the 4th (Gurteen) Sligo Battalion. Probably because of his wound, Molloy had not been put in one of the basement cells.

On 21 May 1921, the *Roscommon Herald* reported that some significant arrests had taken place on 16 May. The report referred to the arrest of Brigadier Dockery, Adjutant Jack Clancy and three others in the County Roscommon village of Cootehill. In the report Dockery was described as chairman of Carrick No. 2 District Council, one of the established local authorities of the time, many of which did not co-operate with the ruling authorities. (He was in jail, too, at the time of his election in 1920.) Jack Clancy was described as a commercial traveller 'for Kenny's of Dublin'. The arrests were made by a cycling party of Auxiliaries during a raid on the licensed premises of William O'Hara. Arrested with Dockery and Clancy were Joe and Willie O'Hara of the Cootehill Company, and the O'Hara's workman, Dominick Mullaney, who was not in the IRA.

Dockery and Clancy, the *Roscommon Herald* report recorded, had been on the run for some months. They had arrived in O'Hara's on bicycles, sought refreshments and had two rifles and two revolvers. The Auxiliaries were stated to have been attracted by a light in the bar.

Escape was immediately in the minds of Dockery and Clancy, with good reason, as will be shown. Reported the *Roscommon Herald:*

> Jack Clancy made a determined effort to escape. He had got loose from his captors and rushed into the fields. Three shots were fired at him and also the contents of a revolver. He had a marvellous escape from being shot down, and he proceeded to take cover behind a ditch. The night, however, was very bright and he was at once surrounded and captured again. In all, there were five prisoners to drive to Boyle.

Contemporary reports and the facts as established by history are not always the same. Micheal O'Callaghan in *For Ireland And Freedom,* his story of Roscommon's contribution to the fight for Irish independence, published in 1964, gives this account of the attempted escape from the Auxiliaries at Cootehill:

> Dockery and Clancy were brought out and put standing against the wall surrounding the church grounds. Only one Auxiliary was left guarding them and when he turned his head momentarily, Dockery decided to make a break for it. He ran and attempted to cross the wall fronting the residence of the parish priest. As he was crossing the wall one of the raiders fired and wounded him in the leg. He fell across the wall and was dragged back to the road.

In a search of O'Hara's place the Auxiliaries found a number of rifles, revolvers and a quantity of ammunition. What they did not find out was that a meeting of North Roscommon officers had been summoned for O'Hara's, to make arrangements for the establishment of a battalion flying column.

The five prisoners, none of whom had possession of weapons at the time of the raid, were beaten up by the Auxiliaries while on their way to Boyle after the arrests. On their arrival in the town they were taken to the RIC barracks in Main Street. There a sergeant named Forde identified Dockery as having taken part in an ambush on an RIC patrol about a mile from Keadue on 20 March 1921, in which three of the patrol were shot dead. Forde was a survivor. As Brigade O/C, Dockery was in charge of the ambush. Clancy was there also but, fortunately for him, he was not recognised. Towards the end of the fight at Keadue, Dockery called on an RIC sergeant named Riley to surrender. Riley turned to fight but Dockery grappled with him and disarmed him. Riley then ran and took refuge in a nearby rectory and Forde clambered out of a ditch where he had taken cover.

Forde surrendered. As the IRA had no means of keeping

prisoners, the two sergeants had to be allowed to go free. Forde recognised Dockery after the ambush and now identified him as 'one of the Keadue murderers'.

With the five prisoners the Auxiliaries handed over to the RIC the rifles and revolvers which they had found in O'Hara's pub in Cootehill. The RIC claimed that these included some of the weapons which had been taken from the patrol after the ambush at Keadue.

That night in the RIC barracks all five prisoners were beaten up again. Mullaney was released next morning and the other four were taken to the military barracks where Dockery and Clancy were put in the basement cells pending their transfer to Dublin. Dockery's position was desperate as he faced trial for murder with the certainty of conviction and execution.

Commandant Jim Hunt and Dick McGrath, who were also in basement cells, were natives of Gurteen, County Sligo. Hunt had been on the run for some time and was arrested at Monasteraden on Tuesday 17 May, the day after the Cootehill arrests were made. With Commandant Sonny Marron of Ballymote, he had been in charge of an ambush at Teevnacreeva on 1 September 1920 in which two RIC men, Constables McCarthy and Murphy, were killed. McGough had also taken part in the action.

Martin Killilea, James Feely, Phil Murray and the others in the rifle range were not as closely guarded as were the men in the cells. Murray struck up a friendship with Corporal George Meadlarkin, a military policeman in the barracks. Meadlarkin, who had married a pretty local girl named Winifred Henry, let Murray know that he was sympathetic towards the IRA.

Then the highlight of the drama followed quickly: the escape of Molloy and Dockery in which Meadlarkin took a significant part. The plan to get Molloy out of the barracks was simple. The prisoners were marched in two batches across the square to the wash-house every morning, and Killilea, Feely and Murray reckoned that it would be comparatively easy for Molloy to get through the wash-house window and into the river. Next stage was to ensure that he would be escorted from the river to a safe place, and so communications must be established with the IRA on the outside.

A boy named Joseph Martin of Oaklands, Boyle (who became postmaster in Wexford town), served Mass in the barracks every morning, and Killilea immediately thought of using him as a courier who would not be suspected by the guards. One of the prisoners, Willie Meehan of Gurteen, approached Martin and the boy readily agreed to help. Meehan slipped him a written message which he concealed in his knickerbockers, the loose-fitting breeches buttoned below the knee, which were then worn by most boys. Martin brought the message to Michael Ward of Green Street, Boyle, and soon it was in the hands of Pat Delahunty. The message was that Corporal Meadlarkin had promised to help in the escape of Molloy and Dockery.

Meadlarkin, like most of the garrison, bought his cigarettes and some other items in a tobacconist shop near the barracks' gate, owned by Miss Margaret Judge who was a member of Cumann na mBan. Pat Delahunty contacted her and she agreed to talk about the escape project with Meadlarkin. She met him almost at once, as there was no time to lose. He gave her valuable information about the layout of the barracks, the prisoners' routine and where and how they were held in the barracks. Then, using the newly established line of communications, Delahunty arranged with Killilea and others on the inside for the escape of Molloy. The plan was masterly in its simplicity. Details had to be finalised without delay.

Delahunty learned that the armed soldiers who escorted the batches of prisoners between the rifle range and the wash-house did not enter the wash-house with them. This was a vital factor in getting Molloy out of the barracks. Killilea, Feely and Murray were satisfied that he could be got out without difficulty. Once he was out it was up to the IRA on the outside to ensure that he was immediately escorted to a safe place. Delahunty reported the situation to Commandant Brennan who, having first surveyed the escape route, then made the dispositions for the IRA party responsible for escorting Molloy from the vicinity of the barracks. The escape was fixed for the early morning of Monday 21 May. Brennan and Delahunty spent Sunday night in Delahunty's house near the barracks.

At six o'clock on Monday morning the first batch of prisoners was escorted to the wash-house by four sleepy soldiers. There were twenty-three in the batch and Molloy was one of them. Inside the wash-house they milled around noisily as usual. While this was going on Jack Downes lifted Molloy to a window in an outside wall. Within seconds Molloy was through the window and in the shallow river. When the prisoners emerged from the wash-house they formed up and were counted. Immediately the soldiers began to argue as to the number of men they had escorted from the rifle range. One stubbornly maintained that there were twenty-three, but he was over-ridden by the other three soldiers who, no doubt hungry for their breakfast, wanted their task finished as quickly as possible. And so twenty-two men were escorted back to the rifle range while Molloy was getting away from Boyle.

The escape was not discovered until the evening roll-call. A big search operation was set in train at once. Lorry loads of RIC, Auxiliaries and the Bedfords swept the town and countryside like a swarm of angry bees. Too late. Molloy was already safely hidden by Seamus Ryan, O/C of the Ballinameen unit. The crown forces never found a trace of him. Embarrassed by the escape, the Bedfords tightened up security in the barracks. Stronger guards were mounted and white patches were sewn on the backs of the prisoners' coats, to serve as targets in the event of another escape attempt. Nevertheless, it was reasoned by the IRA both inside and outside the barracks that the Bedfords would expect the prisoners to be of good behaviour for a while and not to attempt another escape in the immediate future. Despite the security precautions, however, the escape of Molloy was, in many ways, an exercise for the escape of Dockery a few days later.

Obviously, the wash-house trick would not work again. And so the direct participation of Meadlarkin in the escape of Dockery became necessary. He had to open the cell door and he readily agreed to do so. A sum of money was involved, of necessity. Killilea agreed the amount with Meadlarkin and through Miss Judge, Delahunty gave the corporal an assurance that it would be forthcoming. Meadlarkin agreed to divide it as a bribe among the members of the guard on duty on the morning of the escape.

Dockery had to be got out at once as his identification by Sergeant Forde of the RIC was tantamount to a death sentence. Nothing could be done about getting out Jim Hunt, at least not then. His cell was immediately inside the barracks gate and could be entered only through the guardroom. Consequently no money would buy the co-operation of the guard in shutting their eyes to his departure from the premises.

Neither Clancy nor McGough, who occupied two other cells in the basement, was in immediate danger as neither had been identified as a participant in armed attacks on crown forces. About 5.30 on the morning fixed for the escape, just before reveille roused the barracks into life, Meadlarkin walked into the guardroom, palmed the key of Dockery's cell and released the prisoner. He then locked the door and replaced the key on the hook in the guardroom. The members of the guard, their eyes blinded by bribe money, saw nothing. From his basement cell Dockery slipped down a passage towards the south side of the barracks. The passage extended under part of the main building, past what was known as the 'small barracks', then gradually rose counter to the slope of the ground towards the river. As he approached near the river end of the passage, which reached ground level about six feet short of the outer wall of the barracks, Dockery had to bend almost double to keep out of sight of the sentry. He then faced the crucial part of the attempt, which was to cross those six feet of the square and climb the wall while fully exposed to the view of the sentry. Fortune was with him. He covered the ground and got over the wall without being observed. Once he was on the outside the wash-house screened him from the sentry, and he walked down into the river.

For the second time in four days Brennan and Delahunty saw the dawn break as they lay on the damp grass by the bank of the Boyle river. This time there was no mistake. Dockery headed straight towards them.

The battalion commandant and his I/O threw their arms about their brigadier, but there was no time for the further manifestation of their joy. They were still dangerously within reach of the enemy. As before, Batty Reid signalled to the rearguard of Dempsey, Derby and Lohan, and they covered Dockery on his way to freedom.

Meadlarkin quickly came under suspicion of complicity in the escapes, and his life was made hell for him as he was interrogated in Boyle and elsewhere. He was arrested and taken to England where he was kept in detention for about twelve months, during which period he was court-martialled. Conclusive evidence against him was not forthcoming and eventually he was released and discharged from the British army. By then the Treaty had been ratified. Had his part in the escapes been proved he would have faced a long jail sentence if not death by a firing squad.

On his release Meadlarkin returned to Ireland, enlisted in the Free State army and was promoted to sergeant. After his Irish army service he returned to Boyle and farmed at Ballytrasna. Some years later he returned to England where he died. The drama of his part in the escape of Molloy and Dockery will always have a special place in the story of Roscommon's part in the fight for freedom.

'An internee named Murray was the first to trust me,' Meadlarkin said years later. 'He referred me to a Miss Judge in whose shop some of the soldiers used to buy cigarettes. She introduced me to a clergyman and to Mr Delahunty. I told them that Molloy and Dockery were to be executed.'

Three weeks after Dockery's escape all but a few of the prisoners in Boyle military barracks were taken to Rath internment camp in the Curragh from which some of them escaped on the night of 8 September 1921. Clancy and McGough were taken to Mountjoy and held there until after the Treaty had been ratified.

Chapter 19

Fifteen minutes to freedom from Sligo jail

As told to Bill Kelly by Peadar Glynn

The clatter of the falling shovel reverberated through the pre-dawn darkness of the Hangman's Yard and echoed and re-echoed off the walls of Sligo jail. 'Guard-turn out,' bawled an English voice even before the last ringing echo had faded away. The pounding of metal-shod boots down the passageway, the metallic click of rifle bolts and the jingle of military equipment sent icy thrills of dismay through the three men who crouched against a gateway in the yard of the jail. In one dark corner of the yard stood a grim reminder of the fate that awaited the three men they had come to rescue. It was the scaffold. And now because an unfortunately placed shovel had been knocked over, the guard was alerted and it seemed that the would-be rescuers stood an excellent chance of sharing the same fate with the three prisoners, on that scaffold, if they survived the inevitable gun battle in the yard. The man nearest the gate turned to his companions. 'We'll fight them,' he whispered. 'We'll meet in Heaven. Get some cover and be ready for them.'

The man was Billy Pilkington, Commandant of the Sligo

Brigade. Having thus whispered to his two comrades, he snapped back the hammer of his .45 Webley revolver and flattened himself against the wall, scarcely daring to breathe. His comrades, Captain Peadar Glynn and Captain Tom Scanlon, who commanded the Town Company of the Sligo Battalion of the IRA, glided across the jail yard like ghosts; their automatics at the ready, they were in search of cover. Then Glynn vanished and, astounded by his sudden disappearance, Scanlon stopped in his tracks. Whispered words reached him: 'Down here, Tom. I'm down here. There are steps.' Scanlon recovered quickly and went down the steps. The two men crouched below. Though neither of them realised it, they were in the 'drop' beneath the scaffold as they awaited what seemed to be inevitable discovery by the enemy.

In their hole in the ground, Glynn and Scanlon heard the British soldiers, the guard on Sligo jail, charge around the yard. They heard them approach to within a yard of the hangman's 'drop' and pass close to the spot where they had left Pilkington. Vaguely outlined on top of the jail wall were Jack Brennan, Harry Brehony and Paddy Gilmartin, three other members of the rescue squad. Tensed for action, all the IRA men waited, their knuckles white as they gripped their guns; in the space of a hundred heartbeats, they watched as the British soldiers searched the yard. Then the almost unbelievable happened. It was the NCO in charge of the soldiers. 'All right! All right,' he ordered. 'Back in! It must have been an effing cat.'

For fully five minutes after the soldiers had clattered back to the guardroom Glynn and Scanlon remained motionless in their position. Then, following a signal by the brigadier, they crept noiselessly across the yard again and rejoined that intrepid man. By now he had moved through the gate and was at the door to the cell passage. Without a word, as though nothing had happened, Pilkington bent to the task which had been so dramatically interrupted. After a few minutes he turned to his comrades. 'It's no use,' he whispered, 'the key won't work.'

The first bid to rescue Commandants Charlie Gildea, Frank O'Beirne and Tom Deignan had failed. Pilkington, Scanlon and Glynn slipped across the Hangman's Yard, climbed up the rope ladder and down the other side of the wall. Pilkington issued orders rapidly for the dispersal of the men who had been mobilised for the rescue and, with the bitterness of failure in their hearts, they all made their way to their hideouts.

They were to experience similar failure on five more occasions before at last they achieved their objective on 29 June 1921. Never during all that time, however, was there any thought of giving up the attempt.

The first reverse served only to strengthen the determination of Pilkington and before the dawn had broken across Sligo Bay he had given orders for another attempt to be made two days later. The rescue was no easy job but it had to be done. It was May 1921 and the Irish War of Independence was being fought bitterly.

Commandants Frank O'Beirne of Collooney, Charlie Gildea of Tubbercurry, and Tom Deignan of Riverstown were in the hands of the enemy. O'Beirne had already been sentenced to death and Deignan would almost certainly share the same fate. Gildea's position was perilous also. The British had good reason for wishing the end of these three men who were amongst the most active and daring of the band which followed the most daring of them all, Billy Pilkington, the brigadier. At Chaffpool, late in 1920, the Sligo Brigade had hit hard and a district inspector of the RIC died. At Cliffoney the brigade avenged the death of Terence MacSwiney on the very day of his funeral when they attacked the RIC from the Hill of Grange. Four policemen were killed, three wounded and ten rifles were captured.

But IRA losses were heavy too. Vice-Brigadier Frank Carty, previously rescued from Sligo and Derry jails, was back in enemy hands, this time in Mountjoy jail, Dublin. Jimmy Devins, Commandant of the Grange Battalion, with his Vice-Commandant, Eugene Gilbride, and Captain Andy Conway of the Cliffoney Battalion, were in enemy hands also since late in 1920. On their way to attack the RIC barracks at Ballymote, they had driven slap into an enemy patrol and were prisoners even before they had time to get out of the car. Almost as serious as these losses in personnel was the loss of seven of the precious Cliffoney rifles which had been recaptured by the enemy. Commandant Charlie Gildea and Mick O'Hara of the Tubbercurry Battalion had also been captured late in 1920, and Gildea was still languishing in Sligo jail. O'Hara, wounded at the time of his capture, was in hospital under guard.

In the early months of 1921 the enemy intelligence in the Sligo area was just too good, so the brigade ambushed a train at Ballisodare and eliminated their chief intelligence officer. Travelling on the same train was Colonel Dann who commanded the enemy troops in the area. He survived the ambush because he wore civilian clothes, posed as a commercial traveller, and the IRA were unable to identify him positively. And because Dann lived it had now become imperative that O'Beirne and Deignan should be rescued from Sligo jail. Plans to rescue Gildea had been made a few weeks previously.

This was the course of events. Early in May 1921, Brigadier

Pilkington summoned a brigade meeting in the house of Jack Reilly, Gleann Geevagh, to plan the rescue of Gildea. At the head of the table sat Pilkington, tough, quiet-spoken and dedicated, a leader who would allow no man to use strong language in his presence. Grouped around the table were his Battalion Commandants: Jim Keaveney, Sligo; Ned Bofin, Grange; Frank O'Beirne, Collooney; Jack Brennan, Tubbercurry; Tom Deignan, Riverstown; Harold MacBrien, Ballintogher; Sonny Marron, Ballymote; and Joe Finnegan, Gurteen. There also were Captain Peadar Glynn and Captain Tom Scanlon of the Town Company, Sligo Battalion.

The enemy would have given a lot to know about that meeting at Jack Reilly's house, though a raiding party would have found a warm reception there, for these men were the cream of the brigade's fighting elements. They knew that Sligo jail would be a hard nut to crack. They had already taken Frank Carty out of it, but since then the enemy had posted twenty-six officers and men there, to guard the place and the men it held. The jail, on Cranmore, was surrounded by a wall thirty-two feet high and five feet thick. At Chapel Street, less than 200 yards distant, was a strongly held RIC barracks, and across the river at the back of the jail was the military barracks.

The brigadier and Jim Keaveney undertook to deal with the details of the arrangements for the rescue of Gildea, and the battalion leaders set out on the return journey to their areas, to have their men ready at short notice. It wasn't long before the brigadier had learned that the guard who regularly patrolled the passage in the cell block took fifteen minutes to make his rounds. A ladder must be obtained to scale the outer wall of the jail and a rope ladder to get down into the jail yard. Cover parties must be provided and posted, and enemy communications severed. There were many details in need of attention.

Then, within a week of the brigade council meeting, the enemy struck another blow. Commandant Frank O'Beirne was arrested. He was mercilessly beaten up, then court-martialled and sentenced to death for his part in the Ballisodare train ambush, an action in which, incidentally, he had taken no part; but that didn't bother the enemy, for had not Colonel Dann himself identified him as having been engaged!

Within a week of the arrest of O'Beirne, Commandant Tom Deignan was captured. As the keen-eyed Colonel Dann had had a good look at Tom, who had been in the Ballisodare ambush, it was certain that Deignan, too, was booked for the hangman's noose.

It seemed that the fates were operating against the Sligo Brigade. And so it became a vital and urgent matter to get O'Beirne, Deignan and Gildea out of Sligo jail.

The jail faced onto Cranmore Road and its main gate gave access to the cell block on the right. A smaller gate on the left led to the kitchen quarters and laundry, at the back of which was a blank wall that bounded one side of the Hangman's Yard. The yard was bounded also by the external wall of the jail on one side, and by the wall that separated the governor's house and gardens from the cell blocks at the extreme riverside end.

The fourth wall was formed by one side of the cell block, and at the end of this wall was a gate that gave entrance from the Hangman's Yard into a small square space at the end of the passage. From the gate into the Hangman's Yard, on the left, was a door that led into the governor's private grounds and quarters where the military were billeted. Facing the gate that gave into the Hangman's Yard was a door into the cell block, and on the right was a door to the passage along by the side of the cells, which led to the kitchen quarters at the front of the jail. Every fifteen minutes a soldier of the guard unlocked the door from the governor's quarters, patrolled the passage around the cells and then returned to the guardroom.

To reach the cells where the prisoners were held it was necessary to have keys to the gate from the Hangman's Yard and to the door which gave into the cell block that faced it. The rescuers were in luck about the keys. At that time Denis A. Mulcahy of Sinn Féin, the political wing of the independence movement, was awaiting trial in Sligo jail. 'Mul', as he was affectionately known to his friends, was an affable character, friendly even towards the warders – because he wanted an impression of the master-key. He was a resourceful man, too, and he succeeded in impressing a warder's master-key on a cake of soap while the warder was preoccupied. The master-key opened the gate and doors. In addition to his affability and ingenuity, Denis Mulcahy enjoyed yet another great advantage at the time. As he had not yet been convicted he was allowed visitors, and his most frequent visitor was his pretty wife, Mary, an enthusiastic worker in the movement. She brought out the impression of the key and gave it to Brigadier Pilkington who passed it on to Tom Burgess with instructions to make a key as quickly as possible. Tom was foreman in the garage of John Gilbride and for him the cutting of a key was a simple matter under ordinary circumstances. At the time, however, the circumstances were not normal, for several employees at the garage were hostile to the movement; indeed, one of the apprentices was the son of the local head constable. Those hostile elements kept a careful watch on Burgess. Nevertheless, he succeeded in making the key and it was smuggled in to the prisoners by Mary Mulcahy. There was joy on the outside when the prisoners sent out word that the key worked; like the warder's master-key, it opened the locks in the gate and doors.

Pilkington decided that it was time to make the rescue bid. The men of the Town Company were mobilised. Under Brigade Quartermaster Charlie Dolan, and Tom Burgess who was acting company O/C while Tom Scanlon and Pat Gilmartin were on the run, Volunteers Jack and James Monaghan, Paddy Burns, Joe Pilkington, Michael McCrann, Paddy Walsh, Harry Doherty and Tom Currid 'borrowed' the largest ladder available in the yard of Dudley Hanley & Co., a firm of builders providers, on the night of the rescue bid. The ladder had to be taken from Hanley's yard, carried across the main road at a point within fifty yards of the principal RIC barracks at Chapel Street, through the grounds of the Mercy Convent, then for a mile through the fields to the back of the jail. This had to be done during curfew. Pat Scanlon, Tom's father, had made a rope ladder long enough to reach from the top of the jail wall to the ground inside the Hangman's Yard.

Pilkington left nothing to chance. The men of the Town Company, having brought the ladder to the jail wall, were then sent to occupy other positions. Volunteers armed with grenades were posted at the gates of the jail, under the command of Jim Keaveney, Charlie Dolan and Tom Burgess.

James Monaghan, who had been a signaller in the British army before he joined the IRA, was posted on top of a telephone pole to tap the lines, and he also had orders to cut them at once if there was any hint of an alarm. He was perched precariously on the pole throughout each of the seven rescue attempts (yet he was later deemed not to have been on active service!). He listened to all the messages that passed between the enemy posts during the entire operation.

The men of the active service unit, all of whom were on the run, left their billets in the houses of the Scanlon, McSharry and Flynn families of Cairn's View, opposite Sligo cemetery, and then made their way across the fields to the jail where they made contact with Dolan, Burgess and their men. In the party were Brigadier Billy Pilkington, Jack Brennan, Harry Brehony, Jim Keaveney, Paddy Gilmartin, John Joe Sweeney, Tom Scanlon and Peadar Glynn.

The ladder was placed against the outside wall of the jail, and Billy Pilkington and Tom Scanlon climbed quickly to the top of it. They tied the rope ladder to the top rung of the Dudley Hanley ladder and dropped it into the Hangman's Yard. Jack Brennan, Harry Brehony and Paddy Gilmartin, who comprised a covering party, took up positions on top of the wall. In their stockinged feet, Pilkington, Scanlon and Glynn went down the rope ladder into the yard. There followed the incident of the knocked-over shovel and the calling-out of the guard. After the guard had been recalled, Scanlon and Glynn waited until Pilkington signalled that the soldier of the guard had passed on his rounds. Then Pilkington tried to open the gate. The key wouldn't work and so the first attempt had to be abandoned.

Jim Monaghan came down from his perch on the telephone pole, orders were given for the withdrawal of the units which occupied various positions and, in general, all the elaborate preparations were put into reverse. The men of the Town Company took the ladder back through the fields, through the grounds of the Mercy Convent, across the main road, and replaced it in its original position in Dudley Hanley's yard. The ASU men retired to their secret billets in Cairn's View.

After the first futile attempt the key was returned to Tom Burgess and he worked on it again. The second attempt, made a few days later, also ended in failure. So did four other attempts. Seven times in all, the men of the Sligo Brigade went through the ladder routine, Brehony, Gilmartin and Brennan occupied their covering positions on top of the jail wall, and Pilkington, Glynn and Scanlon entered the jail yard. On seven nights a guard walked his rounds without the slightest notion that he was at the mercy of three desperate and armed men. On seven nights Jim Monaghan mounted the pole to his lonely perch, his earphones clamped on his head. And yet, despite this activity in and about the jail during these nights of May and June, the enemy never had the slightest inkling that a rescue was being attempted – a tribute to the skill and the security measures of the Sligo Brigade. Yet the rescue operation might never have succeeded without the assistance of Warder J. Henry, an Irishman who had served in the British army.

Henry became friendly with O'Beirne, Gildea and Deignan and, having seen the British terror in operation in his own country, decided he no longer owed allegiance to the crown. He determined to help the IRA in any way he could.

Once again the men of the Sligo Brigade slipped with polished ease into the routine of breaking into Sligo jail. The date was 29 June 1921. Men of the Town Company had brought the ladder by the now familiar route. Jim Monaghan was up the telephone pole. The ASU men from Cairn's View were ready.

Harry Brehony, Jack Brennan and Paddy Gilmartin took up their accustomed positions on top of the wall, and Pilkington, Scanlon and Glynn went down the rope ladder, crossed the Hangman's Yard and opened the gate into the passage. This time the door to the corridor presented no problem; Warder Henry had already unlocked it. To cover his part in the operation, Henry was securely tied up and left in the passage. O'Beirne, Deignan and Gildea were awaiting the rescue party. When told that they would have to climb a rope ladder, O'Beirne asked: 'What kind of a ladder? Don't you know Gildea weighs two tons all but a pound.' But there was no time for an exchange of banter. The party had to be over the wall and away quickly, for the rounds of the guard dictated that there were only fifteen minutes to freedom in Sligo jail. When O'Beirne got on top of the wall he paused, nevertheless, and observed: 'Tonight, I'm sick of the whole affair; I want free life and I love fresh air.' Breathing his first breath of fresh air in many months, he quickly scrambled down the ladder and, escorted by Harry Brehony and Jack Brennan of the active service unit, he vanished in the darkness.

For the last time the local men took the ladder back to Hanley's yard. Jim Monaghan unhooked his earphones and climbed down the pole. Pilkington, Scanlon, Glynn and the others on the run melted into the friendly darkness. For none of them was the danger past. The War of Independence was not over, and though the Truce was to come eleven days later, neither they nor anyone else knew that.

Michael Collins, who especially appreciated organisation and courage, praised 'one of the best organised operations in the country'.

Chapter 20

Mass escape of internees from the Curragh Camp

by Bill Kelly

One of the most daring and successful escapes by IRA internees was from Rath camp at the Curragh on 8 September 1921. About fifty of them got away by tunnel during that night. In the camp, which sprawled over ten acres, some 1,300 men were held, housed in sixty wooden army huts arranged in four neat rows designated A, B, C and D. The prisoners' compound was rectangular and entirely enclosed by two massive barbed-wire entanglements, each about ten feet high and four feet wide. Between these two forbidding enclosures was a twenty-foot-wide corridor which was patrolled by an officer and six other ranks at irregular intervals, night and day. At each corner of the compound stood a high wooden tower on which machine guns were mounted and manned twenty-four hours a day. Powerful searchlights were played continuously on the prisoners' huts once darkness came down every night, and they also probed the barbed-wire entanglements and the corridor between them.

Among the IRA men interned in the camp were Desmond

Fitzgerald, editor of the daily *Bulletin*, an underground mimeo-graphed news sheet which was distributed to the world Press to counter the official British accounts of the fighting in Ireland; 'Long' Tom Byrne, Commandant of the 1st Battalion, Dublin Brigade; Joe Vize, a staff officer of the Dublin Brigade; Tod Andrews, who was later to become head of Bord na Móna and CIE; Joe Lawless from north County Dublin, who had fought under Thomas Ashe at the Battle of Ashbourne in 1916 and who was to reach the rank of colonel in the Irish army; Tom Moran, Captain of Crossna (County Roscommon) Company, whose brother Paddy was hanged on 14 March, having been convicted, on false testimony, of complicity in the executions of British spies on 'Bloody Sunday' (21 November 1920); Joe O'Connor of the 3rd Battalion, Dublin Brigade; Joe Galvin of Mount Talbot Company, North Roscommon Brigade; Father Smith, Dick Molloy and two Cullen brothers, all from Tullamore; Brophy from Galway; Tommy McCarrick from Tubbercurry in County Sligo; Section Leader Tommy Brabazon of D Company, 2nd Battalion, Dublin Brigade. And there was Jim Brady of the Arigna Battalion, Leitrim Brigade, without whom the escape might never have come off. 'The man who really dug the tunnel was Jim Brady from Arigna,' Tod Andrews told me. 'He really sweated blood on it!'

The camp was believed to be escape-proof – until after 8 September 1921. Prior to that, all attempts at escape had ended in failure. One would-be escaper concealed himself in a laundry van and had got as far as the main gate when he was discovered. Tommy McCarrick hid himself in a latrine until after dark one night but, on emerging and venturing towards the wire, he found himself looking down the barrel of a guard's rifle. Another man attempted to get out buried under a cartload of stinking refuse. Probing bayonets found him. Any prisoner approaching the barbed-wire entanglements was liable to be shot without challenge, the British military had warned – in the notorious Ballykinlar camp James Sloan and James Tormey, both of Westmeath, were gunned down, on 17 January 1921, for going too near the wire.

As it was manifest that there was no way out of Rath camp either over or through the barbed wire, some of the prisoners decided they would try to find a way under it – despite the failure of an earlier attempt at doing so. It was towards the end of April 1921 that the first and unsuccessful attempt to tunnel out was begun. Jim Brady, a former miner, was the only internee with experience of tunnelling. Using makeshift tools, he and Joe Galvin bored down under their hut, which was raised on concrete blocks. After they had reached a depth of about four feet they started to tunnel towards the barbed wire. In the first week of May their tunnel was discovered. A party of the King's Own Scottish Borderers rushed into the compound and made straight for the entrance to the tunnel.

A story persists that the discovery was caused through one of the prisoners having sent a message to Michael Collins to say he would be free in a few days. The message was supposed to have been captured during a raid on one of Collins' offices when Collins himself barely escaped the raiders by climbing through a skylight.

It is a good story but not true. Collins' office at No. 22 Mary Street, Dublin, was raided on 26 May 1921, but he was not there at the time. In fact, he arrived in the street while the raid was in progress, turned into Liffey Street and went on his way. Shortly afterwards, another office he used, at No. 29 Mary Street, was raided. It is also true that, on 12 September

1919, he escaped by climbing through a skylight while a raid on his office at No. 6 Harcourt Street, Dublin, was in progress, but that was long before the first attempt at tunnelling out of Rath camp.

It seems that the tunnel was discovered by one of the 'stool-pigeons' who had been planted in the camp by the British. At all events the military knew exactly where to find the entrance to it.

After the discovery of the tunnel the prisoners were punished by the withdrawal of privileges, and there was a tightening-up of security. Further tunnelling had to be postponed. Soon after the Truce began on 11 July, however, tunnelling was resumed. This time two tunnels were opened. One was known as the Dublin Brigade Tunnel because it was being worked mainly by men of the Dublin Brigade who had managed to get together into the same huts. It was a big and ambitious project. The second tunnel, by men from the west of Ireland and a few from Tullamore, was a smaller unshored boring known as the Tullamore Tunnel or the Rabbit Burrow. Liam Murphy was the unofficial organiser of the Rabbit Burrow enterprise, but the men who did most of the work were Jim Brady and Jim Galvin, helped mainly by Joe Rochford, Joe Shaughnessy and an internee named Regan from Keadue in County Roscommon.

Both tunnels were designed to come up under the outer barbed-wire entanglements at a point parallel with Row D. Though many of the men in the camp knew of the projects, none spoke about them. In Hut 9, Row D, Section Leader Tommy Brabazon knew of the Dublin Brigade Tunnel and was kept informed about its progress. His companions in Hut 9 – Dick Molloy, the Cullens, and Brophy from Galway – were as well informed about the Rabbit Burrow. All were tensed up but they did not discuss the projects even amongst themselves, although they were fully satisfied as to each other's IRA *bona fides*. 'There were too many strangers in the hut,' Tommy Brabazon said, 'and whom you didn't know you didn't trust. There were many in the camp who were not IRA men, and there were a few "stool-pigeons" planted by the British.'

In the hut with Tod Andrews were Jack Knowth and Myles Forde, and with Jim Brady in another hut were Galvin, Regan, Rochford and Shaughnessy. The Rabbit Burrow was started from Brady's hut. For a fortnight Brady chipped away painfully, helped by Galvin, and they were relieved by Rochford and others for short spells. Their tools were a screwdriver and crowbar, and table knives stolen from the dining hall. The problem of disposal of the soil was overcome by hauling it back to the entrance in pillow slips. From the entrance it was discreetly removed in pockets-full and dispersed so that no one would notice it on the trodden surface of the camp compound. There was no air-shaft in the tunnel. The only ventilation was through the entrance and, consequently, the atmosphere at the workface was foul. Rochford and Shaughnessy lasted only an hour at their first attempt after which they emerged choking and gasping for breath. Galvin and Brady, especially Brady, worked on grimly, enduring the foetid smell of damp earth and their own sweat for the most part of each of eleven days until they were almost completely exhausted.

A lookout system was devised to warn the tunnellers of the approach of guards. Despite the difficulties, and they were many, work on the Rabbit Burrow proceeded at an amazingly rapid pace. Inside a fortnight Brady and his comrades had arrived below the inner barbed-wire entanglements. At that point the work became a little easier because they pushed up a small air vent, right under the entanglements, and the atmosphere in the tunnel then became more tolerable. There was little danger of the tiny vent being noticed by the guards.

On Monday 5 September, troops of the East Sussex Regiment began unloading stores – baulks of timber and barbed wire – outside the outer entanglements along the side of the camp where both tunnels were to break surface. Swiftly the word got around the camp: the British were building another concentration camp adjoining the Rath. And so it became imperative that one of the tunnels should be finished and used without delay. The Rabbit Burrow was chosen because it was the more advanced. On Wednesday 7 September, eighteen days after work had started, Brady and Galvin reckoned that they had reached a point clear of the outer entanglements but, when they tentatively pushed a marker through the top soil, observers were dismayed to see that it showed in the corridor between the two entanglements. With renewed energy the tunnellers pressed on with their work. The decision was taken that the escape should be made on the following night, Thursday 8 September.

Because certain officers had to be got out first and because it was never envisaged that the Rabbit Burrow, which was a small-escape project, would be used by all who were included in the escape plans, it became clear that many men would have to remain inside. In Hut 9, Row D, Brabazon, the Cullens, Brophy and Molloy endured the disappointment as best they could. They knew they could no longer count on getting out this time. It was foggy on Thursday night as Liam Murphy told off the men who were to go and gave them their places in the queue. They were to go in batches, with an interval between each batch, so that if anything went wrong at least some men would have a chance to get away.

Brady and Galvin went first. They still had an important job to do: to open the tunnel into the fresh air under the outer entanglements. At 11.30 p.m. they entered the Rabbit Burrow. Scurrying on hands and knees as fast as they could along the narrow passage, within minutes they were at the end of the tunnel which had taken nineteen days of back-breaking labour to complete. Down on top of them came the loose earth as they hacked feverishly at the roof of the tunnel. Quickly they opened a hole that was large enough. Helped by Brady, Galvin got his head and shoulders above ground. The glare of the searchlights, after the black darkness of the Rabbit Burrow, nearly blinded him at first and then filled him with despair. They had miscalculated. Instead of coming up between the second barbed-wire entanglement and near a four-feet-wide ditch which had been cut by the British after the failure of the first attempt (May 1921), the tunnel opened in the corridor between the two lines of entanglements. Quickly recovering from this shattering discovery, Brady and Galvin crawled towards the outer entanglement, flattening themselves against the cold surface of the corridor as anxious eyes watched from the darkened interior of internees' huts.

'Halt! Who goes there?' Suddenly the chilling challenge ripped the silence of the night. It was followed immediately by the more ominous metallic sound of a machine gun being cocked in the nearest of the wooden observation towers. Tensely, Brady and Galvin waited, hoping against hope that the sentry had not seen them. Seconds passed and the challenge and the sound of the cocking handle seemed to hang in the air. The two escapers knew the score well: anyone seen approaching close to the barbed wire would be shot. They also knew that the guards had orders to shoot to kill. They braced themselves for the worst. Then relief. Glorious, heart-filling, incredible relief. 'Visiting Rounds' came the answer to the guard's challenge – from the side of the tower removed from where the escapers lay.

The incident of the challenge happened at a psychological moment, saved the lives of Galvin and Brady and made possible the mass escape. By an extraordinary quirk of fate the military patrol was approaching the tower just as the two internees were cutting their way through the outer barbed-wire entanglements. The officer thought that the challenge was directed at his patrol, and the arrival of the patrol distracted the guard. None of the military spotted Galvin or Brady. The patrol moved on.

Using a wire-cutter that had been appropriated from a British working party, Galvin and Brady quickly cut a passage through the entanglements, and then returned to Brady's hut to report.

It was well after midnight when the first pair of internees got clear of the camp. By then the fog was quite thick. Back in Brady's hut, at the tunnel entrance, Liam Murphy was directing pairs of internees in the order of their going. Once they were outside the barbed wire, the escapers set off in little groups in search of friendly shelter. Out they went. After Galvin and Brady went Vize, Lawless, Byrne, Andrews, Knowth, Forde and Moran. About fifty got away. Among the many left behind in the camp were Captain Tommy McCarrick, Captain Joe O'Connor, Section Leader Tommy Brabazon and Lieutenant Dick Molloy. McCarrick and O'Connor made a later escape bid, were caught, court-martialled and transferred to Kilkenny jail. With many other prisoners they succeeded in escaping from Kilkenny, using the tactics which had been successfully employed in Rath camp. Desmond Fitzgerald, as a TD, had been released in August with thirty-seven other members of Dáil Éireann who had been held in various jails and internment camps.

Some of the escaped prisoners wandered around in the fog for hours. At one time a party of them, having lost their bearings, found themselves back at the outer barbed-wire entanglements. Brady and Galvin made their way to Newbridge and from there to Dublin. Moran headed west and reached the safety of his own area. Knowth, Forde and Andrews moved more or less blindly through the fog. The going was tough. Andrews had boots, the other two were in their bare feet. Their luck was in. Eventually they reached Sallins railway station and an attendant gave them shelter until a train came along. He flagged down the train and handed them over to the guard who set them down safely in Dublin.

Roll call in the camp at seven o'clock next morning, Friday 9 September, disclosed the absence of the escapers. Immediately a large-scale search was mounted. Lorries of Tans, Auxiliaries and regular military swept through Kildare and the neighbouring counties, but not one escaper was recaptured. The network of friendly houses was widespread. In fact, at the time there were only a few houses in the country, except in the north-east, where a man wanted by the British would not be sheltered gladly.

Back in the camp the internees had their privileges withdrawn for some time. But they didn't mind. Many of their comrades had got free. Perhaps their own chance would come later. Summing it up, Section Leader Brabazon said: 'If the bigger Dublin Brigade Tunnel had been finished, we could have emptied the camp. But it wasn't to be. The fog, too, could have proved the undoing of the lot that got out. Yet, ironically enough, four days later, by which time it was estimated the big tunnel would have been completed, rain poured down all night and kept the guards under cover. We'd have got a thousand out that night instead of fifty.'

The British were coy about releasing details of the escape. The Irish newspapers carried the bare bones of the story on Saturday 10 September, but reported that British GHQ had told them that any statement must come from the Curragh Command. Curragh Command had told them to seek information from GHQ. Apparently the details were eventually provided by IRA sources. On Monday 12 September the full story of the tunnel and the escape was published in *The Freeman's Journal* and delighted the heart of separatist Ireland.

Chapter 21

Escapes from Kilworth Camp

by Florence O'Donoghue

Kilworth military camp and rifle range occupy an extensive area on both sides of the main Cork-Dublin road halfway between Fermoy and Mitchelstown. In 1921 the camp held about 250 IRA prisoners housed in six huts. The area occupied by these huts on the western side of the main road, together with the sheds and yards behind them and the recreation ground in front, was completely surrounded by a high barbed-wire fence. Another similar fence separated the sheds and yard from the prisoners' compound. Two sentries patrolled the area around the sheds and yards day and night, one beat being on the inner side of the wire between the compound and the sheds, and the other inside the outer wire fence on the northern side.

Plans for escape were being made by some of the prisoners in July when the Truce came and, as there were no immediate releases, these plans were continued. One method alone seemed feasible if a substantial number of prisoners were to escape – a tunnel. A hut was selected from which the tunnel would start. To reach as far as the outer barrier of barbed wire would necessitate boring for a distance of over 200 yards. The alternative was to bore a shorter tunnel to a point under the floor of the sheds at the rear of the huts, find a means of egress from the sheds and from the yards behind them, and a means of cutting through the final wire barrier.

This was the plan decided on. It was made possible by the invaluable assistance which the prisoners got from a civilian employed in the camp by the British, a west Cork man named Murphy. In the course of his work as a carpenter he was frequently in and about the huts and, once the prisoners had enlisted his assistance, he gave them the information, the tools and the help which made the escape possible.

Murphy provided accurate measurements of the distance from the inside of the selected hut to the point under the floor of the shed where the tunnel would come to the surface; he arranged to have the nails drawn in one of the sheets of corrugated iron in the outer wall of the shed, and to supply the prisoners with a tool for cutting the outer wire barrier. In a false bottom in his carpenter's tool box he brought in the few small tools with which the prisoners had to work.

Cutting the tunnel was of necessity a slow and tedious job. It had to be carried out with great caution, practically under the eyes of the camp authorities. A major difficulty in any such effort is the disposal of excavated material. In Kilworth this was done by utilising the seven-inch space between the inner and outer sheeting in the wooden walls of the hut. A board on the inside was very carefully removed and replaced after each bucket of earth had been dumped inside.

Various preparations had to be completed before the actual excavation commenced. First a trap-door had to be cut in the floor of the hut. This was so skilfully done by Wat Furlong, a carpenter from County Wexford, that it was never observed in the course of the weekly hut inspections from July to October, when the prisoners escaped. It had, of course, to be taken up every time a man went down to work in the tunnel and when he returned. It was kept closed except when someone was entering or emerging, or when the excavated earth was being taken out.

The subsoil proved to be clay, not too difficult to dig, but as the tunnel progressed the roof leaked whenever there was rain, and there was an ever-present danger of collapse although the initial shaft was sunk to a depth of six feet. The tunnel itself was cut only large enough for a man to creep through. Conditions inside it were such that each man working in it would immediately attract attention by the state of his clothes if precautions had not been taken.

A tailor amongst the prisoners made a suit of sorts from a couple of old blankets, and this was worn by each man in turn during his spell in the tunnel. Only one man could work there at a time and only one implement was available – an old, worn entrenching tool. As the months passed and the tunnel slowly grew in length, means had to be found of drawing the excavated earth from the point at which the man was working back to underneath the trap-door. A piece of sacking and a rope were used for this purpose.

The prisoners kept two look-out men on constant duty while work was going on in the tunnel. A constant watch was kept to ensure that everything in the hut looked normal if there was an unexpected visit by an officer or NCO. The two British military sentries on duty were kept under observation for any indication that their suspicions had been aroused. When the tunnel extended beyond the huts, these sentries were marching over it day and night, and one danger was that the roof would collapse under their constant tread. It had to be shored up with cut bed-boards at one point.

Slowly the work went on without arousing the suspicions of the camp authorities, and at last it was judged to have reached a point under the floor of the selected shed. The work of the long months of preparation was now ready to be put to the test. Its urgency was emphasised because the British had commenced to remove many of the prisoners to Spike. Already some huts were empty, but fortunately not that from which the tunnel had been dug.

One other preparation had to be made. Contact with the nearest IRA company outside the camp was necessary so that the escaping men would be met and taken to places of safety. The surrounding country was unfamiliar to most of them.

At this point Bill Allen came into the picture. He lived near the camp and supplied milk to the garrison. Inside a can of loose milk he brought in a note in a small sealed bottle. Glanworth Company would be on duty to take over care of the prisoners when they got through the outer wire. A final checkup with Murphy to ensure that the floor of the shed had been cleared at the right spot, and that the nails had been drawn in the sheet of corrugated iron in the outer wall of the shed, and all was ready.

Lights-out was at 10 p.m. At 10.30 Maurice Cronin, Jim Quirke and John O'Reilly went through the trap-door into the tunnel. They were given three minutes' start on the main group, to enable them to break through the last few inches to the shed floor, find and remove the loose sheet of corrugated iron, and cut the outer wire barrier. All went well; their calculations of distance and direction had been accurate. They came up at the right point in the shed floor, they found the loose sheet of corrugated iron and removed it, and Maurice Cronin cut the wire. They had moved and worked almost without noise. The sentries marching over the tunnel had not been alarmed.

One by one, the men in the darkness inside the hut went down into the deeper darkness of the narrow tunnel. Most of them left their boots behind. The long procession of earth-stained men emerged onto the shed floor, were guided through the hole in the wall and to the gap cut in the wire to the freedom of the fields outside. They were free – between thirty-five and forty of them.

Maurice Cronin, a native of nearby Rockmills, needed no guide. He knew the country well and took Quirke and O'Reilly with him. The Glanworth Company took charge of the remainder of the men and took them to places of safety. None was traced or recaptured, although the British used bloodhounds on their trail when the break-out was discovered.

After this escape the remaining prisoners were, with one exception, transferred to Spike Island. Johnny Leahy, a native of Gortroche on the slopes of the Ballyhooley mountains, had been captured a few days before the Truce by crown forces from Kilworth camp. For some unknown reason he was detained in one of the four punishment cells in the guardroom. He was still there when the last prisoners in the huts were transferred to Spike. A simple but ingenious plan to rescue him was worked out by the Glanworth Company.

Leahy was allowed visitors in the presence of the guards, but supervision was not always strict and it was possible to suggest the proposed plan to him. Bill Kearney and John Leamy had a look at the layout of the camp, and Bill Allen was able to tell them the location of the medical officer's dispensary and the hours at which the military doctor normally attended. To give the plan a chance of success the prisoner had to feign illness on an agreed day.

The main road bisected the camp. The medical officer's

dispensary was on the opposite side of the road from the guardroom and about 150 yards down on the Fermoy side. It was anticipated that the prisoner, on requesting medical attention, would be taken from the guardroom to the dispensary. The M/O's session normally started at 10 a.m. Success depended on accurate timing and on the assumption that Leahy would be out of the guardroom and on the road to the dispensary at 10 a.m. In a final check of the plan John Leamy went on a visit to the prisoner with Leahy's sister and cousin. While parcels which they brought were being examined by the guard, Leamy told Leahy what was proposed, instructed him to report ill on the morning of 12 October and checked his watch with the guardroom clock.

Bill Kearney got a loan of an old Ford car from Ned Gallagher, then postmaster at Glanworth. Owen Curtin, who had driven the car for Liam Lynch in the capture of General Lucas, was detailed to drive it. On the evening of 11 October, Kearney, Leamy, Curtin and Dick Smith met at Mahony's public house about half a mile north of the guardroom. That was to be their starting point next morning. Leamy gave Kearney the watch which had been synchronised with the guardroom clock that day. They estimated the time it would take to drive from Mahony's to the road block which the military maintained thirty yards north of the guardroom, be passed through it and be in a position between the guardroom and the dispensary at 10 a.m. A minute or two, one way or the other, could mean the difference between success and failure. It would not be possible to stop; the best that could be hoped for was a slow down or a burst of speed, depending on where the prisoner was when they were passed through the road barrier.

In the event, luck was with them next morning. The Ford,

with Curtin driving and Kearney in the back seat, left Mahony's with an allowance of one minute to get through the road block. Dick Smith followed later on a bicycle, so that if the rescue succeeded he could go at once to Ned Gallagher and advise him to report that his car had been stolen. Just as the car passed through the barrier its occupants saw Johnny Leahy, escorted by an unarmed corporal, on the road ahead on the way to the dispensary.

As the Ford came abreast of the corporal and his prisoner, Curtin slowed down, Kearney opened the door and Leahy made a dash from his escort and jumped into the car. The excited shouting of the corporal attracted the attention of some other soldiers on the road. They threw some sacks of potatoes and loaves of bread which they were carrying in front of the car. Curtin managed to avoid the potato sacks and scatter the bread. They were through, but another hazard remained – there was a Black and Tan post less than a mile ahead. However, a crossroads intervened where they could get off the main road. At the best speed the Ford would do, Owen Curtin raced to Molly Barry's cross, turned right off the main road, then across Ballinhown Bridge and Bonnban railway crossing to Patrick Kirby's at Johnstown. From there Johnny Leahy crossed the fields to his home, and the last prisoner was out of Kilworth camp.

Chapter 22

Rescue of Linda Kearns MacWhinney from Mountjoy jail

by Lochlinn MacGlynn

Linda Kearns MacWhinney wrote of her time in jail: 'All this time, no matter where I was, my sole thought was to escape.' She has left at least two records of her prison days and of her escape: one in an edited version, another entirely in her own words. If they differ at some points, such is memory and the effect of time and space.

On the Wednesday of Easter Week 1916 Nurse Linda Kearns started a Red Cross hospital in an empty house in North Great George's Street, Dublin. Soon the casualties were arriving there. Republican soldiers, some women and a British soldier, but next day Nurse Kearns had an ultimatum from a British officer: make the hospital strictly military (for British soldiers only) or close it. She closed it and turned to doing dispatch work in those dangerous streets and to helping the republicans in other ways at every opportunity.

In 1917, when the brave effort of Easter Week was only beginning to have its real practical success, she was available again when called on. She was again a dispatch-carrier engaged on such journeys as Dublin to the west with a dispatch between the leaves of a 'sevenpenny' novel. And so, through many adventures, to a November night in 1920 when, with three IRA men, she was on her way to an action. About midnight she drove a car that contained 'all the rifles and ammunition which our column possessed'. These she listed as comprising ten rifles, four revolvers and 500 rounds of ammunition 'to be exact'.

Suddenly, as they came to the top of a small hill about a mile outside Sligo, there was a flare of lights. Among the shouts that followed she could hear: 'Halt!'

Could she drive through this challenge? She drove on as far as possible. She got near but there was no chance to break through. British army lorries blocked the road. They were right across it and the only thing for her to do was stop.

Next stop after that was Sligo jail. She began her experience of handcuffs on journeys from one jail to another: to Derry jail, to Armagh jail, five months later to a 'destination unknown' which turned out to be Liverpool and Walton jail. 'Good gracious,' she remembered hearing an onlooker say when, handcuffed, she was being put on the ship for Liverpool, 'thirty policemen to take one prisoner to Liverpool'.

Perhaps the authorities guessed that, handcuffs or no hand-cuffs, the magic thought 'escape' was always in Linda's mind. In fact, the reality of being free had just eluded her on several occasions. Without her knowledge rescue had been tried in Sligo. She was moved from Armagh just before the day her rescue was to be attempted there. When, after a month in Liverpool, she found herself in Mountjoy jail, Dublin, the prospects for escape looked brighter.

'Much more freedom was allowed to political prisoners in

Mountjoy than in any of the other jails I had been in,' she recalled. 'We were permitted to have our cells open from 6 to 7 p.m. every evening, and I decided to plan an escape to be attempted at this hour of the day.'

It was late in the year, late autumn and dark at the required hour. Visitors and parcels were allowed. One of the visitors was Nurse Josie O'Connor and she brought an unusual visitor just released from a British convict prison. Linda took him to be an IRA man who had finished his sentence. But he wasn't. She and her companions had escaped before they knew that the ex-convict, who had brought a letter from Father Dominic, a patriotic Capuchin friar, was indeed an ex-convict and had not been a political prisoner – he was an ordinary prisoner who had been serving his sentence in the same jail as Father Dominic. His part in the escape was a fascinating one. But, as Linda did in telling it, let us keep some of his role until near the end of the story.

Mountjoy was less terrible than what she called 'the horrors of Walton'. When a friend saw her after Walton and on her way to Mountjoy, this friend said with tears: 'Oh, Linda, they have nearly killed you.' In Mountjoy she found the doctor courteous and kind; there was also, of course, the discipline of the jail. None of the little 'kindnesses' that came her way, as compared with her ordeal in Walton, made her love this jail any the more. She wanted to be out. She had always wanted to escape. Her chance came when Nurse Josie O'Connor and the ex-convict brought her an innocent-looking flask of hot beef-tea. She needed the nourishment but, even more, she needed the big piece of dental wax the flask contained. With it she got a 'perfect impression' of the key which opened the door from the corridor to the grounds. She had noticed that when there was considerable noise in the corridor during 6–7 p.m., when the cells were permitted to be open, the guard on the prisoners was less strict. Noise made by the prisoners indicated that they were busy with ordinary affairs; silence might indicate that they were planning something, or perhaps had already planned it and were gone.

The next piece of 'equipment' to reach her was a cake. It contained a note with a plan of the back of the jail and the wall. 'There was also,' she recalled, 'a suggestion that a rope ladder could be thrown over if I would risk it and if I could get out into the grounds. The note had a narrow escape: the cake was cut right across before I received it.'

One of her facilities at Mountjoy was permission to send out some clothes to be laundered. Sewed up in these went her plan and the wax impression of the key. A version of Linda's memoirs, edited by Annie M.P. Smithson the novelist, was published in 1922 with the title *Leaves From The Diary Of Nurse Linda Kearns*. In it Linda referred to two keys, not one. Two duplicate keys, she wrote in that account, had to be made 'similar to the ones of the two doors of the corridor through which we would pass'. In this account, too, she said the dental wax had to be kept in a thermos flask to be soft and ready for use.

The differences in these two accounts are an indication of how difficult it is to establish details, once and for all, in the accounts of events of those years (memory is fallible, details are forgotten); but Linda's early diary (1916–1921), the account used by Miss Smithson and published in 1922, describes the two keys in detail. In this account, Linda recalled:

One of the keys was an easy one to manage, as nearly every wardress had a duplicate of it on her bunch of keys, and this was often left out of her hands on the table, etc., but of the second key there were only three duplicates in the whole prison, and so to get its impression was a very difficult task. However, suffice it to say that at last I had the impression of both. The keys were then made, and handed to me during another visit.

In her other account, when the details had been either blurred or sharpened in her memory, Linda herself said:

> Then Nurse O'Connor came again and brought me a chicken well stuffed, and in this I found a key, made from the impression I had sent out. At the first opportunity I tried it but, alas, it would not fit. You can imagine my sorrow. If only I had a tool of any sort to file it. I had an idea of trying to exchange the key with the one carried by the wardress, if I could do it without her knowledge, but this I considered risky as they were not all alike in appearance.

Leaves From The Diary Of Nurse Linda Kearns includes no mention of a key not fitting; it describes how two keys were made, not one. And, in that account, the escape seemed simple: 'Slither, Linda, slither!' said the voice of a friend, when a rope ladder had been got over the wall and into the jail. 'And I slithered – to freedom!' added Nurse Kearns.

One key or two keys, it was not all that simple. In her own more detailed account where only one key is mentioned we see that not even one key was required in the end. When she found the key would not fit, she was, she tells us in this account, 'very disappointed and depressed'. She consulted Eithne Coyle, one of the three who were to make the escape with her. This account, incidentally, is the more careful one. In the earlier account, for instance, she had not been able to fill in the Christian name of one of the three who escaped with her; in the later account, with its one key, she remembered they were Eileen Keogh, with Kathleen (not Mary, as in the 1922 account) Burke and Eithne Coyle. Or perhaps it was in the editing, from a diary, that the name of Miss Keogh could not be found in full.

Anyway, the idea of making this particular escape came to Linda from a male political prisoner. He was serving twenty years. When she found that a window of her corridor could be opened a little she was able to communicate with him when he was in the male exercise yard below. 'Up Sligo!' was his first greeting.

She was then in the hospital and another male prisoner (under sentence of death) who came to have a wound dressed brought notes which he gave to a hospitalised political prisoner on exercise under the window. 'A stone and a good aim did the rest, and I got a regular mail! It was this correspondent who gave me the first idea of trying to escape, for which I have to thank him.'

In the *Leaves From The Diary* in 1922 she goes on to describe how 'as I left I carefully locked the corridor doors with my duplicate keys', but in her later account it is stated that, after her discussion with Eithne Coyle in whom she confided, they thereafter 'organised the thing together, and it provided us with a great deal of amusement'. She added:

Ideas were put up and cast aside. Eventually the plan was decided on. We were assured by the friendly wardress that on whatever evening we would decide to make a bid for freedom, the door would not be locked. Eithne and I practised all sorts of stunts during exercise. We were a source of amusement to the sentries.

They were, of course, training for the escape bid – creeping silently on gravel, climbing on each other's shoulders, throwing stones over the wall. In the opinion of some they were going 'potty'. This account is less detailed about the amusing 'setting' for the escape. By now, Linda Kearns had been transferred from the hospital to the cells where it was easier to contact her companions, and as part of their preparations they staged these odd 'games'. On the evening planned for the escape the game was football – Cork versus the rest of Ireland. As seven o'clock came near, the excitement mounted – and not because of the game alone. In the *Leaves From The Diary* it is stated simply:

> Ten minutes before the hour one of us slipped away, and we others followed at intervals of a few moments each. I was the last to leave, and as I departed I got a good kick at the ball and gained a goal for the rest of Ireland.

Then she described how she locked the corridor doors behind them with the two duplicate keys.

According to that brief account a small scent bottle was thrown at the pre-arranged spot, the rope ladder was thrown over the wall to them, and they were away; but for the sake of history her later account, which is in more detail, must be given. According to this, the message she sent out was that they would be in the grounds at 6.20 p.m., and she marked the spot with an 'X' on the drawing she had received earlier.

That very afternoon she and Eithne Coyle (who had been in Mountjoy longer than Linda and had given her the very necessary name of one of the friendly wardresses) told the others, and Eileen Keogh and Kathleen Burke decided to go with them.

But how to evade the sentries? Two soldiers were always circling the jail inside the wall. So Linda 'timed them' and decided that only three or four prisoners could get over the wall in safety while the patrol was 'absent'. The wall was twenty-five feet high. To reach it, give the pre-arranged signal (which in the 1922 account is described as a small scent bottle thrown over the wall) and climb a rope ladder, between the 'passing' of the patrol, was no mean assignment for four women supposed to be playing a football match.

Girls who were left behind gave the impression that the escapees were still in their cells. They called on them to come out and finish the game, but Linda and her three friends were then involved in a much more exciting game.

Perhaps only one or two could get away. Eithne Coyle volunteered to go to the grounds with them, hold the ladder, and if she failed to make it herself (before the soldier came round), she would 'start a game of hide-and-seek in the grounds, and so cover our departure and give us time to get away'. She was doing the shortest sentence, so she insisted on being the last. Linda's was the longest sentence; then Eileen Keogh and next Kathleen Burke, and in this order as many as possible of the four would make the escape bid.

In her later account of the escape the scent bottle of the earlier memories has become a stone: 'We four slipped out into the November dusk, closed the door behind us and got to the wall. I threw a stone over.' Stone or scent bottle, it brought an immediate response. A string with a weight attached to it came over the wall. And the soldier was heard approaching.

The girls crouched close to the wall, a breathless interlude, until he was out of sight. It took all four to get the ladder moving over the wall, but in the process they ignored the cutting qualities of the rough top of the wall and so found themselves with a piece of string in their hands – and no more. The string had been cut through and the ladder had dropped down on the wrong side of the wall.

A step, voices, perhaps one of the soldiers coming again. The girls hid themselves in a shadow but the step halted and, Linda thought, the soldiers had perhaps stopped to talk as they met on their rounds.

To the wall again. A penknife attached to a string was lowered to them. The noise of the penknife against the wall was exaggerated by the tension. 'I was sure,' wrote Linda, 'it was heard all over the jail.' After the string came the rope ladder.

A rope ladder hangs so close to a wall that it is extremely difficult to get a grip on it with fingers and feet, but Linda managed it. At the top of the wall she could see nothing, but felt a rope which apparently went down the other side. And it was then she heard her friend Josie O'Connor whispering: 'Slither, Linda, slither!'

At the lower end of the rope was Tim Ryan of the IRA, who took her across the canal to the bridge at Berkeley Road. Dr Oliver St John Gogarty was waiting in a car and Tim Ryan told him to wait three more minutes – if no other escapee had turned up by then he should drive off as fast as possible. One turned up immediately. She was Kathleen Burke who came 'with young Donnelly, who, I heard later, was in the Fianna'. Making a detour round the city, Gogarty brought them to Earlsfort Terrace, where they fully enjoyed the hospitality of Miss O'Rourke, a relation of Mrs Gogarty. And Linda has recalled the luxury of that hospitable reception:

We had coffee, baths and she put us to bed in the most lovely bedroom. I never realised before what a lovely feel a satin eider-down has, and how restful and soothing ironed linen sheets are.

Her hands were torn from her struggle with the jail wall and her 'slithering' down the rope. Gogarty dressed them. She and Kathleen Burke were thinking of their companions, Eileen Keogh and Eithne Coyle. Gogarty realised this and was soon on his way in search of news of the other two. It was good news. They had escaped also and were in the home of Dr MacLaverty.

Linda and Kathleen remained a few days in Earlsfort Ter-race. A Dublin Castle official, Arthur ('Andy') Cope – the Assistant Under-Secretary for Ireland – told Gogarty: 'They'll be caught in Grafton Street in a few days; they won't be able to resist the shop windows.' After that warning it had to be 'the country' for the girls. So Linda sent a message to Joseph O'Connor, later a judge, who was working with Michael Collins. He took Linda, Kathleen and Eithne to a convent. Eileen Keogh went to Gorey. Then, after a few days, Tim Ryan arrived at the convent with an urgent message from Collins: they were to leave the convent at once because they had been 'given away' and the military were *en route* to arrest them. Collins had got the tip-off from one of his many contacts and Tim Ryan, on his motor-bike, was enabled to get to the convent ahead of the military. And it was at this stage that Linda and Kathleen learned that the ex-convict who was involved in their escape was not in the IRA and had informed the British authorities of their whereabouts – there was a reward for information about them. On leaving the convent the girls were then taken to Dugget's Grove, Carlow, the location of an IRA training camp. There they took charge of the housekeeping, organised a small first-aid hospital and did other good work, as Linda had been doing when it all began in her first-aid post in George's Street in Easter Week. They nursed the wounded and exhausted – among them some prisoners who, after the Truce, had escaped from Kilkenny jail and remained in the training camp until the general release following the declaration of an amnesty on 12 January 1921.

They hated leaving the convent but had found valuable work to do elsewhere. 'The nuns were darlings,' Linda recalled later, 'and such patriots.'

In her account of the escape, written at different times and subject to the vagaries of memory, the essentials are the same; and in all of them the luxury of that first night of freedom in Earlsfort Terrace with Kathleen Burke emphasised, by contrast, the miseries of the days in jail.

In the account published in 1922, the path from the jail is smoothed over:

Once outside the grey walls of the prison ... we drifted away in the kindly gloom, and we could only clasp each other's hands and whisper again and yet again: 'Is it true? Are we really free?'

Perhaps space did not permit, or the years of her diary did not make safe the writing of accounts such as that of crossing the canal, but Annie M.P. Smithson, with the novelist's sense of contrast, did give us, from the diary, Linda's account of that first night of freedom:

We shared the same room that night in a friend's house, and how delightful everything seemed. She had a visitor in her spare bedroom, but that visitor insisted on giving us the room; and oh! the cool, clean linen, the eiderdown, even the very wallpaper, and the dainty supper-table and such glorious coffee! – all were a pleasure untold to our poor, starved senses, sick and weary of the eternal greyness of prison walls and days. How we talked that night! Going over every detail of our escape, and laughing heartily over some of them. Of luggage we had none; I came away with a nail file and a fountain pen! But this mattered, indeed, little in comparison with the stupendous fact that we were once more free, even though that freedom had its limitations.

Here was material for the romantic novelist, and Annie M.P. Smithson was a very popular one. She has said she kept to Linda's words 'as far as possible', but who would blame her if she adorned the story with a romantic phrase here and there!

The memoirs of 1922 were dedicated to Éamon de Valera as 'a very slight tribute of the respect and affectionate regard in which he is held by the joint authors'. And with their dedication they gave this appropriate quotation from Terence MacSwiney, the man whose defiance of the prison system, by his marathon hunger strike, had earned the respect of the world: 'Not all the armies of all the empires of the earth can crush the spirit of one true man.' Or, it need hardly be added in the light of Irish history, of one true woman.

Chapter 23

Second escape from Spike Island

by Florence O'Donoghue

Because of its strategic position dominating the entrance to Cork harbour, the history of Spike Island in the 163 years between 1775, when the British government acquired it, and 1938 when it was restored to the nation, is largely a record of defensive fortifications and convict prisons. In 1847, the famine year, it was first used as a prison and by 1850 it held 2,000 convicts, some of them confined in the dark, damp underground cells which may still be seen, and in one of which John Mitchel was held a prisoner in the last days of May 1848.

For thirty-six years, up to 1883, in this fortress of British conquest the prisoners were used as a slave labour force in the reconstruction of the harbour defences and other works. They built the headland forts and the fortifications on the island itself. They enlarged Haulbowline by reclamation from its original twenty-two acres to its present sixty-nine acres. They built the causeway and footbridge, now no longer existing, joining Spike to Haulbowline, which was used for many years in moving the prisoners to and from their work. There is at Mount Melleray a painting used as a stage backdrop which shows this causeway and footbridge joining the two islands. It is recorded for the year 1861 that 'the amount of work performed last year on the fortifications was nearly equal to the entire expense of the prison'.

During those thirty-six years in this grim fortress, where discipline was harsh and sentences long, many a prisoner must have had thoughts of escape but none succeeded in evading or outwitting the vigilance of its military guards. Not until the War of Independence, when the island was once again used by the British government as a place of internment for Irishmen who had challenged its usurpation in arms in defence of their established Republic. The story of the first escape from Spike, that of three officers of Cork. No. 1 Brigade, is told elsewhere in this book.

After the Truce, in July 1921, there were about 500 prisoners on the island. As the negotiations in London dragged on, it was manifest that the British government did not intend to release any IRA prisoners pending the outcome. To many it appeared possible that the struggle would have to be resumed, and it is not surprising that thoughts of escape should have agitated the minds of men restless and chafing at the inactivity and boredom of internment.

The prisoners were housed in two blocks, each of two storeys and designated A and B. These buildings, the great square in front of them and most of the other buildings on the island were ringed about completely by a forty-foot-wide moat. On either side of it ramparts faced with cut-stone walls rose to a height of eighteen feet. The top of the inner rampart provided a wide platform on which sentries were posted day and night. A barbed-wire fence topped it and searchlights had been set up at strategic points. In addition, a motor launch with an armed crew made a continuous tour of the island. To escape from the fortress without aid seemed impossible. But the officers who discussed it, under cover of camp council meetings, thought they saw a glimmer of hope for a limited number to get away. Close attention was given to the routine of the sentries, the time at which the searchlights came on in the shortening evenings, the tides and the phases of the moon. They concluded that the best time for the attempt would be just as darkness fell.

In the plan which they were slowly working out, it would be necessary first to evade the count of prisoners which was made at 4 p.m. daily when they were locked up, to provide a secret means of exit from A block, to get through or over the inner wall, then across the moat and over the second wall under the noses of the patrolling sentries. Having got so far they would still be on the island. They still would have to face the hazards of a dash from the shadow of the outer wall to the water's edge in the intermittent darkness between the sweeps of dazzling searchlights, the hazards of possible sentries on the pier, of the circulating launch, and, above all, take the chance of finding a boat with oars unlocked in which to cross the mile-and-a-half of water to the mainland. It took two months to mature the plan and it worked successfully.

It would have been impossible to get over the inner rampart on which the sentries patrolled. The key to success was a disused passage through this rampart from the back of A block into the moat. It had been filled with barbed wire, and over a period the prisoners put all sorts of rubbish into it. When they were ready to attempt the escape they complained to the authorities that this was a danger to health. In the process of cleaning out the passage most of the barbed wire was removed. A hole was made and concealed in the wall at the back of A block from which the passage to the moat could be reached. A cat-ladder was made from a light plank, chair rungs and electric light flex. On 10 November preparations were completed.

Six of those making the attempt were in A block, Bill Quirke being the only one from B block. He went sick that afternoon and was concealed in A block while another prisoner took his place in his bed in B block. A trap-door had been cut in the floor of the top storey. The prisoners there were always counted first, and on this evening when the top-floor count was completed one of them dropped through the trap-door to the lower floor to be counted there again and keep the tally right. So far all went well.

About 5 p.m. the seven escapees went through the hole in the wall at the back of A block and into the passage leading to the moat. Their comrades inside immediately replaced the stones. It was necessary to wait in the passage until the vital few minutes between dusk and the switch-on of the searchlights. Waiting tensely, they could hear the tramp of the sentry over their heads, and his call, 'No. 4 post, all correct.' Their timing proved to be very accurate. As the sentry turned on his beat the first pair, carrying the cat-ladder, dashed across the moat, placed the ladder against the wall and in a minute were over on its outer side. At intervals, as the direction of the sentry's beat allowed, the others slipped across, climbed the ladder and got safely over. All seven were now outside the outer wall of the moat – Bill Quirke, Moss Twomey, Tom Crofts, Dick Barrett, Henry O'Mahony, Paddy Buckley and Jack Eddy. They had just removed the ladder and concealed it when the searchlights came on. In fact, they concealed it so well that it was not found until the following evening, and it was only then that the means by which they had escaped was discovered.

But they were still a long way from freedom. The sweeping searchlights and the armed launch were intimidating obstacles, and if they could not find a boat their attempt would fail miserably. They had been told about a boat that was beached on the island and they had a rough idea of its location. Very slowly, evading the searchlights which seemed to illuminate every blade of grass, they made their way to where they thought the boat should be. They found it, but found, too, that it was far too heavy to be lifted to the water's edge. This was an acute disappointment, but, having got so far, it made them all the more determined to find a means of getting off the island.

The night was dark, wild and stormy. They crept for shelter into an old disused outhouse while they discussed their next move. Despite the risk of sentries on or near the pier they decided to work their way round to it. Elsewhere there seemed to be no possibility of finding a boat. They were making good progress when they heard the motor launch and had to take cover until it passed. They got to the pier. Searching quietly, first on one side and then on the other, they found that the few boats there were locked and chained. Some distance further out, however, they could see dimly the outlines of a boat at anchor. Jack Eddy swam out to it, came back and reported that it was anchored by a rope. Silently he swam out again and with a pocket knife began to cut the rope. The knife slipped from his half-frozen hands and he had to sever the remaining strands with his teeth. He pushed the boat in. There were no oars, but after another search they found a pair under the pier. Bits of furze sticks served as rowlocks. All now piled into the boat. Evading the searchlights and the motor launch, they pulled away from the island as quietly as possible, and, helped by Henry O'Mahony's local knowledge, they came safely ashore at about 10 p.m. near the Belmount Hutments at Cobh.

Chapter 24

Escape of seven from Mountjoy jail

by Patrick Rigney

Having passed unscathed through the Rising of 1916 when, as a boy of fifteen, I carried dispatches for the Volunteers, it was my bad luck to be captured, in July 1921, three days before the Truce with the British began. Following the reorganisation of the Volunteers in 1917, I joined the ranks and at the time of my capture had six months' service with the active service unit of the Dublin Brigade IRA.

With the intensification of the war with Britain in the early months of 1921, the ASU was formed and it comprised men picked from the 1st, 2nd, 3rd and 4th battalions. The unit was organised in sections corresponding with the battalions, and each section operated as such in its own battalion area and adjoining county districts. I served with number four section.

For large-scale operations all four sections of the entire fifty-strong unit were employed.

The ASU gave full-time service to the IRA. As a unit member I took part in about forty attacks of various kinds, in and around Dublin, on British regular military, Black and Tans, Auxiliaries and members of the enemy intelligence groups. During an ambush on a party of military staff officers in Camden Street

I was badly wounded in the leg but escaped capture with the assistance of one of my comrades; so, when I was taken prisoner later and sentenced to fifteen years' penal servitude I thought my luck was out permanently.

Having received instructions to remove some military goods from a laundry at Inchicore on 8 July 1921, I went there with Paddy Kelly and Joseph O'Toole, both of whom also belonged to the fourth section ASU. We first commandeered a Ford van at Dolphin's Barn and then set out for Inchicore. It was planned that we would link up there with an advance party which, prior to our arrival, would have occupied the laundry building, secured the manager and staff and cut the telephone wires. Having burst through a military patrol which attempted to stop us at Inchicore Bridge, we arrived without further incident at the laundry where, to our dismay, we did not find the advance party – for their part in the job. The laundry was situated no more than about 150 yards from Kilmainham jail where, at that time, there was a half-company of British soldiers on duty. Immediately beyond the jail was the Royal Hospital, also strongly guarded. We knew that exact timing and the best use of every second were vital to the success of our mission and that, consequently, there was no point to our delaying in the hope of being joined later by our comrades. It was evident from the moment of our arrival at the laundry that our plans had miscarried in some way. We decided to drive down the road, pass the jail gate and reconnoitre the position.

As we cleared a bend of the road which had limited our view to twenty yards or so, we were appalled to see, bearing right down on us, a party of military numbering about twenty-five with an officer at their head. They were coming at the double, rifles at the ready, and, as soon as we were sighted, the officer shouted a command to halt. O'Toole and myself cocked our guns. Kelly was driving and we told him to accelerate and burst through the military as he had done with the patrol we met on the bridge. He thought the decision unwise and pulled up. By doing so he undoubtedly saved the lives of all three of us.

Kelly saw that, this time, we had no chance of getting through the military which, it was learned later, comprised picked sharpshooters stationed in Kilmainham jail. We subsequently learned that the military in Kilmainham had been alerted by the manager of the laundry who had smartly eluded the advance party of our comrades, succeeded in reaching the jail and raising the alarm just prior to our arrival at the laundry. We had driven straight into serious trouble.

The raid on which we were engaged that day was one of many minor operations carried out daily in the city during that period. Because rumours were current that negotiations for a truce had commenced, IRA headquarters had issued instructions forbidding major operations until the outcome of the negotiations was known. We were to maintain the fighting spirit and morale of the men on active service, however – always an important consideration during a period of inactivity, however long or short. Small engagements of the type planned for the laundry at Inchicore were sanctioned for this purpose.

On our surrendering to the military we were immediately treated to some abuse and threats by the young and seemingly inexperienced officer in charge. As some of the troops wanted to shoot us out of hand, it was a distinct relief to hear the officer order our removal to the comparative safety of Kilmainham jail. On our arrival there we were abused and threatened again, and then locked up in the basement cells where we were kept without light or exercise for three days. During that period the only breaks in the monotony were the meal times and the frequent visits of the guards who came in to curse us from time to time. Often during those three days and nights I reflected on the strange turnabout of events which resulted in my occupying a cell in Kilmainham, for I had been one of a party which had waited many nights outside the jail to take part in the rescue of Frank Teeling, Simon Donnelly and Ernie O'Malley (14 February 1921).

On the fourth day following our arrest we were brought to Arbour Hill detention barracks. There, some weeks later, we were summoned before a court martial. We were charged with being in possession of firearms, fully loaded, cocked and ready for instant use; with commandeering a motor van, and with attempting to seize military goods at the Inchicore laundry. We refused to recognise the court and were returned to Arbour Hill after the trial. Some days later we were informed that each of us had been sentenced to fifteen years' penal servitude.

When the officer who had brought me the 'joyful tidings' of my sentence had left the cell I began to think over my situation. Peace negotiations between representatives of the Irish republican and British governments were then in progress. If agreement were reached, which would satisfy in full the aspirations of Irish republicans, we would be liberated; otherwise it was certain that hostilities would be renewed and that we would be sent to a penal establishment here or in England. I made up my mind to escape at the first opportunity.

As convicted criminals in the view of the British, we were not left long in Arbour Hill detention prison. In Mountjoy jail, our next 'home', we were placed in A wing with IRA men who had been captured in circumstances similar to our own and sentenced to long terms of imprisonment. There was no political treatment for prisoners in A wing: no visits, food parcels, papers, books, cigarettes or any other such comforts were allowed, but it was possible to get smokes occasionally, conveyed through friendly sources, from our comrades in D wing. Prisoners in D wing were receiving political treatment and, after some weeks, our demand for similar treatment in A wing was conceded by the jail authorities. We learned later that our friends outside had won for us this amelioration of our conditions by their incessant agitation.

As soon as possible I sent word to my mother, through a friendly warder, asking her to get about half-a-dozen hacksaw blades, bake them into a cake and attempt to pass the cake through to me on her next visit to Mountjoy. This she did without a hitch. Immediately afterwards I set to work on the first part of my escape plan, which was to saw through the bars and frame which guarded my cell window. Once I had cut a space large enough for me to get through the window I intended to improvise a rope of prison blankets and sheets of sufficient length to enable me to get from my cell on the third landing, to the ground floor outside A wing. This, I reckoned, would be the easiest stage of my escape bid.

I would next have to slip stealthily from A wing, through B wing and so to D wing. I had decided that an attempt to scale the boundary wall could best be made at the end of D wing. At that point, even if I were so fortunate as to steer clear of warders in attempting to get to it, I would certainly have to reckon with an armed Auxiliary. I meant to provide myself with some means of dealing with him. And so I planned to carry with me a large piece of the iron window-bar, steal up on the Auxiliary guard, spring on him and beat him unconscious.

It was not a particularly promising plan and its implementation was made more difficult because of my troublesome leg wound. Fortunately it did not become necessary for me to try it. Seven of my A wing comrades of that time, who did attempt to get out the way I have described, had actually got through to the end of D wing when they were discovered by the Auxiliary guard. They were given a bad time by the guards and afterwards transferred to jails in England where they were held until the general amnesty after the Treaty.

At the time when I was cutting through the cell window bars I was approached one day by a non-political prisoner named Fitzgerald. He was considering ways of escaping and talked to me about them. I had known him only as a wardsman whom I saw occasionally working on D wing. His duties were to keep the landings clean, remove waste matter, collect dirty linen and replace it with clean linen, and do other menial work of a like kind around the jail. He told me that in the course of performing these tasks he had access to most parts of the jail. This had enabled him to acquire an intimate knowledge of the routines and regulations. He had got to know the warders and their hours on and off duty, and had taken a special interest in those who were posted to the basements; he could tell me the exact movements of the military and Auxiliary guards, the hours they changed and all sorts of minute details concerning the characters of the men and their habits. This information he had compiled for his own use, with view to attempting an escape at the first opportunity.

As I did not know Fitzgerald, I was suspicious of his interest in me on the first day when we met. On our next meeting, however, I listened attentively to his account of arrangements which he had made in the meantime. We then parted, having agreed that there was a sporting chance of four or five men making a getaway.

Fitzgerald, with the help of friends outside and an accomplice inside, had succeeded in getting in a .45 revolver and a few rounds of ammunition. He had arranged also for a second revolver to be smuggled in later. Thus armed, and disguised with some Auxiliary 'glengarries' which he would make for us from prison blankets and the wool that binds them, an escape would be attempted.

From that time onwards I was in constant contact with Fitzgerald. In due course he told me that he had got in the second revolver but had received no more ammunition. We then agreed to make the attempt, using the available materials and weapons. For some days afterwards we discussed in detail the merits of different plans which he suggested for our escape.

At last fate more or less decided our plan of action. About the third week in November a party of Auxiliaries from some part of the provinces arrived at Mountjoy and, on the assumption that they were complete strangers to the military guards, we decided that the long-awaited time had come for us to make our break. The next decision was to pick the men who would come with us. After much consideration we chose Davis and Troy. In the event, seven men actually made their escape.

At four o'clock, on a typical evening in the last week of November, all four of us who were about to make the break assembled in my cell on the third floor of A wing. It was five minutes before locking-up time. Just before the attempt began I slipped across to the cell occupied by the O/C of prisoners, a dear friend of mine, and told him what we were about to do. He was not optimistic about our chances of getting away but, as we parted, he breathed a fervent prayer for our success.

Back in my cell I found that our company had been joined by three more of the prisoners – O'Brien, Keating and Keegan. They had learned what was afoot and no force of persuasion on our part would deter them from coming with us. Although they had not an item of disguise amongst them, we eventually had to consent to their joining us in the attempt. The additional hazard which this development introduced can be readily appreciated; in fact, it nearly ruined the enterprise when we got to the outer main gate.

The original party of four had each been provided with a trench coat and leggings. With these and our 'glengarries' made by Fitzgerald, we looked the part of Auxiliaries sufficiently well to pass all but the closest inspection. Some preliminaries had to be arranged before the seven of us left my cell. Because of the unexpected addition of O'Brien, Keating and Keegan to our party, all seven had to be quickly rehearsed in the parts they were to take in the work about to be done. As we had only a few rounds of ammunition, the empty chambers of the revolvers had already been filled with candle grease to prevent their emptiness from being detected in case we had to present them.

Everything settled, we moved off. Fitzgerald, with his knowledge of the jail routine, knew that we could count on getting out of A wing unchallenged at this hour. On reaching B wing basement we were just in time to capture the warder on duty and relieve him of his keys. With his own keys we locked him in a cell, having sternly warned him against making any attempt to attract attention. We had not reached the end of the basement, however, when our prisoner began to kick the cell door and make a frightful noise which, we were sure, must be heard by the guards at any minute. While this performance caused us some very anxious moments it also brought forth a supreme effort by Troy. Without any previous experience of dealing with prison locks, he succeeded in unlocking the double-locks on the seven doors, each at the first attempt, and this enabled us to take our first steps towards freedom without any loss of time. The doors led by a passage to the reception steps outside A wing, a short distance from the main gates. On our arrival at the reception steps we paused briefly before beginning the final stage of our escape bid.

The evening seemed specially sent by providence to shield us from watchful eyes. A seasonable November fog had just come down as Fitzgerald, leading our party, walked from the cover of the reception steps. With his trench coat, leggings and 'glengarry' he looked the part of an Auxiliary to perfection; but, perhaps, the neatest touch to his disguise was a lighted cigar stuck between his teeth in characteristic 'Auxi' fashion. We had yet to get through three gates at the main entrance. Gate! This we sang out nonchalantly to the British Tommy on guard as we approached the two inner gates. He jumped-to with alacrity and smartly swung the gates open to allow us to pass. We filed out with our heads in the air.

A stroke of luck was immediately ahead of us. It was usual for an armed Auxiliary to be on duty inside the main gates and we anticipated an encounter with him, to get possession of the keys. To our great relief he was not there. Instead, his box was surrounded by a number of warders who were going off duty, and amongst them was the warder who held on his belt the keys we wanted so badly. But this time our request for 'gate' was met by the uncompromising response: 'You're not going out there!'

The significance of the retort was instantly obvious. It could only mean that we had been detected. The warders must have recognised the three men in civilian dress and so, within sight of freedom, was our escape bid to be doomed to failure? All seven of us reacted similarly and simultaneously. We set upon the warders. I was next aware that Troy had used the right key first time again as he triumphantly turned the lock of the outer main gate. Like seven wild men we pushed the gate open and burst through.

The guards opened fire on us and we discharged our few rounds at them, in defiance. Not that we had any chance against them in an exchange of fire, as they occupied covered positions and had rifles and plenty of ammunition. Our only hope was to dash down the straight drive to the North Circular Road at once – about 150 yards distant. Away with us, down that straight. As there was no shelter we offered a fair moving target to the enemy within Mountjoy. The miracle was that none of us was hit. I dragged along after the others. As my bad leg prevented me from keeping up with them, they soon outstripped me. When at last, panting and exhausted, I reached the North Circular Road, I was alone. My position was fairly desperate, for I knew that our pursuers would come up with me at any minute. Then I saw a motor-cyclist calmly filling his carbide lamp, seemingly oblivious of the sensational happenings in the neighbourhood. Although he was a complete stranger I quickly made up my mind to ask his help to get away. I was in a position where I had to gamble my chance of liberty and so, limping up to the unknown man, I rapidly explained my predicament. He listened quietly, never said a word but jumped on his bicycle, motioned me on to the back and swept me across the city to within a few yards of my home. And so, thanks to the courage of my unknown helper, I was being welcomed by an overjoyed mother, brothers and sisters, while the British were hunting all over the city for my comrades and myself. My stay at home was brief in the extreme. Within minutes I was on my way to greater safety with old friends in County Dublin.

Some days later, when I thought it safe to venture abroad, I was walking through a lonely part of the city and came suddenly face-to-face with one of the Auxiliaries who had been guarding me in Mountjoy. Before I had time to think of escape, he walked up to me and, thrusting out his hand, said 'Hello, Paddy, that was a pretty cool little stunt you fellows pulled off the other day.' And, having offered his congratulations on our performance, he turned and walked away.

Chapter 25

The tunnel out of Kilkenny jail

by Bill Kelly

The time was November 1921. The place was Kilkenny jail, a mid-nineteenth-century building in which many IRA prisoners were being held. Since early autumn their numbers had been swelled by the transfer of would-be escapers from Rath camp at the Curragh, whence more than fifty prisoners, having tunnelled their way towards freedom, got out of the camp in the early hours of 9 September; and by seventy-two men from Spike Island, among them Edward Punch and Jimmy Murphy of Limerick, who were under sentence of death, and others who were serving long sentences.

Martin Kealey of Kilkenny, Commandant of the prisoners, viewed the new arrivals gloomily, for their coming had resulted in a considerable tightening up of security. Military had been drafted into the jail to reinforce the regular warders and RIC guards who included Black and Tans. And this was no help to a break-out bid that Kealey had almost ready for the word go when the new men were brought in.

Amongst the prisoners from the Curragh was Tommy McCarrick of No. 1 Company, Tubbercurry Battalion, Sligo Brigade. Sentenced to twelve months for trying to escape from the camp, he was only a few days in Kilkenny when he proposed to Martin Kealey that they should tunnel their way out as the Curragh men had done. Kealey was immediately interested; he had originally planned that the prisoners would attempt to break through one of the disused underground punishment cells and scale the walls during darkness. The security measures which followed the arrival of the prisoners from other parts had upset that plan. There were, however, enough determined men in Kilkenny jail to try any means of escape, and the tunnel was a definite possibility. Among them were Joe O'Connor, 'Little Joe', Commandant of the Dublin 3rd Battalion; Seán Quilter of Tralee (Adjutant of the prisoners), Bill Donoghue of Carlow, Jerh Ryan of Horse and Jockey, Mick Meaney of Down, Dave Gibbons of Armagh, Ned Punch of Limerick, Michael Burke of Glengoole, who had survived ninety days of hunger strike in Cork jail at the time of Terence MacSwiney's long martyrdom in Brixton; Patrick Power of Carrick-on-Suir, Tom Brennan of Waterford, Willie McNamara of Clare, Tom Hyland of Laois, Éamon Balfe of County Wexford.

The long-disused punishment cells in Kilkenny jail were deep underground and extended beyond the area of the occupied cell block. They were filled with loose earth. Gratings which formerly allowed light to filter into them had been removed and replaced by flower beds. The entrance to these cells had been boarded up. Not long after McCarrick had talked to Kealey this entrance was reopened by the prisoners and the opening carefully concealed. It was the first step in the escape bid.

Spiral stone steps led down to the underground cells, but a working party of prisoners which had gone below found that they could not shift or break down the keystone of the wall in order to commence their tunnel. McCarrick and O'Connor thought they could deal with the stone. They first forced their way into the condemned cell and, with a saw fashioned from a knife, hacked out an opening about two feet square in a wall and sawed through a joist. They then found that they, too, could neither break nor move the keystone with their improvised tools. Accordingly, the boards at the entrance were carefully replaced and the nails broken off at the head. Dust was showered over the wood so that only a most minute examination would reveal that the timber had been tampered with.

An iron bar was obtained from somewhere and a new attempt made on the keystone. Prisoners formed a living shield as another opening was being made in the wall of the condemned cell, and then McCarrick and O'Connor, using the bar as a lever; succeeded in prising loose the stubborn stone.

Already some of the edge had gone off the recently improved security measures so that, despite the unusual activity among the prisoners, none of the warders, the guards or Governor John Boland noticed anything out of the ordinary. Boland had been chief warder in Mountjoy in 1917, when Thomas Ashe died as a result of bungled forcible feeding whilst on hunger strike. There was some feeling against Boland amongst the prisoners on that account, but they had no complaints about his treatment of themselves and they did not demonstrate against him. Feelings apart, because of the tunnel job they had to go through the movements of being model prisoners, in the hope of lulling their jailers into a false sense of security.

Now that the keystone had been dealt with, the excavation of the tunnel could be commenced as soon as the tough bars of one of the underground cells had been removed. McCarrick and O'Connor again went into action. Hour after hour they sawed away monotonously through the tough steel until at long last the bars were severed and the prisoners thus had access to the underground cells into which earth had been shovelled when the gratings were removed after the punishment cells had ceased to be used.

Martin Kealey had taken control of the operation. He appointed Bill Donoghue to be the officer in charge of the overhead section engaged in it, and Tommy McCarrick in charge of the underground working parties.

The tunnellers had the usual problem of disposing of earth without leaving any significant trace of their industry. They also had to drive the shaft straight and true, shore up the working and attempt to ensure an adequate supply of fresh air. Kealey arranged that three shifts of three men each would work from eight in the morning until six in the evening, and he had no problem about getting volunteers for the task. First the loose earth in the underground cell where they opened the tunnel had to be disposed of, after which it was necessary to prop up an area beneath a rectangle of earth in the yard where a flower bed had been made. Some of the prisoners willingly donated the centre-boards of their plank beds to prop up this sector.

While on the job, whether working on the surface or in the tunnel, the men wore old clothes so that no vigilant warder or guard would spot traces of earth in their ordinary clothes. A rope was made from strips of cloth and a disposal bag was improvised from pillow cases. One man at a time chipped away at the face of the earth with a knife or sharpened spoon or some other makeshift implement. When he had filled the bag with earth the rope was used to haul it back to the opening. The bag was emptied and the earth carefully placed in another disused underground cell. Bill Donoghue's team had look-outs posted to give warning of any approach by warders while McCarrick's men chipped away and disposed of the earth.

It was exhausting work and dangerous too, for the tunnel, some three feet high by two feet wide, was not shored up adequately at any point. And so there was the ever-present danger of a cave-in. As the prisoners were unable to improvise an adequate ventilation system the atmosphere in the tunnel became foul very quickly. Perspiration dripped from the body of the man at work on the face of the shaft and soon he was drenched in his own sweat. Even in the mornings, before work had begun, the tunnel smelled of perspiration, sweat-sodden clothes and damp clay.

Monday 14 November almost brought disaster to the escape bid. Father Delahunty, CC, Callan, who had served nearly twelve months of a two-year sentence, wanted out of jail without delay; so did Seán Quilter of Tralee and Seán Power of Waterford. They had got themselves transferred to the hospital wing into which they had managed to have a hacksaw blade smuggled. They had sawn through their window-bars and were preparing to bid farewell to Kilkenny jail when an alert warder discovered their handiwork and put an end to the enterprise. Surprisingly, Governor Boland merely had them sent back to the cells and imposed no other punishment. Warders and guards, however, alerted by the attempt, were especially vigilant for some time afterwards. The guard was doubled and guards were also placed outside the jail for the first time. This was serious. There was an immediate meeting of the prisoners' leaders to consider the situation caused by the placing of guards (military in full battledress) outside the walls. Escape was virtually impossible as long as these guards remained. Commandant Kealey then sent for Alderman de Loughrey, Mayor of Kilkenny, and pointed out to him that the placing of guards outside the walls was a breach of the Truce. He requested him to protest to the military authorities in the city. De Loughrey did so and, following his intervention, the military guard outside the walls was withdrawn. And so this threat to the escape was removed.

Often the tunnelling routine was interrupted by spot searches. The work went on, nevertheless, and after about fifteen days the prisoners thought they must be near the outer wall.

Then the leaders conferred. Better to come up fifteen feet beyond the outside wall rather than one foot inside it. This was obvious. So they decided that tunnelling should continue for a few more days. Then the diggers came on bones which suggested that the tunnel was running through the graves of some long-dead convicts. They dug doggedly on. On the nineteenth day their puny implements uncovered solid stone and they knew then that they had reached the outer wall of the jail. Four feet of solid stone ahead. Yet, by Monday 21 November they had taken the tunnel ten feet outside the wall. A poker pushed upwards to test the depth showed that the exit end of the tunnel was just six inches below surface. They had got through.

A conference was hastily convened and Commandant Kealey and his officers decided that the break should be made about six o'clock on the following night, shortly after the changing of the guard. To wait longer would increase unnecessarily the risk of discovery of the tunnel. Even now could they be sure that the enemy was not already aware of its existence, and would they break through only to face a ring of soldiers or police? These were amongst the questions which agitated the minds of the prisoners as they turned into bed that Monday night. All of them were quieter than usual and few slept more than fitfully with the thought of freedom so near at hand.

Covert glances and winks were exchanged at breakfast next morning. It was the day on which they would be free of the grey walls of Kilkenny jail from which no prisoner had ever escaped. But would they? Their confidence was badly shaken by a whispered piece of news that was circulated rapidly and sent a thrill of apprehension through the men who were waiting impatiently for six o'clock. The news was that a new governor had taken up duty that very morning. John Boland was being transferred to Dundalk jail (he was suspended as a result of the escape) and his place in Kilkenny had been taken by Captain Burke. This could upset the escape plan. The new man might change the usual routine of the jail during the take-over process, and the plan depended on the established routine being observed.

All day long the men were in a fever of suspense as they went about their usual tasks and parades. They caught glimpses of Burke as he and Boland inspected buildings and installations. The warders were exceptionally active to impress the new governor with their keenness and efficiency, and there was an air of briskness in Kilkenny jail that had not been about the place for some time. A new broom sweeps clean, thought Kealey. Would this one sweep away the hopes of freedom?

At last the long day turned to dusk and the prisoners, in a ferment of suppressed excitement, began to drift in ones and twos towards the assembly point. Suddenly an alarm was flashed from man to man and all dispersed as unobtrusively as they could. Governor Burke was having another inspection. It was just six o'clock, the time scheduled for the escape to begin. Nobody knew what the inspection presaged. Could it mean that the tunnel had been discovered? Was the new governor about to introduce rules which would foil the jail break? The inspection could mean almost anything. Silently and suspiciously the prisoners watched as the governor made his rounds with considerable thoroughness. Then he checked the lighting and the arrangements for the night watch. After that he was gone. It was then nearly seven o'clock. The escape bid was almost an hour behind schedule, but the friendly darkness of the November night would cover the movements of the prisoners for more than a round of the clock.

At a signal from Kealey the job was on. Down into the underground cell the prisoners filed, each told off for his position in the queue. In the lead was McCarrick. Scurrying along on hands and knees in the darkness, he quickly covered the fifty yards length of the tunnel and then, without delay, broke through the thin upper layer of clay. It was almost 7.30 when he got his head above ground and felt the first of the cool night air on his face. As he took a quick look round he momentarily froze in shock, for the exit hole was less than twenty yards from the main gate of the jail in St Rioch's Street. Quick as a flash McCarrick recovered and dashed across the road to the shelter of a terrace of houses. Fast on his heels came Bill McNamara and two others, carrying dummy pistols made of wood; it was their job to hold up anyone who approached the jail gates. They at once took up positions and waited tensely.

Women from the nearby houses came over and helped pull the escaping prisoners out of the hole. Out they came: Martin Kealey, Larry Condon of Fermoy, G. O'Halloran of Kilkenny, J. Keogh and G. Connelly of Youghal, Seán Power of Waterford, Pat Power and Willie O'Mara of Carrick-on-Suir, Bill O'Leary,

George Kirwan and Seán Kelly of Tullamore, Ned Punch and Timmy Murphy of Limerick. Father Delahunty came out too. So did Seán Power and Seán Quilter of Tralee; their sentences had nearly expired but Quilter was served with an internment order on the previous Saturday.

In quick succession the men emerged while McNamara and his two colleagues stood guard with their dummy revolvers.

Out came Mick Burke, the hunger striker from Glengoole; Mick Meaney, Tom Hyland, Tom Leonard, Larry Fraher; T. Barry, D. Connelly of Westport, Dave Gibbons of Armagh, Power of Clonea, Crohan of Naas, Kearns of Limerick, Jerh Ryan of Thurles. Out they came, forty-three in all.

Some prisoners who had not worked on the digging came feet first, and feet first also they were pulled out into St Rioch's Street by local women and some other prisoners. One man brought along a suitcase which, at one stage, effectively blocked the tunnel and caused delay as well as earning for him the curses of some of his comrades who were held up in the tunnel until the blockage was freed.

Jerh Ryan of Horse and Jockey, and Mick Murphy had remained in the jail as a rearguard to deal with inquisitive warders who might chance on the scene. More than half the men had already gone when a warder named Tom Power, having noticed a number of his charges going into a cell and seemingly remaining inside, decided that there was something unusual going on. Moved to investigate, he saw what was happening. The look of amazement on his face quickly gave way to one of resentment and concern when he realised that the prisoners were on their way out. 'Aw, lads, you shouldn't do this while I'm on,' he said plaintively. Then Murphy's brawny arm reached out and encircled his throat, effectively cutting off further speech.

Perhaps he had some reason for resentment because, not only had he been friendly towards the prisoners, he had even given them a key from which to make an impression as part of the earlier escape plan. Be this as it may, he was a warder and must not be allowed to interfere. Quickly he was trussed up but the noise of the scuffle had alerted a guard who shot a Verey light into the night sky. RIC and warders rushed down the corridor to the trouble spot. Maurice Walsh of Limerick was unlucky, for he was in the tunnel when it collapsed ahead of him. He edged his way back into the cell where he was pounced upon by the police and warders.

Immediately that the Verey light flared in the darkness the prisoners divided into parties of eight or ten and made off with all speed. Bill Donoghue of Carlow, who had some vague knowledge of the local topography, led Tommy McCarrick and seven others through the fields. They forded the River Nore and struck across country. At length they came to a farmhouse and decided to take a chance and ask for food. Donoghue and McCarrick cautiously approached the house and knocked gently on a window while the others flattened themselves on the ground. A girl's voice enquired who was there. Donoghue asked if she would give them a drink of water. 'Wait until I dress,' replied the girl, and the two men then signalled their companions to approach nearer to the house.

Minutes later the girl enquired: 'Who are you?' Back came the reply: 'Escapers from Kilkenny jail.'

'If that's true, I'll get you some supper,' said the girl. She opened the door to admit the men. They had been fortunate in their choice of house. The girl was Kitty Teahan, sister of a local brigade officer who afterwards became a senator. Her brother was, in fact, at a brigade meeting and he arrived home about 1 a.m. after the fugitives had been given a meal. He led them to brigade headquarters which was reached about five o'clock in the morning of Wednesday 23 November. Later that day the party was divided and the men were taken to safe houses where they lay low for some weeks.

A countrywide search was set up immediately that the escape was discovered by the authorities. Hundreds of soldiers and police were employed in the operation, and on foot and in lorries they scoured the countryside. But the escapers had vanished. They were in adjoining counties enjoying a well-earned rest and the protection of the local brigades.

The British estimated that eight tons of clay had been excavated from the tunnel and that the prisoners must have spent more than two months at work on it.

The Treaty was signed in London on 6 December. Ironically, two days later a general order was made for the release of all internees, and so the former prisoners of Kilkenny were able to return to their homes with impunity. Soon afterwards they received from the British the belongings which they had left behind in Kilkenny jail.

The Authors

Piaras Béaslaí. Historian, playwright, poet and journalist, Piaras Béaslaí, Liverpool-born, was one of the founders of the Irish Volunteers and was second-in-command to Commandant Ned Daly in the 1st Battalion area during the 1916 Rising. Court-martialled after the rising, he was sentenced to three years' penal servitude. On 17 June 1917, he was one of 120 sentenced prisoners released from Lewes prison and welcomed with wide acclaim in Dublin next day. On the resumption of the War of Independence he was on the headquarters staff IRA as director of publicity and editor of *An t-Óglach*, the secret underground journal of Óglaigh na hÉireann. Arrested on 4 March 1919, he was charged with making a seditious speech and possessing incriminating IRA documents. Sentenced to two years' imprisonment, he and nineteen other IRA prisoners escaped from Mountjoy jail, Dublin, in broad daylight, less than four weeks later. He was recaptured in May of the same year and held first in Birmingham and then in Strangeways jail, Manchester. On 25 October, he and five other IRA prisoners escaped from Strangeways. Piaras Béaslaí spoke for the Treaty in the Dáil, of which he was the member for East Kerry since the general election of December 1918. In the Civil War he fought on the Free State side and became a major-general in the National Army. In 1926 his massive two-volume work on his great friend Michael Collins was published: *Michael Collins and the Making of New Ireland*. He wrote in both Irish and English and was much in demand as a writer and lecturer on the War of Independence, on which subject, following his retirement from the army, he contributed many articles to the *Irish Independent* and *The Kerryman*. He was in his eightieth year when he died in 1965.

SIMON DONNELLY. A plumber by trade, Simon Donnelly was a lieutenant in C Company, 3rd Battalion, Dublin Brigade, when he turned up at his company's mobilisation point on Easter Monday 1916. His company captain refused to turn out, so Commandant Éamon de Valera had to promote Donnelly to be captain, there and then. Throughout Easter Week he fought in Boland's Bakery, and at one stage led a diversionary action to take pressure off the bakery which was de Valera's command post. After the surrender he was sent to Wakefield detention barracks and held there from 6 May until the release of the unsentenced prisoners in December 1916. He became vice-commandant of the 3rd Battalion, Dublin Brigade IRA, under Commandant Joseph O'Connor – known to his men as 'Holy Joe'. Captured by the enemy on 10 February 1921, he was beaten up by Auxiliary intelligence officers in Dublin Castle and then moved to Kilmainham jail. A few days later he sensationally escaped from Kilmainham with Ernie O'Malley and Frank Teeling. He opposed the Treaty and fought with the republican forces in the Civil War. When hostilities ended, he rejoined the family plumbing business. He took a leading part in the founding and organisation of the Old IRA which helped towards ending much of the bitterness between pro-Treaty and anti-Treaty elements. Simon Donnelly died in 1966.

GEORGE GERAGHTY. A mason by trade and a native of Roscommon, George Geraghty joined the 1st Battalion, Dublin

Brigade, Irish Volunteers, and fought with his battalion in the 1916 Rising. After the surrender, he was first held in Richmond barracks, Dublin, but some days later was transferred to Wakefield detention barracks in England. Released in the general release of unsentenced prisoners in December 1916, he resumed soldiering when the Volunteers were reorganised in 1917. He was arrested in Roscommon at the time of the so-called 'German Plot' in May 1918, deported, and held in Usk jail in south Wales. With three other 'German Plot' prisoners – Frank Shouldice, Barney Mellows and Joe McGrath – he sensationally escaped from Usk in January 1919. From then until the Truce he fought with the Dublin Brigade. George Geraghty took the Free State side in the Civil War and fought in the National Army. On leaving the army he emigrated to England and died there in 1970. He and Frank Shouldice collaborated in writing the account of the escape from Usk jail for this book.

Professor Michael Hayes. Son of an IRB man, Michael Hayes was born in Dublin, on 1 December 1889. He was appointed an assistant to the Professor of French at University College, Dublin, in 1912. He was a strong supporter of the pre-Truce Sinn Féin and a close personal friend of its founder, Arthur Griffith. In 1913 he joined C Company of the 3rd Battalion, Dublin Brigade of the Irish Volunteers, and in the Rising of 1916 he fought in Jacob's factory, under his friend and UCD colleague, Commandant Thomas MacDonagh. In the general election of December 1918 he was director of elections for Professor Eoin MacNeill in the National University constituency. His residence at No. 49 Longwood Avenue, Dublin, was raided by British military, in November

1920, and Richard Mulcahy, Chief-of-Staff of the IRA, escaped by a hair's breadth, but Hayes was arrested. Following a period in Mountjoy jail and Arbour Hill military detention barracks, he was interned in Ballykinlar camp, County Down. Prior to this, in 1920 also, he had secured an MA in French by thesis, with first class honours. While still interned he was, in 1921, elected to the second Dáil as a member for the National University, and was released under the Truce, in August 1921, to attend the Dáil. He voted for the Treaty and became Minister for Education. On the death of President Griffith, in August 1922, Hayes was made Acting Minister for Foreign Affairs. From 9 September 1922 until March 1932 he was Ceann Comhairle (Speaker) of Dáil Éireann. In 1929 he was called to the Irish Bar. He was a member of the Seanad Éireann Cultural Panel from 1938 until his retirement in 1965; Leader of the Opposition, 1938–48; Leader of the Seanad, 1948–51, 1954–57. He was for many years chairman of the Standing Committee and National Council of Fine Gael. In 1932 Professor Hayes was appointed university lecturer in modern Irish language and literature; Professor of Modern Irish, 1951–60. He was a member of the Royal Irish Academy, and of the Senate of the National University. He retired from UCD in 1960. He contributed articles and reviews, particularly on the 1916–23 period, to *Studies* and other publications. He died in 1976.

BILL KELLY. A freelance writer, Bill Kelly was thoroughly read in the 1916–23 period in Irish history in which he was a diligent researcher for some ten years. Most of his published work dealing with that period was based on personal interviews with men and women who had made recent Irish history. It was published mainly in the form of newspaper articles such as 'Death of a Field Marshal', the story of the shooting of Sir Henry Wilson in London. Bill Kelly served for six years as a radio journalist in the newsroom at Radio Éireann, was editor of *Golfing in Ireland*, the shortlived *News Record* and other periodicals. He was assistant editor of *Waterfront News*, the Dublin port paper. He contributed articles to many newspapers and magazines in Britain and Ireland, and was probably best known as a sports writer through his weekly soccer column in *The Sunday Press*, which he wrote for many years. In the course of his work for this book he interviewed scores of people in many parts of the four provinces.

JOSEPH LEONARD. A Dublin man and an electrician by trade, Joe Leonard was twenty years of age when he fought in the 3rd Battalion, Dublin Brigade, Irish Volunteers, in the 1916 Rising. After the surrender he was deported and held in Wakefield detention barracks, and was released with the unsentenced prisoners in December 1916. In 1917 he was arrested for drilling and served a sentence in Mountjoy jail where he took part in the hunger strike which ended with the tragic death of Thomas Ashe who was killed by forcible feeding. He was one of the first members of 'The Squad' which was formed in July 1919 and attached to the intelligence department. It consisted of about twelve men who were specially selected for difficult and dangerous jobs. These men were required to give their services whole-time to the IRA and were paid the wages they had been earning in their civilian jobs. From the formation of 'The Squad' until the Truce, Joe Leonard took part in scores of engagements in Dublin, including the attack on Lord French, the Lord

Lieutenant, and his escort at Ashtown, County Dublin, on 19 December 1919, and the attempt to rescue Seán MacEoin from Mountjoy jail, on 14 May 1921. The first barracks taken over from the British, in 1922, was Beggars Bush, the headquarters of the Auxiliaries, and Joe Leonard was one of the Irish army officers who marched in at the head of their men. He took the Treaty side and, in the Civil War, fought in the National Army with the rank of commandant. Later he was promoted to colonel. He died in 1961.

FIONÁN LYNCH. A south Kerryman born in 1889, Fionán Lynch was a teacher, university graduate (BA in Celtic Studies and Higher Diploma in Education) before taking part in the 1916 Rising as a captain in the Four Courts garrison (1st Battalion) area. Sentenced to death after the Rising, the sentence was commuted to ten years' penal servitude. On release he resumed his activities and was in Belfast jail in revolt against prison treatment, in 1918, when he was elected TD for South Kerry. He was co-secretary to the Irish delegation who signed the Treaty which he supported. He held high command in the National Army during the Civil War and fought mainly in the south. He was Minister for Education in the Provisional Government and later Minister for Fisheries during the Cosgrave regime. When Fianna Fáil took office, in 1932, he became Deputy Ceann Comhairle. He qualified as a barrister and practised. In 1944 he retired from politics on appointment as a judge of the Circuit Court. He died in June 1966.

SEÁN MACEOIN. As the young blacksmith of Ballinalee, Seán MacEoin was one of the most noted of the IRA guerilla leaders during the War of Independence. He was vice-brigadier and director of operations, Longford Brigade, from September 1920 and by 1 November his brigade was fully organised and his flying column was ready for action. He was also Longford County Centre of the IRB and (later) Connaught Provincial Centre. While a prisoner awaiting trial in Mountjoy jail, in 1921, he was elected a member of Dáil Éireann. In the words of Professor Michael Hayes, he 'had shown not only great courage, but also ingenuity, military knowledge and a capacity for taking responsibility'. By his successful defence of the village of Ballinalee, 1–8 November 1920, notably on 3 November, against a British force which comprised eleven lorries of Black and Tans, he became a national hero. The Tans withdrew in great disorder under cover of darkness, leaving pools of blood, military equipment, revolvers, thousands of rounds of .303 ammunition, and loot which they had taken from Granard some hours earlier. MacEoin's men, who had commenced the engagement with sixty rounds apiece, ended up with 500 or more rounds each.

On 9 January 1921, a district inspector of the RIC named McGrath leading a party of ten Black and Tans surrounded MacEoin who was alone in a cottage near Ballinalee where he had his headquarters. MacEoin shot his way single-handed through the eleven of the enemy and escaped, but McGrath was fatally wounded.

On 2 February, at Clonfin near Ballinalee, MacEoin with eighteen men of his column attacked a motorised party of about twenty Auxiliaries. The enemy fought bravely but were forced to surrender after the engagement had continued for an hour. They had lost three men killed and twelve wounded. MacEoin complimented the survivors on their fine fight and set them free. He secured medical aid for the wounded.

By now, his successful exploits against the British had made him one of the most wanted men in Ireland in their book. In March Cathal Brugha, Minister for Defence, summoned him to Dublin, a city of which he then knew very little and which was teeming with British spies and touts. The train on which he set out on the return journey to Longford was intercepted by the British at Mullingar. MacEoin tried to shoot his way out of the trap but was seriously wounded, captured and badly beaten up in Mullingar RIC barracks. Next day he was taken back to Dublin under heavy military guard. In King George V Hospital (now St Bricin's) he was guarded in his room by an Auxiliary, a warder, a military sergeant and a deputy governor of Mountjoy jail. An armed sentry was posted near the entrance to his room. In one visitor's view, MacEoin gave the impression of 'a caged and wounded lion'. Recovered from his wounds, he was transferred to Mountjoy, tried by court martial for the 'murder' of District Inspector McGrath and sentenced to death – despite evidence of his chivalry as volunteered by three Auxiliaries who had survived the fight at Clonfin, and a plea for mercy from the relatives of McGrath.

His situation greatly grieved Michael Collins who conceived several plans to save him from the gallows; one attempt, the most daring and spectacular, only just failed. (MacEoin himself collaborated with Professor Michael Hayes and the late Colonel Joe Leonard in writing the story of that attempt, which is included in this book.) The execution of IRA prisoners was suspended by the British Cabinet in June, but MacEoin was still awaiting execution when the Truce became operative at noon on 11 July. The British, to enable their proposals for a settlement to be put before the Dáil, released thirty-seven TDs whom they were holding in jails and internment camps. But they still held MacEoin: a cabinet decision. Collins was furious. He insisted that if MacEoin was not released there should be no meeting of the Dáil. De Valera agreed and threatened to break off negotiations with the British. MacEoin was released. He took the Treaty side and soon after the establishment of the National Army in 1922, he joined the army with the rank of major-general. He was for a time GOC Western Command. On the outbreak of the Civil War, however, he left this post for one on the field of action which was more agreeable to him. He remained in the army until 1929. A year later he retired from the reserve of officers with the rank of lieutenant-general. He was Minister for Justice and Minister for Defence, respectively, in the coalition governments of 1948–51, 1954–7. In 1959 he contested the presidential election in opposition to de Valera and polled 417,536 votes to 538,000. He withdrew from politics following defeat by a single-figure margin in the general election of 1965. He died in 1973.

LOCHLINN MACGLYNN. A battalion intelligence officer in the IRA in his teens in Donegal, Lochlinn MacGlynn was brought to Dublin at the age of twenty by Seán MacBride, to be assistant editor of *An Phoblacht*, which he later edited. In the early years of the Second World War he ran the Press Office of the Curragh Command (Defence Forces) but went back to civilian life mid-war. He became London editor and features editor of the Irish News Agency, which was wound up in 1957; was information representative in Ireland for one of the major European organisations for over ten years, and, in 1969, at the height of the Northern Ireland crisis, he was sent abroad by the Irish government as a Press attaché. Journalist, author and radio writer, his features were syndicated widely in the US, and in translation on the continent. His short stories were broadcast by the BBC, published in *The Bell, Irish Writing, Irish Bookman* and in such overseas publications as *Short Story International* (US) and *Argosy* (Britain).

FLORENCE O'DONOGHUE. Major Florence O'Donoghue was an exceptionally competent and diligent military historian whose writings are distinguished by minute accuracy and exhaustive research. In addition to *Tomás MacCurtain: Soldier and Patriot*, his fine biography of Brigadier Tomás MacCurtain, first republican Lord Mayor of Cork, he has done a similar service for General Liam Lynch with *No Other Law* (the story of Liam Lynch and the IRA, 1916–23). He edited *The IRB and the 1916 Rising* by Diarmuid Lynch, and also wrote the foreword and some preliminary chapters. His services as a lecturer and consultant were much sought, particularly on the momentous period in Irish history from the formation of the Irish Volunteers (1913) to the end of the Civil War (1923). He was secretary of the Military History Bureau set up by the Irish government in the late 1940s. A member of the pre-1916 IRB, O'Donoghue joined the Irish Volunteers in Cork in 1914. He became adjutant and head of intelligence in the Cork No. 1 Brigade, IRA, and adjutant in the 1st Southern Division which was formed in 1921 under the command of General Liam Lynch. He took no part in the Civil War. When, in 1940, a national emergency was declared, he joined the Irish army with the rank of major and was appointed intelligence officer for the Southern Command. Born in Rathmore in County Kerry, Major O'Donoghue was seventy-two at the time of his death in December 1967.

Donal O'Kelly. Son of a distinguished County Galway family, Donal O'Kelly went to live in Dublin at an early age and became involved in the movement for Irish freedom. He was a member of the staff of the Department of Local Government during the lifetime of the first Dáil and was arrested in 1921. Following the acceptance of the Treaty he joined the National Army and fought in the Civil War. He left the army in the general demobilisation, in 1924, but, at the outbreak of the Second World War, he rejoined and served throughout the national emergency. On leaving the army again, in 1946, he resumed his career as a journalist and writer, and edited a number of periodicals, including *Hibernia*. He was employed by the Irish University Press, was the author of a number of works, and has had twenty-four translations from the French published, including two volumes by the celebrated Daniel Rops.

Paddy Rigney. As a fifteen-year-old Fianna boy, Paddy Rigney was under fire in the South Dublin Union area, in 1916, where the 4th Battalion, Dublin Brigade, fought under Commandant Éamonn Ceannt. He helped carry the first badly wounded Volunteer from Marrowbone Lane to the Protestant infirmary. Because of his youth he was sent home after the surrender. When the Volunteers were reorganised, in 1917, he joined the 4th Battalion, Dublin Brigade, and from 1919 (by which time the Volunteers had become the IRA) until January 1921 he took part in several operations against the enemy. He was a member of the brigade's active service unit from the time of its formation early in 1921. The ASU gave full-time service to the IRA, and, as a unit member, Rigney participated in about forty attacks in and around Dublin, on British regular military, Black and Tans, Auxiliaries and intelligence agents. At the burning of the Custom House in Dublin, on 25 May 1921, he was in one of the groups which provided protective cover for the men who destroyed the building. During an attack on enemy elements in Camden Street (then known as 'the Dardanelles') he was badly wounded in a leg but escaped capture. Three days before the Truce (11 July) he was captured following an unsuccessful raid and some weeks later, was court-martialled and sentenced to fifteen years' penal servitude. In November he and six other prisoners made a daring escape from Mountjoy jail. He opposed the Treaty and joined the republican force which, under Rory O'Connor, occupied the Four Courts. With Ernie O'Malley and Seán Lemass he escaped from the National Army after the surrender of the Four Courts. During the Civil War he led a republican column in County Wicklow, but was wounded again and recaptured in 1922.

DESMOND RYAN. The noted writer and historian, Desmond Ryan, was born in Dulwich, London, and came to Ireland with his family at an early age. In 1907 his father, W.P. Ryan, founded *The Peasant*, an Irish-Ireland paper with leanings towards social reform – it lasted until 1910. Desmond, who was the literary executor of Pádraig Pearse of whom he was a pupil in St Enda's College and beside whom he fought in the GPO in 1916, had inside knowledge of the historical events about which he wrote. After the Rising he was held in Stafford detention barracks from May to December 1916. He wrote *The Man Called Pearse*, a biography of Pearse, and his book *The Rising*, the complete story of Easter Week, went through three editions. He also wrote *The Story of a Success*, a history of St Enda's College. His other best-known works include *Michael Collins and the Invisible Army* (Anvil); *Unique Dictator*, a study of Éamon de Valera; *Remembering Sion; The Phoenix Flame*, a study of Fenianism and John Devoy; *Seán Treacy and the Third Tipperary Brigade IRA* (Anvil). With William O'Brien, one time General Secretary of the Irish Transport and General Workers' Union, he edited the two volumes of *Devoy's Post Bag*, the letters and papers of the Fenian John Devoy. Ryan worked as a journalist on *The Freeman's Journal* and, at the end of the Civil War, he returned to England where he lived until 1959. Back in Ireland again, he made his home in Dublin. He died in 1964.

FRANK SHOULDICE. As a Volunteer in the 1916 Rising, Frank Shouldice fought in the 1st Battalion area, under Commandant Ned Daly. With two other Volunteers, he was positioned high up in the top floor of Jameson's Malt House, from which position the three exercised a most effective command of much of the North King Street area, scene of some of the most intense fighting of Easter Week. In the final British assault on the Volunteer positions there, two battalions of the South Staffords suffered heavy casualties. After the surrender, Shouldice was first lodged in Richmond barracks, Dublin, and was shortly afterwards deported to Stafford detention barracks in England where he was held until the general release of the unsentenced prisoners in December 1916. He was arrested in the big round-up ('German Plot') of Sinn Féin and Volunteer leaders in May 1918, and held in Usk prison until his escape with Geraghty, Mellows and McGrath in January 1919. He afterwards fought in the west of Ireland until the Truce, but took no part in the Civil War. He became a civil servant and lived out his retirement in Dublin.

AUSTIN STACK. Born in Tralee, in 1880, the son of a prominent IRB man, William Moore Stack, Austin was an uncompromising republican. Having won earlier fame as a footballer, he was commandant of the Kerry Brigade of the Irish Volunteers when the attempted gun-running, as a prelude to the 1916 Rising, failed through the premature arrival of the German arms ship, *Aud*. Sentenced to death, which was commuted to penal servitude for life, Austin underwent the first of his many prison experiences. He led revolts against the prison system in the struggle for political recognition and treatment. A prison wrecker as well as a prison breaker, he suffered the pains of hunger strike five times, the last for forty-one days. While in Belfast jail, in 1918, he was elected TD for West Kerry and was subsequently the Minister for Home Affairs who set up the Dáil courts. He opposed the Treaty and did not enter Leinster House with Fianna Fáil. He held ministerial offices in the republican government and was the Hon. Secretary of Sinn Féin from 1917–1929, when he died from ill health brought on by prison hardships.

Index

MERCIER PRESS

Irish Publisher - Irish Story

We hope you enjoyed this book.

Since 1944, Mercier Press has published books that have been critically important to Irish life and culture. Books that dealt with subjects that informed readers about Irish scholars, Irish writers, Irish history and Ireland's rich heritage.

We believe in the importance of providing accessible histories and cultural books for all readers and all who are interested in Irish cultural life.

Our website is the best place to find out more information about Mercier, our books, authors, news and the best deals on a wide variety of books. Mercier track the best prices for our books online and we seek to offer the best value to our customers, offering free delivery within Ireland.

Sign up on our website or complete and return the form below to receive updates and special offers.

www.mercierpress.ie
www.facebook.com/mercier.press
www.twitter.com/irishpublisher

Name: _____

Email: _____

Address: _____

Mercier Press, Unit 3b, Oak House, Bessboro Rd, Blackrock, Cork, Ireland